# Troubled Youth
in
Treatment Homes

# Troubled Youth

# in

# Treatment Homes

## A Handbook of
## Therapeutic Foster Care

EDITED BY

Pamela Meadowcroft

AND

Barbara A. Trout

Child Welfare League of America
Washington, D.C.

CHILD WELFARE LEAGUE OF AMERICA, INC.
440 First Street, NW, Washington, DC 20001-2085

CURRENT PRINTING (last digit)
10 9 8 7 6 5 4 3 2 1

*Cover design by Sherry Howard*
*Text design by Rose Jacobowitz*


PRINTED IN THE UNITED STATES OF AMERICA

# Contributors

BRAD BRYANT, M.P.A., Director, Research and Training, People Places, 1215 N. Augusta Street, Staunton, VA 24401

PAT CAMPBELL, M.S.W., Director of Social Services, People Places, 1215 N. Augusta Street, Staunton, VA 24401

BERNIE FABRY, Ph.D., Director Home Places, The Pressley Ridge Schools, Pittsburgh, PA 15214

EILEEN MARY GREALISH, M.Ed., Director of Model Implementation, PRYDE, The Pressley Ridge Schools, Pittsburgh, PA 15214

NANCY GROSS, Director, Youth Homes, Belmont Regional Center, 700 Parkwood Avenue, Charlotte, NC 28205

ROBERT P. HAWKINS, Ph.D., Professor, Psychology Department, West Virginia University, Morgantown, WV 26506

RÓBERT J. JONES, Ph.D., Director of Research and Evaluation, The BIABH Study Center, Professional Parenting Program, 204 Avery Avenue, Appalachian University, Morganton, NC 28655

WM. CLARK LUSTER, M.Ed., Executive Director, The Pressley Ridge Schools, Pittsburgh, PA 15214

PERCILLA J. LYNCH, M.Ed., Director, PRYDE Maryland, The Pressley Ridge Schools, Columbia, MD 21044

PAMELA MEADOWCROFT, Ph.D., Deputy Executive Director, The Pressley Ridge Schools, Pittsburgh, PA 15214

ROBERT SNODGRASS, Ph.D., Executive Director, People Places, 1215 N. Augusta Street, Staunton, VA 24401

GARY TIMBERS, Ph.D., Director, BIABH Study Center, Professional Parenting Program, 204 Avery Avenue, Appalachian University, Morganton, NC 28655

PAMELA WEAVER, M.A., Director, PRYDE Pittsbugh, The Pressley Ridge Schools, Pittsburgh, PA 15214

# Contents

# Foreword

IN HER 1982 STUDY, *Unclaimed Children,* Jane Knitzer reported that, of the three million severely emotionally disturbed children in this country, two-thirds do not receive the services they need, and countless others receive inappropriate services, often in excessively restrictive settings. Those findings were not new. The Joint Commission on the Mental Health of Children in 1969 and the President's Commission on Mental Health a decade later both concluded that troubled children were not receiving needed services, and that, in particular, community-based services were lacking. Most recently, the Office of Technology Assessment of the United States Congress concluded that while mental health problems are often tragic for children, "an even greater tragedy may be that we currently know more about how to prevent and treat children's mental health problems than is reflected in the care available." Study after study and report after report have called for comprehensive, community-based, family-focused systems of care for troubled children and youths, and the development of such systems is now becoming a national goal.

What types of services should ideally constitute a community-based system of care? A project sponsored by the National Institute of Mental Health, Child and Adolescent Service System Program (CASSP) described the desired system of care, how it might be organized, what components should be included, and what principles should guide service delivery. The resulting monograph, *A System of Care for Severely Emotionally Disturbed Children and Youth,* by Beth Stroul and Robert Friedman, provides a framework for planning and is considered a blueprint for change. The model presented in this monograph is based on a philosophy of comprehensiveness and is organized into major service dimensions, each corresponding to an area of need for the child and family. The mental health dimension consists of a range of nonresidential services—prevention, early identification and intervention, assessment, outpatient treatment, home-based services, day treatment, crisis services—and a range of residential services—therapeutic foster care (TFC), therapeutic group care, therapeutic camp services, independent-living services, residential treatment services, crisis residential services, and inpatient hospitalization. It is important to recognize that all of the components are interdependent; the effectiveness of each service depends upon the availability and effectiveness of other services.

The model presented in this monograph is more than a network of service components. Instead, it represents a philosophy about the way in which services should be delivered to children and families. One of the principles most relevant to this volume is the notion that "emotionally disturbed children should receive services within the least restrictive, most normative environment that is clinically appropriate." The concept of "least restrictive environment" has received a great deal of attention in the adult mental health field, with court decisions and policies mandating an individual's right to treatment in the least restrictive environment. Children and adolescents too should be served in as normal an environment as possible. Too often, children are removed from their homes when intensive services and support could keep the family intact. Of course, out-of-home placements are needed in some cases; it is not always in the child's best interests to remain with the family. Too often, however, children are placed in more restrictive settings than they actually need. These placements are made simply because the less restrictive services and settings are not available.

Therapeutic foster care is considered the least restrictive of the residential services. TFC programs try to approximate closely a natural environment, providing treatment in a family atmosphere and allowing youngsters to attend public schools and remain involved in community activities—which does not mean, however, that only less severely disturbed youngsters can be served in therapeutic foster homes. TFC programs report that they successfully serve some of the most severely disturbed youngsters in home settings—some youngsters who were rejected or ejected by the most restrictive, highly supervised institutional settings. TFC programs effectively serve children with a wide variety of problems and labels, including emotional disturbances, delinquency, substance abuse, handicaps or severe medical problems, and mental retardation. Currently, TFC programs are emerging to serve infants and young children with AIDS.

The three programs profiled in this book (PRYDE, People Places, and Professional Parenting) have been pioneers in therapeutic foster care. Each of these programs evolved from other types of programs—a residential treatment center, a special education and partial hospitalization center, and a group home. Program developers recognized the vast potential inherent in providing treatment in home settings. They have demonstrated that it is, indeed, possible to provide intensive and effective treatment in these home settings to youngsters considered the most disturbed and disturbing. They have demonstrated the effectiveness of this treatment approach in strikingly different environments, ranging from inner-city Pittsburgh to rural areas in Virginia, West Virginia, and North Carolina. Perhaps most important, they have demonstrated that highly intensive treatment does not necessarily require highly restrictive settings.

This book provides a picture of how several TFC programs operate. It is a comprehensive presentation, covering every facet of organizing and operating a TFC program from recruitment and training of treatment parents to working with biological families to evaluating the program's effectiveness, enabling others to benefit from the experience and expertise of these well-established programs.

The evidence presented within this volume and elsewhere clearly justifies an expanded investment in TFC programs. It is critical, however, to recall that no one service modality can meet the multiple and changing needs of troubled children and their families. TFC services must be placed within the context of a larger system of care, one that provides a comprehensive array of services and effectively coordinates service delivery. The availability of TFC services within a system of care will not eliminate the need for more restrictive treatment environments such as hospitals or residential treatment centers. TFC services will, however, ensure that youngsters have an opportunity to receive intensive treatment in more natural, less restrictive settings.

BETH A. STROUL
*Consultant*
*Child and Adolescent Service System Program (CASSP)*
*Technical Assistance Center*
*Georgetown University Child Development Center*

# I

# Therapeutic Foster Care: Past and Present

BRAD BRYANT

AND

ROBERT D. SNODGRASS

SINCE THE EARLY 1950s AND with increasing frequency more recently, a model of care and treatment has been developing to meet the needs of children who require the structure that characterizes an institutional program but who could benefit from the richness and normalizing influence of a family environment. A variety of titles have been used for such programs, including special foster care, specialized foster care, treatment family care, and professional parenting, to name only a few. Within recent years, therapeutic foster care (TFC) seems to be the preferred label among mental health audiences and will be the term generally used in this volume. Regardless of what they call themselves, however, these new programs all share a common and explicit focus on exceptional children. All are designed to serve youngsters with special problems and handicaps who, until recently, were referred routinely to more restrictive group

*1*

home or institutional settings considered better equipped to deal with their problems.

Therapeutic foster care programs in fact draw heavily on the treatment technologies developed in more restrictive settings, but apply them in the true family environment that is found in the traditional foster family home. These new programs, however, are distinguished from traditional foster family care by their emphasis on planned treatment or re-education of children and adolescents toward the development of effective and responsible interpersonal and social behavior, carried out in the home by foster parents who serve as the primary treatment agents. In a sense, TFC today is something of an adaptive hybrid, combining elements of residential treatment programming and the foster family environment into what may be described as a model of foster family-based treatment. This model offers an alternative to both the traditional foster family home and the institution for youngsters who are not appropriately or adequately served in either type of program.

Foster family care traditionally has provided nurturant custodial care to dependent children and has been successful in that mission for most youngsters it serves [Pardeck 1982]. In general, however, foster family care has failed to provide stability and consistency for "special-needs" children, particularly those described as having emotional or behavioral disturbances [Trasler 1955; Bergen 1955; Eisenberg 1965; Pardeck 1982]. These children have been referred to institutions. TFC programs share a common concern with preventing the institutionalization of this more difficult client group. It is hardly surprising, then, that these programs should differ in many important theoretical and practical respects from the more traditional foster family approach, despite the similarity in setting. Likewise, given the sharp environmental differences between foster family and institution, it should be expected that foster family-based treatment will also present important contrasts to the institution despite similarities in purpose, population, and approach. The intent of this chapter is to identify in broad terms the differences and commonalities shown by these program types, and in so doing to describe general distinguishing features of an emerging model of TFC.

It is, in a sense, misleading to refer to TFC as an "emerging model." Therapeutic foster care is not an entirely new concept, although there appear to be significant differences between early and more recent programs. Nor are all current TFC programs so alike that a single "correct" and fully articulated model may be said to exist at this time. Even among the three TFC programs on whose experiences this volume is based, clear differences in practice are apparent. A broader sample of TFC programs yields an even broader range of differences. What is most surprising, however, is not that differences appear across individual programs separated by both time and location, but that so many of these programs begun in isolation appear to share common perspectives and approaches.

The nature of the challenge has largely dictated the nature of the response, as shown by the continuities that can be seen between early TFC programs and more recent efforts. Before attempting present definitions, then, it may prove instructive to review *(1)* the early development of TFC as "special foster care" and certain dynamics that have favored its evident, recent expansion; *(2)* parallel developments in the field of behavioral psychology; and *(3)* philosophical and practical commonalities that brought three independently evolving enterprises into contact with one another.

## Early Development of Special Foster Care

Early special foster care programs emerged out of necessity, often on an ad hoc basis to fill a clear gap in services to disturbed children. The Baltimore Family and Children's Society, for example, in 1951 created its "specialized foster-family care program" because the city at that time did not have a local residential treatment center for behavior problem children and could not afford to build one [Waskowitz 1954]. More typically, in the 1950s and early 1960s, special foster care programs were initiated by psychiatric hospitals and residential treatment centers to serve children who no longer required institutional care but who were unlikely to find stability in their own or regular foster homes [Bryant 1980].

Such institutionally sponsored programs were designed primarily to serve a transitional aftercare function for children who already had been treated with some success in a more structured setting. The function of the special foster home actually was little different from that of a regular foster home. The major difference lay with the pronounced management problems presented by a more disturbed and disturbing population of children. Whatever continuing therapy the child required was provided by professionals at the parent institution, or, as in the case of the Baltimore program, by private therapists in their offices.

In contrast to later programs, the role of the foster parent in early special foster care was simply to persevere in caring for difficult children until the youngsters were ready, as a result of the professional therapy, to return to their own homes or to more traditional foster families. In fulfilling their assigned role, foster parents were asked not to serve differently but to serve more. Case managers similarly continued to act as support givers, service coordinators, and placement overseers, but were required to carry out these functions far more intensively with each family and child. To allow greater intensity of services, however, early programs evolved certain fundamental structures that continue to characterize much of therapeutic foster care practice today.

In supportive services to parents, for example, special foster care developers recognized from the outset that foster parents would need far more supervision and contact with professional staff than ordinarily was provided. Early programs consistently required a minimum frequency of weekly or biweekly visits to foster homes, particularly during the first several months of placement. Professional staff members, usually caseworkers, provided round-the-clock on-call backup to foster parents so that consultation was available at all times from a staff member familiar with their child. Caseloads were therefore reduced substantially so as not to exceed a maximum of ten to 15 children per worker [Bryant 1980].

Although the foster parent role did not change qualitatively, agencies did recognize the added demands of parenting disturbed children. Foster parents as a rule were paid roughly twice the standard foster care board rate as an incentive to persevere with more difficult youngsters. The maximum number of children that could be placed in any one home also was lower than in traditional foster care, although policy differed somewhat in this respect from one program to another [Bryant 1980].

In the 1950s and early 1960s, then, special foster care could be characterized as more an intensification than a fundamental alteration of the traditional foster family model. Still, contemporary contributors to the literature on special foster care were almost uniformly enthusiastic about the success of their programs in managing severely disturbed clients [Naughton 1957; Bohman 1957; Reinhold and Farragher 1967; Rice and Semmelroth 1968; Wildy 1975]. Clear outcome or other evaluative data for these programs, however, were seldom collected. The Baltimore program mentioned above does offer one notable exception. Discharge data gathered over a three-year period were promising, considering that the client population was composed of children explicitly targeted for more restrictive residential treatment. Of the 51 children served during that time, only six were discharged to institutional settings [Waskowitz 1954].

Despite positive accounts, though, early programs were few and relatively short-lived [Bryant 1980]. For the most part, an implicit division of functions prevailed at the time, in which traditional foster family care was viewed as appropriate for "normal" children but not for those requiring special training or treatment. Conventional wisdom left little room for perceiving any type of foster family placement, even with intensified services, as appropriate for handicapped, especially emotionally disturbed children. With a few exceptions, research clearly indicated that these children usually failed to achieve stability in foster homes [Bergen 1955; Trasler 1955; Eisenberg 1965]. Specialized institutions were considered better suited to meet their needs or at least were preferable on less explicit but more cosmetic grounds [Wolins and Piliavin 1964].

## Later Program Developments

The 1960s presented a fundamental challenge to assumptions favoring the separation of handicapped persons from "normal" society. The confident idealism of the Kennedy generation, shaped by the issues and emotions of the civil rights cause, produced a radical movement for deinstitutionalization of mental patients, low-risk offenders, and children placed in treatment-oriented or correction facilities. Philosophical and political pressure eventually translated to legal action as legislatures and courts began to advocate certain basic principles associated with de-institutionalization as requisite guidelines for educational and residential placement decisions.

Due largely to the early leadership efforts of the National Association for Retarded Children, beginning in 1950, the principles of "normalization" and "integration" of exceptional persons into community living gained legal recognition in the Mental Retardation Facilities and Community Mental Health Centers Construction Act of 1963. The act produced a dramatic expansion of community mental health services alongside widespread closures and cutbacks in congregate care facilities [Matsushima 1977]. In the early 1970s, normalization and integration were extended to the public school classroom via the practice of "mainstreaming" exceptional children in regular classes wherever possible [Smith and Neisworth 1975]. Mainstreaming itself was a practical outcome of the passage in 1973 of Public Law 94-142, the Education for All

Handicapped Children Act, which sought to guarantee special education to handicapped children in the "least restrictive" environment appropriate to the individual need of each child [Ballard and Zettel 1977].

Drawing on the precedent established with P.L. 94-142 in education, a 1974 federal court ruling in the case of *Gary vs. the Louisiana Department of Health and Human Resources* (DHHR) applied the principle of least restrictive setting to the arena of residential placements for handicapped children. In this court suit filed on behalf of all Louisiana children placed in out-of-state institutions by the DHHR, the court defined a continuum of residential services based on restrictiveness of setting that extended from the parental home through foster family and group home to institution as the most restrictive placement option. Interestingly, the state's response to the court's ruling for the plaintiff was to create a large-scale program of special foster care to provide the least restrictive treatment option possible for children ordered returned to Louisiana from specialized institutional placements [Louisiana DHHR 1977].

This historical example serves to highlight the clear conceptual parallels to be found between special education and special foster care programs during the late 1960s and early 1970s. Both were developed at that time to fill service gaps to handicapped children perceived as poorly served by traditional approaches. Children exhibiting emotional/behavioral problems have tended to fail in regular classrooms and, as a group, experience the highest frequency of re-placements in foster family care [Pardeck 1982]. Rather than determining that these youngsters could not be served in public schools and private homes, however, practitioners in special education and special foster care sought to alter established practice to meet the special needs of troubled clients. The shared aim was to maximize the normalizing influence of mainstream educational and community settings through integration.

Theory, however, ultimately had to be validated in practice. Special education and special foster care programs had to show that they could manage behavior and promote adaptive change in children who in the past had proven too disruptive for the regular school and community settings in which they now were to be served. This challenge required creative development of tools and techniques as well as a no-nonsense, buck-stops-here kind of commitment to observable results. Both program types were thus required to assume a degree of responsibility for client change that had not been assumed before in either public school classroom or foster family home.

In fact, direct accountability for change in clients has distinguished some later special foster care programs from earlier efforts, which tried to maintain difficult children in families while change or treatment efforts were undertaken elsewhere. As noted earlier, the early programs were transitional supplements to institutional services. Later programs were designed increasingly as alternatives to more restrictive residential treatment and care.

The later programs that defined their purposes more broadly as treatment also differed in several practical respects from earlier efforts. Accountability for planned change required that foster parents and case managers assume qualitatively different roles. Both jobs became far more proactive as the primary locus of treatment and change efforts shifted from the therapist's office to the foster family home, and the primary agent of treatment became the foster parent rather than the professional therapist.

Although this transition was philosophically in keeping with the deinstitutionalization movement and the companion concept of least restrictive care, the aspirations of advocates for direct treatment by foster families were ahead of their methods for implementation. The therapies of the day, the so-called "talk" therapies, required extensive training, normally at the graduate level. Also, they focused on attitudinal and cognitive change rather than on the kinds of behavioral deficits and problems that characterized the youths who were to be served by therapeutic foster families. Moreover, they worked best for individuals who, unlike the troubled and troubling children in TFC, were highly verbal and self-motivated. Finally, they were intended and best suited for the one-to-one environment of the clinic or counseling center. What was needed in TFC was a technology of treatment appropriate for troubled children and adolescents that was so logical, straightforward, and compatible with good typical parenting practices that it could be reasonably taught to, and implemented by, foster parents, with hope of beneficial results.

In fact, a treatment technology that met all of these requirements had been evolving concurrently with, but separately from, special foster care. It went by various names at various stages of its own development: operant learning theory; behavior modification; social learning theory; and, more recently, applied behavior analysis. It had its origins in the experimental psychology laboratories of the 1940s and 1950s, but by the time it was needed in the foster care arena, it had been applied to a broad range of human behavior problems. One branch of the behaviorist approach was of particular interest to TFC advocates: Achievement Place or, as it later became known, the teaching family model, a comprehensive and carefully planned method of treatment designed to be implemented by married couples (called teaching parents) in group homes for delinquent or otherwise difficult youths.

The first Achievement Place homes, one for boys [Phillips 1968] and one for girls [Wolf et al. 1976] were opened under the auspices of the University of Kansas in the late 1960s. The subsequent expansion of the teaching family model was remarkably swift. By the mid-1970s, dozens of similar programs were operating around the nation (they now number in the several hundreds). The National Teaching-Family Association (NaTFA) was chartered in 1977 and, over the years, a substantial quantity of materials—journal articles, books, manuals, technical reports, and audiovisual aids—has been issued [James et al. 1983]. But it was the substance more than the scope of the teaching family model that attracted the attention of those who envisioned the foster family home as the nexus of treatment for problem children. The model was elegant in its simplicity, it was designed for use by surrogate parents in group homes for difficult children, and it represented a logical extension of effective parenting skills.

Systematically in some cases and inadvertently in others, the methods and also the language and philosophy of the teaching family model began to find their way into the thinking and activities of those pressing forward with treatment-oriented foster care programs. In the Wisconsin Treatment Home Program begun in 1968 and Boston's Treatment Alternatives Project in 1972, foster parents were viewed more as professional colleagues, direct treatment agents, than as volunteer caregivers [Bauer and Heincke 1976; Gruber and Heck 1977]. Reflecting social learning theory, behavioral family therapy, and the teaching family model, the treatment process was seen to occur most powerfully in the foster home environment, which clearly had the greatest day-to-day influence on what and how children learned. The term "foster parent" was replaced by more descriptive terms such as "treatment parent," "professional parent," "parent counselor," "parent therapist," or "teaching parent," the last borrowed directly from the teaching family model [Phillips et al. 1972]. Just as the group home was to some an effort to make residential treatment more family-like, therapeutic foster care went all the way by providing residential treatment in a true and naturally occurring family setting. Preservice foster parent training, rarely provided in earlier programs, became a standard feature where foster parents were expected to undertake a direct treatment function [Larson et al. 1978; Levin et al. 1976].

Corresponding changes occurred in the role of the case manager. In TFC, case managers developed and monitored specific treatment plans implemented in the home by foster parents. The plans normally were developmental or learning-based and may be compared conceptually to the Individual Educational Plans required in special education programming today. Case managers also served as treatment parent trainers, providing continuing, individualized instruction and consultation to parents in the home. Carried out under the supervision of psychologists or clinical social workers, this treatment planning and training function went far beyond the traditional casework tasks of providing general supervision and emotional support to parents [Bryant 1980].

Concern with evaluation and measurement issues grew logically as well. In the professional literature of the late 1960s and the 1970s, the number of articles on special foster care increased significantly, including basic program descriptions and limited program evaluative data [Bryant 1980]. Alberta Parent Counselors reported the use of written instruments to evaluate client progress, along with broad measures of general program performance [Larson and Allison 1977]. The California Family Care Program demonstrated that only 7 percent of retarded children placed in development-oriented special foster care were returned to institutions after one year, as compared to 25 percent of those placed in more traditional maintenance-oriented foster homes [Mamula and Newman 1973]. Client discharge data collected by the Treatment Alternatives Project, the Alberta Program, and the Treatment Home Program supported the belief that special foster care could function as a workable alternative to more restrictive treatment settings for a wide variety of handicapped and disturbed youngsters [Gruber and Heck 1977; Larson and Allison 1977; Bauer and Heincke 1976].

Elements of an identifiable therapeutic foster care model were beginning to emerge by the early 1970s, although very little communication seemed to take place among representative programs. Judging from the enthusiastic tone of discovery typical of publications at the time, new programs still began in relative isolation, reinventing the wheel on a trial-and-error basis.

Even without the benefit of collaboration, however, new wheels appeared to emerge more or less round—that is to say, while later TFC programs did differ widely in such areas as treatment orientation and pre-service training content, the broad distinguishing features were shared by most programs described in the literature [Bryant 1980]: an explicit focus on planned behavior change, a qualitatively new and proactive role for treatment foster parents and case managers in the change process, pre-service training for treatment parents, and an emphasis on evaluation and accountability. It should be noted, however, that programs closely resembling earlier special foster care efforts continued to appear in the 1970s despite some disappointing data from those where pre-service training and extra pay to foster parents were not supplemented by intensive case management and continual training [North Carolina Division of Youth Services 1979].

Promising outcome data alone did not guarantee longevity even for programs that could clearly document success. Budget cuts and termination of grant funding closed a number of apparently thriving programs, including the Alberta and Boston projects mentioned [Larson et al. 1978; Gruber and Heck 1977]. One particularly promising public program in Iowa's Department of Social Services District 10 essentially was closed down following an administrative reorganization and the subsequent loss of key personnel. This closure occurred despite documented savings of over $300,000 realized during the three-year pilot period due to the relative cost efficiency of TFC over more restrictive treatment settings [Iowa DSS 1980].

Given these examples of TFC programs that have failed due to funding problems or despite funding advantages, it is somewhat ironic to note that, at a time of heightened public concern over the costs of human services, cost arguments generally have favored TFC over other residential treatment options. In the literature of the period, TFC programs established as alternatives to institutional treatment from the late 1960s to the mid-1970s consistently reported per diem costs ranging from one-half to two-thirds the expense of institutional care [Bryant 1980]. A more recent investigation of relative operating costs further indicates that TFC enjoys clear advantages over group home and institutional programs with regard both to per diem costs and to direct and indirect start-up costs as well [Bryant 1984].

## Growth of the Therapeutic Foster Care Model

Practical and conceptual factors have converged over the past two decades to lend TFC increasing appeal. In addition to the considerations already mentioned, TFC offers clear advantages with regard to treatment effectiveness.

Practical developments in treatment technology, both behavioral and psychodynamic, have increasingly supported the value of therapy in a family setting [Haley and Hoffman 1967; Hawkins et al. 1966]. Alexander and Parsons [1973], among others, demonstrated success, beginning in the late 1960s, in treating delinquent children in their own families using the parents as therapeutic agents. The profound influence of environmental factors in establishing and maintaining attitudinal and behavior patterns has been demonstrated in a variety of studies [Brown 1971; Stewart and Garth 1978]. Social learning theory has argued on that basis that the treatment of various psychological disturbances should take place in a setting most closely approximating that to which the individual must return or adjust permanently, in order to maximize generalization of therapeutic progress to natural settings [Bandura and Walters 1960]. Since most children will enter or return to family situations, treatment conducted in a true family environment would appear to have clear advantages over other therapeutic settings.

Living in a therapeutic foster home may be viewed as a training experience for the development of basic parenting skills. Given the profound role played by imitative learning in children's development generally, children exposed to effective parenting models should be better able to learn adequate parenting skills themselves [Bandura 1971; Bandura and McDonald 1970; Heilbrun 1970; Love and Kaswan 1974; Knopf 1979; Weinberg 1980]. This point seems particularly relevant today as growing numbers of children enter care because of parental neglect and abuse [Shyne and Schroeder 1978]. The pathology of family disorganization characteristic in such cases tends to be repeated in successive generations [Young 1964]. A strong argument can be made on that basis in support of interventions that can break this chain of failure, offer acceptable alternative parent models to children, and foster the familial attitudes and skills required for successful, non-abusive parenting in later adult life.

A therapeutic family setting offers the advantages of positive modeling by all family members. More congregate residential settings, on the other hand, suffer from a reverse dynamic. Institutions and, to a lesser extent, group homes, usually are plagued with the disruptive effects of negative peer influence related directly to the number of clients treated in a single setting. For reasons relating primarily to efficiency and management considerations, congregate programs tend to admit relatively homogeneous populations or to arrange internally subgroups of residents whose problems and general characteristics are similar. The result is to maximize peer influence, allowing continual and extensive peer reinforcement of ordinarily unacceptable social behavior. It has become increasingly evident over the years that children in institutions may acquire further maladjusted behavior patterns that make successful functioning in the community even more difficult [Snodgrass 1977].

Empirical evidence indicates that mild retardation of a non-organic nature may be overcome or substantially reduced through stable, stimulating, and consistently nurturant living conditions [Heber 1972]. A TFC placement can offer such care without setting an exceptional child apart as deviant. It allows a child to relate to an average variety of other children with regard to age, intelligence, and social skill levels. Studies comparing children reared from early life in institutions with children in foster or own homes have shown that institutionalized children tend to display relative deficits in intelligence, long-range development, school readiness, and interpersonal relations, and to exhibit more stereotyped, self-stimulating behaviors [Duehrrson 1967; Braginsky and Braginsky 1971]. Institutional care has been criticized further for failing to provide adequate learning or coping situations for children and for producing the hospitalism and apathy characteristic of institutionalized mental patients [Robinson and Robinson 1976].

Developments over the past two decades in the theory and practice of treatment for handicapped children clearly favor a model of care centered in a naturally occurring family setting. The failure of regular foster family care to provide stability and continuity to disturbed children, however, left a gap in services to this population that was filled only partly by the many group home programs appearing through the 1960s and early 1970s. Although the group home represented an important advance over more restrictive institutional care, it suffered to a lesser extent, as mentioned above, from some of the same liabilities as larger congregate settings. Given the current strong emphasis in the child welfare field on the issue of permanence in child placement, one of the most significant of these liabilities has become the inability of group home programs to offer long-term placement to children who cannot return, for various reasons, to their own families. As TFC programs have begun to demonstrate the capacity both to treat disturbed children effectively in minimally restrictive, normalizing environments, and to provide continuing long-term family placement for those who need it, the unique potential of the therapeutic foster care model has become increasingly apparent. It might be expected, as a result, that TFC as a program type will continue to grow in the years ahead as the preferred placement alternative for the majority of disturbed children and youth.

## Contributing Programs

If TFC is likely to expand, then guidelines for program development are needed now. In the past, as mentioned earlier, therapeutic foster care programs began in relative isolation, without the benefit of the experience of other practitioners. In 1983, at least one exception to this characteristic isolation resulted in informal contacts between a number of individual programs on the East Coast of the country through the catalyzing efforts of the National Institute of Mental Health's (NIMH) Center for the Study of Violent and Anti-Social Behavior.

For a year and a half, representatives from therapeutic foster care programs in Virginia, North Carolina, and Pennsylvania, as well as staff members from NIMH, met to compare experiences, program developments, and evaluative data. The collaboration not only directly helped the participants themselves, but suggested that broader communication could aid the general development of the model. Under the guidance of Dr. James Breiling of the NIMH staff, plans for a collaborative writing effort involving experienced, high-quality TFC programs were formed. The present volume represents the combined input of three principal contributing sites from the original group: Virginia's People Places, begun in 1973; North Carolina's Professional Parenting Program, launched in 1979; and Pennsylvania's PRYDE program, begun in 1981.

People Places, Inc., a private, nonprofit child-placing agency located in rural Staunton, Virginia, began as a weekend adjunct to a five-day residential treatment center program for emotionally disturbed and behaviorally disordered children and adolescents. Since many children in the institutional program had no placement resource available on weekends, the residential staff adapted foster family care to the special treatments needs of disturbed children. Pre-service training, in-home consultation, and intensive support were provided to treatment parents who were expected to carry out individual behavioral treatments plans with the same child each weekend.

Early in the program, the staff began to recognize that children appeared to make more significant gains and exhibit fewer problem behaviors during their weekend foster home visits than in the treatment center. By the end of 1973, the program had been extended to offer full-time foster family-based treatment to children as an alternative to institutional placement. The treatment center's chief of residential services left the institution to become director of the family-based program, and several direct-care staff members from the center became the first program managers to design and supervise individual treatment programs in therapeutic foster homes. By 1976, People Places was serving 65 children from Virginia in its full-time therapeutic foster care component and operating its own special education school for those foster children who needed a special school setting.

A 1977 People Places's study offered the first, and quite encouraging, follow-up evaluation of clients discharged from treatment-intensive TFC [Snodgrass and Campbell 1981]. In 1980, the agency published the first comprehensive review of the development of special foster care in the United States and became active in research, training, and the production of program materials concerning the model [Bryant 1980].

The Professional Parenting program was developed by the Bringing It All Back Home (BIABH) Study Center at Appalachian State University in rural Morganton, North Carolina. The BIABH Center itself began as a demonstration project in the early 1970s to establish a network of group home programs for delinquent youths based on the teaching family model of group home care discussed above. Several of the center staff members, in fact, had been active in the original development of the teaching family model and were directly familiar with the organization, treatment technology, and evaluation of that approach [Timbers et al. 1973; Fields et al. 1976]. Despite successful development of the group home network, the BIABH staff recognized certain inherent limits to the group home model itself. Most significant was the fact that group homes cannot serve as permanent placements. An implicit but fundamental assumption of the teaching family model was that the group home program could sufficiently remediate the problems of clients and their families during a time-limited period of intervention so that clients would return home. Substantial problems remained, of course, for children who did not progress enough and for those children whose families were so thoroughly fragmented and pathological as to preclude any eventual return.

Focusing initially on children who required both treatment and long-term or permanent placement outside their own homes, BIABH developed its Professional Parenting program, employing specially trained and supervised foster parents as long-term treatments agents. Much of the training format for group home "teaching parents" was adapted to the pre-service training needs of professional parents, and staff members familiar with group home treatment strategies were employed as consultants to treatment parents on 24-hour call. The Professional Parenting program has grown to serve as a direct alternative to more restrictive residential treatment for children from North Carolina and no longer is limited to augmenting the group home program. The program serves a population of 42 children from three offices, Asheville, Winston, and Morganton, North Carolina.

Pennsylvania's Pressley Ridge Youth Development Extension (PRYDE) is one of several treatment services for emotionally disturbed and disturbing adolescents at The Pressley Ridge School. Begun in 1832, Pressley Ridge over the years has developed a widely respected special education and partial hospital program for 120 disturbed youngsters from school districts throughout the Pittsburgh area and surrounding counties. In addition, Pressley Ridge operates a sizable wilderness program in a nearby area of southwestern Pennsylvania, as well as a status offender program for 20 adolescent boys and girls in West Virginia.

Before the development in 1981 of the PRYDE program, Pressley Ridge also provided residential services to 50 troubled adolescent boys and girls in a cottage program located at the main Pittsburgh campus. In 1980, however, the staff began to consider placement alternatives. The treatment disadvantages of group residential services for its population were increasingly apparent as the level of disturbance in new admissions and the costs grew higher. This escalation was the result of contemporary efforts in the child welfare field to keep less troubled youth in their own homes or in regular foster care, and to refer only the most troubled youngsters to residential treatment. In keeping with Pressley Ridge's ecological approach to treatment programming [Hobbs 1982], the staff sought a replacement for Pressley Ridge's cottage component that could be at once less restrictive than traditional residential services, equally treatment-intensive, and significantly more cost-effective.

In mid-1980, program developers began designing a program of foster family-based treatment that would be highly systematic, accountable, and intensive according to a simple, coherent treatment approach [Hawkins and Luster 1982]. The staff spent about six months obtaining start-up funding through foundations and grants, drafting a version of the pre-service training for treatment parents, and orienting local agencies and others to the new program. PRYDE's early commitment to accountability of treatment and documentation of program components has continued to produce a wide array of foster parent and staff training materials, as well as program evaluation data. The program itself has expanded rapidly since its inception. It serves 100 children, primarily an inner-city, urban population from its Pittsburgh and suburban offices; 50 children of rural, small-town populations from three offices in West

Virginia, and 50 children of urban and small-town areas through its office in Columbia, Maryland.

## Commonalities among Contributing Programs

The three programs whose development is profiled above have much in common. All three were designed as treatment programs for severely disturbed children and youth. Despite important differences in implementation, all three are committed to a particular treatment technology. Each program employs applied behavior analysis and takes a learning-based approach to client treatment and behavior change. Each was attracted initially to the foster family as a vehicle for treatment because of the unique advantages that environment offered over more artificial and restrictive settings with regard to social modeling, normalizing influences, and opportunities for maximum generalization of treatment gains. Because a learning-based approach to treatment places particular emphasis on the power of the environment in shaping and maintaining adaptive change, all three programs are strongly committed to deinstitutionalization of treatment services for clients who can be served safely in normal community settings. All three programs are private, nonprofit agencies that work with children who are among the most disturbed and disturbing children of those who can be managed in community settings. Each, for example, has worked with autistic or diagnosed psychotic children, physically assaultive and hostile youths. All have developed out of more restrictive treatment-oriented settings and represent adaptations of the technology of applied behavior analysis to a naturally occurring family environment.

## Contrasts

Although the similarities are notable, the programs differ clearly in several aspects. People Places, Professional Parenting, and PRYDE West Virginia are located in small cities in the rural South, while the PRYDE Pittsburgh office operates in a large metropolitan area. People Places, Professional Parenting, and PRYDE West Virginia serve a statewide population to maintain a viable census size, while PRYDE Pittsburgh and the suburban PRYDE Sewickley and Columbia, Maryland, offices serve a smaller geographical area of denser population. People Places and Professional Parenting, with 50 and 40 children, are moderate-sized operations, while PRYDE's 200 children represent a large model. Even larger TFC programs, however, such as Minneapolis's PATH program and Philadelphia's Concern do exist, serving hundreds of children.

The three programs present other demographic differences as well. About half of PRYDE Pittsburgh children and foster parents are black; roughly one-fourth of People Places clients and treatment parents are black; that figure is only 10 percent for Professional Parenting and lower still for PRYDE offices located in West Virginia. PRYDE Pittsburgh, headquartered in a large city, and its rural sister program, PRYDE West Virginia, report less difficulty in recruiting parents than do the other two rural programs.

Further contrasts exist in such areas as degree of formal structure, data keeping and reporting, treatment programming, and other organizational features. Professional Parenting, for example, tends to serve only those clients in need of long-term family placement. PRYDE more frequently provides shorter-term treatment to youths who may return to their parents and consequently provides intensive services to the parents. For those youths for whom return home is not possible, however, continued, longer-term placement in their PRYDE homes remains an option. People Places often combines shorter-term treatment with permanent foster family placement in a treatment parent home. Subsequent chapters describe such contrasts in detail where they appear to represent significant alternatives or additional practical information to program planners and practitioners. For the most part, however, a more generic description of practice is employed where individual program differences are minimal.

Although each program has specific reasons for doing what it does, there are no empirical outcome measures available at this time to indicate that one approach is to be favored over another. Rather, the clear contrasts among the programs are likely to be of significant value in themselves as examples of the diversity and breadth of alternatives possible within the framework of what appears to be a rather rapidly growing and promising model of TFC.

## REFERENCES

Alexander, J.F., and Parsons, B.V. Short-term behavioral intervention with delinquent families: Impact on family process and recidivism. Journal of Abnormal Psychology: 291–225, 1973.

Ballard, J., and Zettel, J. Public law 94-142 and section 503: what they say about rights and protections. Exceptional Children 44: 177–184, 1977.

Bandura, A., ed. Psychological Modeling. Chicago: Aldine-Atherton, 1971.

————, and McDonald, FJ. Influence of social reinforcement and the behavior of models in shaping children's moral judgments. In Fitzgerald, H.E., and McKinney, J.P. (eds.), Developmental Psychology: Studies in Human Development. Homewood, Illinois: The Dorsey Press, 1970.

————, and Walters, R.H. Social Learning and Personality Development. New York: Holt, Rinehart and Winston, 1960.

Bauer, J.E., and Heincke, W. Treatment family care homes for disturbed foster children. Child Welfare LV: 478–489, 1976.

Bergen, M.L. Reasons for removal of children from foster home placement. Unpublished M.S.W. thesis, Catholic University of America, 1955.

Bohman, J.L. Methods of recruiting foster homes and ways to enable foster parents to help children. Child Welfare XXXVI: 741–750, 1957.

Braginsky, D.D., and Braginsky, R.M. Hansels and Gretels: Studies of Children in Institutions for the Mentally Retarded. New York: Holt, Rinehart and Winston, 1971.

Brown, D. Behavior Modification in Child and School Mental Health: An Annotated Bibliography on Applications with Parents and Teachers. Rockville, Maryland: National Institute of Mental Health, 1971.

Bryant, B. Special Foster Care: A History and Rationale. Verona, Virginia: People Places, 1980.

————. Special foster care: Evaluation of an alternative to institutions for disturbed children. Unpublished master's thesis, University of Virginia, 1984.

Duehrsson, A. The development of children in residential and foster care. In Dinnage, R., and Kellmer Pringle, M.L. (eds.), Foster Home Care: Facts and Fallacies. New York: Humanities Press, 1967.

————. Parent counselors: A community treatment program for disturbed youths. Child Welfare LVII: 47–52, 1978.

Eisenberg, L. The sins of the fathers: Urban decay and social pathology. American Journal of Orthopsychiatry 4: 243–248, 1965.

Fields, S.; Maloney, D.M.; Maloney, K.B.; Timbers, G.D.; and Jones, R.J. Evaluating the Satisfaction of Consumer Groups Involved with Group Care for Adolescents. Western Carolina Center Papers and Reports, 6(4). Morganton, North Carolina: Western Carolina Center, 1976.

Freeman, H. Foster home care for mentally retarded children: Can it work? Child Welfare LVII: 113–121, 1978.

Gruber, A.R., and Heck, E.T. The treatment alternatives project. Association for the Advancement of Behavior Therapy Newsletter 4: 13, 18, 1977.

Hampson, R. Selecting and training foster parents as therapists: Community care for handicapped children. Unpublished master's thesis, University of Virginia, 1975.

Haley, J., and Hoffman, L. Techniques of Family Therapy. New York: Basic Books, 1967.

Hawkins, R.; Peterson, R.F.; Schweid, E; and Bijou, S.W. Behavior therapy in the home: Amelioration of problem parent-child relationships with the parent in therapeutic role. Journal of Experimental Child Psychology 4: 94–107, 1966.

Hawkins, R.P., and Luster, W.C. Family-based treatment: A minimally restrictive alternative with special promise. In Behavioral Treatment of Youth in Professional Foster

*Homes,* chaired by E.L. Phillips. Symposium presented at the American Psychological Association convention, Washington, DC, 1982.

———; Peterson, R.F; Schweid, E; and Bijou, S.W. Behavior therapy in the home: Amelioration of problem parent-child relationships with the parent in therapeutic role. Journal of Experimental Child Psychology 4: 94–107, 1966.

Heber, R., et al. Rehabilitation of Families at Risk for Mental Retardation: Progress Report. Madison, Wisconsin: The University of Wisconsin, 1972.

Heilbrun, A.B. Parental model attributes, nurturant reinforcement, and consistency of behavior in adolescents. In Fitzgerald, H.E., and McKinney, J.P. (eds.) Developmental Psychology: Studies in Human Development. Homewood, Illinois: The Dorsey Press, 1970.

Henderson, H. Redeploying corporate resources toward new priorities, In Starchild, A. (ed.), Business in 1990. Seattle: University Press of the Pacific, 1979.

Hobbs, N. The Troubled and Troubling Child: Reeducation in Mental Health, Education, and Human Service Programs for Children and Youth. San Francisco: Jossey-Bass, 1982.

Iowa Department of Social Services, District X. A Three Year Report of the Specialized Foster Home Program. Cedar Rapids, Iowa: Iowa DSS District X, 1980.

James, L.; Mahoney, D.; Thompson, L.; Watson, E.W.; Brooks, L.E.; Blase, K.; and Collins, L. Teaching-Family Bibliography. Boys Town, Nebraska: Father Flanagan's Home, 1983.

Knopf, I.J. Childhood Psychopathology: A Developmental Approach. Englewood Cliffs, New Jersey: Prentice-Hall, 1979.

Larson, G., and Allison, J. Parent Counsellors: Evaluation—Outcome. Calgary, Alberta: Alberta Social Services and Community Health, March 1977.

———; ———; and Johnston, E. Alberta parent counselors: A community treatment program for disturbed youths. Child Welfare LVII: 47–52, 1978.

Levin, S.; Rubenstein, J.S.; and Streiner, D.L. The parent-therapist program: An innovative approach to treating emotionally disturbed children. Hospital and Community Psychiatry 17: 407–410, 1976.

Louisiana State Department of Health and Human Resources. Specialized Foster Care Program. Baton Rouge, Louisiana: DHHR, 1977. Mimeographed.

Love, L.R., and Kaswan, J.W. Troubled Children: Their Families, Schools and Treatments. New York: John Wiley & Sons, 1974.

Mamula, R.A., and Newman, N. Community Placement of the Mentally Retarded. Springfield, Illinois: Charles C. Thomas, 1973.

Matsushima, J. Child welfare: Institutions for children. In Turner, J.B. (ed.), Encyclopedia of Social Work. Washington, D.C.: National Association of Social Workers, 1977.

Naughton, F.X. Cementing the gains of residential treatment through foster care. Child Welfare XXXI (10): 1–3, 1957.

North Carolina Division of Youth Services. What They Need Is Love: Second Annual Report on Community-Based Alternatives in North Carolina. Morganton, North Carolina: DYS, 1979.

Pardeck, J.T. The Forgotten Child: A Study of the Stability and Continuity of Foster Care. Washington, D.C.: University Press of America, 1982.

Phillips, E.L. Achievement Place: Token reinforcement procedures in a home-style rehabili-
    tation setting for "pre-delinquent" boys. Journal of Applied Behavior Analysis 1:
    213–223, 1968.

————; Phillips, E.A.; Fixsen, D.L.; and Wolf, M.M. The Teaching Family Handbook.
    Lawrence, Kansas: University of Kansas, 1972.

Reinhold, P.E., and Farragher, M.E. Specialized services for maintaining severely disturbed
    children in public schools within the community. American Journal of Orthopsychia-
    try 37: 314–315, 1967.

Rice, D.L., and Semmelroth, S. Foster care for emotionally disturbed children. American
    Journal of Orthopsychiatry 38: 539–542, 1968.

Robinson, N., and Robinson, H. The Mentally Retarded Child. New York: McGraw-Hill,
    1976.

Shyne, A.W., and Schroeder, A.G. National Study of Social Services to Children and Their
    Families. Washington, D.C.: Children's Bureau, 1978.

Smith, R.M., and Neisworth, J.T. The Exceptional Child: A Functional Approach. New
    York: McGraw-Hill, 1975.

Snodgrass, R.D. Specialized foster care: A model for serving handicapped children. Paper
    presented to the convention of the Virginia State Federation for Exceptional Children,
    Roanoke, Virginia, October 1977.

————, and Campbell, P. Specialized foster care: A community alternative to institutional
    placement. Paper presented to the Association for the Advancement of Behavior
    Therapy, Toronto, Ontario, November 1981.

Stewart, M.A., and Garth, A. Psychological Disorders of Children: A Handbook for
    Primary Care Physicians. Baltimore, Maryland: Williams & Wilkins, 1978.

Timbers, G.D.; Timbers, B.J.; Fixsen, D.L.; Phillips, E.L.; and Wolf, M.M. Achievement
    Place for pre-delinquent girls: Modification of inappropriate emotional behavior with
    token reinforcement and instructional procedures. Paper presented at the American
    Psychological Association, Montreal, Quebec, August 1973.

Trasler, G. A study of success and failure of foster home placements. Ph.D. thesis,
    University of London, 1955.

Waskowitz, V. Foster family care for disturbed children. Children 1 (4): 9–18, 1954.

Weinberg, S.J. The transmission of psychopathology through four generations of a family.
    In Williams, G.J., and Money, J. (eds.), Traumatic Abuse and Neglect of Children at
    Home. Baltimore, Maryland: The Johns Hopkins University Press, 1980.

Wildy, L. The professional foster home. In Foster Family Care for Emotionally Disturbed
    Children. New York: Child Welfare League of America, 1975, 1–8.

Wolf, M.M.; Phillips, E.L.; Fixen, D.L.; Braukmann, C.J.; Kirigen, K.A.; Willner, A.G.;
    and Schumaker, J.B. Achievement Place: The teaching-family model. Child Care
    Quarterly 5(2): 92–103, 1976.

Wolins, M., and Piliavin, I. Institution or Foster Family: A Century of Debate. New York:
    Child Welfare League of America, 1964.

Young, L. Wednesday's Child. New York: McGraw-Hill, 1964.

# 2

# Describing the Children Served in Treatment Homes

GARY TIMBERS

THE PREVIOUS CHAPTER DESCRIBES two significant trends from which emerged therapeutic foster care (TFC). One trend was to make foster care more professional, and the second was to shift away from the notion that treatment could be provided only in secure residential settings. The emerging model brought together the nurturing and quality of life that can be found in a carefully selected program family and combined it with a treatment program carried out by the program parents, sustained by training and ongoing support activities.

The questions that remain to be answered are those usually asked of any new child service program: What kinds of children does it serve and how well does it serve them? This chapter examines a set of preliminary data from a sample of children in three TFC programs as a way of answering those questions. The data include both demographic and behavioral characteristics of the children, an assessment of the problems that distinguish their biological families, a review of the typical histories of previous placements from which these children emerge, and, finally, information concerning the success of TFC in interrupting the child-care revolving door to which they have given poignant meaning.

## The Study Sample

Information on client characteristics was solicited from each of the three core programs. For purposes of uniformity, each program submitted data from client records (which, in many instances, may not be complete) on all children who were in placement one or more days during the same specified 12-month time period. To be included in the study sample, a child may have been admitted to the program either before or during the period, as long as the child was in placement for at least one day during that time. Thus, the groups included children who were admitted before the period but were discharged during it, children who were both admitted and discharged during the period, and children who were admitted during the period and continued in the program after the period had ended.

This procedure produced a study sample of 76 children for one PRYDE site (Pittsburgh), 73 children for People Places, and 35 children for Professional Parenting. All subsequent discussion here is addressed to these three groups of program clients.

### Sex and Race of Children

PRYDE admitted about equal numbers of males and females; People Places admitted about two-thirds males and one-third females; and Professional Parenting admitted slightly more females than males (refer to table 1).

PRYDE served a much larger population of black children during the sample interval than did the other two programs. Sixty-five percent of the children served by PRYDE were black, compared with 16 percent and 9 percent, respectively, for People Places and Professional Parenting. Although the black population of Allegheny County (the primary service area for PRYDE Pittsburgh) is only 12 percent of its total population, that program reported excellent success in recruiting black parents from the densely populated Pittsburgh metropolitan area and therefore was able to meet the needs of many urban black children who were referred.

## TABLE 1
### *Sex and Race of Children*

| | %<br>PRYDE<br>($n = 76$) | %<br>People Places<br>($n = 73$) | %<br>Professional<br>Parenting<br>($n = 35$) |
|---|---|---|---|
| *Sex* | | | |
| Male | 51 | 66 | 43 |
| Female | 49 | 34 | 57 |
| *Race* | | | |
| Caucasian | 34 | 77 | 91 |
| Black | 65 | 16 | 9 |
| Other | 1 | 7 | 0 |

People Places and Professional Parenting are located in semirural areas of central Virginia and western North Carolina with relatively small black populations and, consequently, the number of black program families, as well as black children placed, reflects this.

### *Age of Children*

Are the children admitted by the three core programs entering out-of-home placement for the first time or are they veterans of out-of-home placement? Table 2 reports the ages at which the children were first removed from their own homes. For all three programs, there were children for whom removal occurred at birth and also interprogram consistency at the other end of this range: 16 years was the maximum age of first removal for PRYDE and People Places, 15 years for Professional Parenting. On average, People Places children were first removed from their homes at age eight and PRYDE and Professional Parenting Children at average ages of nine and nine and one-half, respectively.

Both People Places and Professional Parenting had infants in their programs. This situation occurred for People Places because a girl in a nearby psychiatric hospital gave birth, and an emergency placement for the infant was offered by that program. Professional Parenting had accepted a pregnant teenager into placement and, when the baby was born, the professional parents supervised the mother's care of the infant. Ultimately, custody was removed from the mother, and the child stayed in the Professional Parenting home until he was adopted. The youngest

## TABLE 2
### *Age of Children*

|  | PRYDE (n = 76) | | People Places (n = 73) | | Professional Parenting (n = 35) | |
|---|---|---|---|---|---|---|
|  | Range | Average | Range | Average | Range | Average |
| Age First Left Home | 0–16 | 9.0 | 0–16 | 8.0 | 0–15 | 9.5 |
| Age Entered Program | 3.9–17.1 | 12.5 | 0–18.9 | 12.0 | .67–17.3 | 13.0 |

admitted to PRYDE was three years, nine months. For all three programs, the oldest children admitted were in their late teens.

The average age at entry into the programs was 12 years for People Places, 12½ for PRYDE, and 13 for Professional Parenting. By subtracting the age at which a child first left home and the age a child first entered one of the programs, information about the amount of time a child was in other residential environments can be derived. The amount of time from first placement to placement in one of the three programs ranged from three and a half years for PRYDE and Professional Parenting children, to four years for People Places children.

### *Previous Placements*

In what kinds of environments were these children before placement in a therapeutic foster home? Each program submitted data on the frequency and type of previous placements for each child in its study sample. As a rule, a child's placement in one of the three programs was not the first placement. All 35 Professional Parenting children and all 73 People Places children had had at least one previous placement. Three of 76 PRYDE children entered TFC without a previous placement. The largest number of previous placements for a single child was seven for PRYDE, 11 for People Places, and 16 for Professional Parenting. The average number of placements per child was 3.8 for People Places, 4.7 for Professional Parenting, and 2.5 for PRYDE.

The number of different types of placements per child is also revealing. Of the 11 categories of placements, PRYDE children had an average of 2.4 types of placements, People Places children had an average of 2.2 types of placements, and Professional Parenting, 3.2.

The previous-placement data reveal patterns both among and within programs: 57 percent of the PRYDE children experienced previous placements in emergency shelters, 29 percent in group homes, 26 percent in foster homes, 24 percent in psychiatric institutions, and 22 percent in child-care institutions. Professional Parenting children most often had previous placements with relatives (77 percent), foster homes (71 percent), emergency shelters (40 percent), group homes (39 percent), and child-care institutions (31 percent). Most common previous placements for People Places were foster homes (69 percent), psychiatric institutions (27 percent), group homes (25 percent), and relatives (22 percent). Although percentages were relatively small compared to other types of placements, all three programs had children from failed adoptive placements (refer to table 3).

The most striking features of this information are the high number and variety of previous placements these children experienced. Perhaps this finding is symptomatic of a combination of the level of difficulty of the children, the families' problems, and the failure of existing programs to meet their needs. The modest diversity among programs is probably due simply to differences in the availability of placement alternatives across sites, or to incomplete records.

When these data are reviewed with the information about the length of time that had lapsed since first removal from the own home and placement in one of the three core programs, a consistent picture de-

## TABLE 3
### *Previous Placements of Children*

| Type of Placement | % PRYDE ($n = 76$) | % People Places ($n = 73$) | % Professional Parenting ($n = 35$) |
|---|---|---|---|
| Adoptive home | 1 | 11 | 20 |
| Relatives | 16 | 22 | 77 |
| Foster home | 26 | 69 | 71 |
| Emergency shelter | 57 | 17 | 40 |
| Group home | 29 | 25 | 39 |
| Child-care institution | 22 | 21 | 31 |
| Wilderness camp | 3 | 0 | 0 |
| Jail/Secure detention | 4 | 14 | 9 |
| Juvenile corrections institution | 5 | 3 | 11 |
| Psychiatric institution | 24 | 27 | 11 |
| Other | 4 | 15 | 0 |

velops. Children are removed from their homes, a variety of different types of placements are attempted over a period averaging three to four years, they are not successful, and, finally, the child is referred to a TFC program.

## Problems of Biological Parents

The role of dysfunctional parents in raising children who develop problems is well documented (see chapter 8, in this volume). Thus, it is no surprise that children entering the three TFC programs come from families characterized by multiple and serious problems. Data on biological parents were collected by a review of each child's files, including social histories, psychological evaluations, and other file notes. Since the data were collected per child, if either parent had a particular problem, it was counted. Marital discord, histories of alcohol and substance abuse, and histories of emotional or psychiatric disturbance were present in many of the parents (refer to table 4). Also documented were findings of parental physical and sexual abuse of their children.

## History of Abuse Toward Child

Many of the children in each of the three programs had been victims of either physical or sexual abuse (refer to table 5). Data were collected by counting the number of children who had either confirmed or suspected histories of abuse described in their case files; however, cases of suspected abuse often do not appear in case files because of state child abuse laws on documenting this information. The actual proof of sexual abuse is sometimes not pursued in courts because a lesser charge can accomplish the same legal end (i.e., removal of the child from the parent) with less difficulty. Nevertheless, a scrutiny of each child's records for reasonably clear evidence that the child had been victimized revealed that approximately one-half of the children in each of the three programs had been victims of physical abuse. About one-half of the children in PRYDE and Professional Parenting, and one-fourth of the children in People Places, had histories of being sexually abused.

## History of Pre-Referral Problems

Assessment of a child's history of pre-referral behavior problems was difficult because of the widely varying depth and content of docu-

## TABLE 4
### *Problems of Biological Parents*

| | % PRYDE (n = 76) | % People Places (n = 73) | % Professional Parenting (n = 35) |
|---|---|---|---|
| Alcohol or substance abuse | 39 | 23 | 51 |
| History of emotional disturbance or psychiatric hospitalization | 26 | 26 | 54 |
| Marital discord | 41 | 55 | 77 |
| Imprisonment | 24* | 12 | 20 |
| Felon/miscreant | 18 | 19 | 14 |
| Unemployment | 54** | 17 | 63 |
| Physical or sexual abuse of children | 39 | 44 | 54 |
| Child neglect or dependency ruled by court | 89 | 23 | 43 |
| Child abandonment | 18 | 18 | 14 |
| Deceased | 11 | 18 | 29 |

Note: *These data were collected per child so that either one of a biological parent with a particular problem could be counted.*

*n = 37 (remaining, "don't know")

**n = 33 (remaining, "don't know")

mentation and uncertainty as to the degree to which persons contributing to the referral information actually knew the children. In some cases, documentation was poor and content covered only the few months before placement in the program; however, the opposite was also occasionally the case. Some files, for example, contained extensively detailed descriptions of both the child's problems since birth and those of the biological families. In the more detailed case histories from all three programs, it was not difficult to identify 20 behavior problems per child. By contrast, more brief or cursory histories often failed to note even the children's most significant problems.

Twenty-five problem behavior categories were identified. Data compilation was carried out by program staff members for Professional Parenting and People Places and was based on referral information, social histories, and psychological evaluations provided by referring agencies. PRYDE data are based on a 15-item problem area checklist provided by

## TABLE 5
*Suspected or Confirmed History of Abuse in Children*

|                | %<br>PRYDE<br>($n = 49\star$) | %<br>People<br>Places<br>($n = 73$) | %<br>Professional<br>Parenting<br>($n = 35$) |
|----------------|:---:|:---:|:---:|
| Sexual abuse   | 50  | 27  | 51  |
| Physical abuse | 57  | 45  | 51  |

*Information only available for 49 children

Allegheny County Children and Youth Services and completed by the children's caseworkers some time before referral to PRYDE.

The most striking observation on the history of problems is the severity and variety of problems that are evident among the children served by the three programs (refer to table 6). Furthermore, most children have experienced multiple problems. PRYDE children presented an average of 6.2 problems per child; People Places, 7.4 problems per child; and Professional Parenting, 11.3 problems per child.

Some problem behaviors are common across all three programs. For example, various types of school problems, histories of verbal and pha-tion on the history of problems is the severity and variety of problems that are evident among the childr and peer relationship problems are all frequently reported at rates ranging from 40 percent to 80 percent. As revealing as these kinds of behaviors are in demonstrating the level of difficulty the children served by each of the three programs presented, some of the less frequently reported problems are, when they occur, extremely difficult, and also demonstrate the flexibility of the three programs in providing care for children with severe problems. For example, medical problems are not frequently reported, but the three programs have served children who have spina bifida, cerebral palsy, and AIDS. Similarly, low percentages were reported for self-destructiveness, which includes such serious problems as head banging, cutting, and self-mutilation.

The individual problems in each category represent a management challenge for any caretaker. But, on average, a child referred to any of the three programs is characterized by multiple sets of problems ranging from simply difficult to extremely difficult, thus magnifying the management task.

## Adjudication as Delinquent or Status Offender

Apart from the foregoing data, each program's sample of children was also reviewed to determine how many children had penetrated the juvenile justice system to the point of formal adjudication. Because juvenile cases are often informally diverted from adjudication even though the child has committed a juvenile offense, the data reported in

TABLE 6
*Pre-Referral Behavioral Problems of Children*

| Problem | % PRYDE ($n = 76$) | % People Places ($n = 73$) | % Professional Parenting ($n = 35$) |
|---|---|---|---|
| Incorrigible | ★ | 33 | 69 |
| Peer relationship problems | ★ | 44 | 80 |
| Overly dependent | 45 | 6 | 29 |
| Poor self-concept | 56 | 51 | 86 |
| Depression/withdrawal | 35 | 30 | 63 |
| Destruction of property | 20 | 33 | 37 |
| Medical poroblems (physical) | 7 | 14 | 20 |
| Medical problems (psychological) | 1 | 25 | 9 |
| Drug abuse/experimentation | 12 | 22 | 34 |
| Encopresis/enuresis | 13 | 21 | 11 |
| Hallucinations/delusions/mood swings | 25 | 8 | 20 |
| Hyperactivity/autism | 15 | 26 | 14 |
| Runs away | 21 | 33 | 54 |
| Truancy | 11 | 11 | 37 |
| School (social) | 27 | 58 | 74 |
| School (academic) | 37 | 47 | 63 |
| School (learning disability) | 3 | 37 | 37 |
| Suicide attempts/threats | 9 | 14 | 26 |
| Self-destructive | 5 | 11 | 17 |
| Sexual problems | 25 | 33 | 54 |
| Tantrums | 36 | 44 | 57 |
| Verbally/Physically aggressive (adult) | 73 | 40 | 51 |
| Verbally/Physically aggressive (child) | 73 | 45 | 71 |
| Dishonest behavior | 53 | 41 | 83 |
| Mentally retarded | 11 | 12 | 31 |
| Average number of problems per child | 6.2 | 7.4 | 11.3 |

★These problem areas were not definable from referral data.

this section underrepresent the actual frequency of such offenses. Categories of status offense (offenses not illegal if the person were an adult, e.g., running away, truancy, out of parental control) and delinquent offenses (felonies or misdemeanors if committed by an adult) were used for People Places and Professional Parenting. Since Pennsylvania has no formal adjudication of status offenders, PRYDE could not indicate those children who are labeled status offender by the courts because youngsters engaging in status offenses are more commonly adjudicated dependent/neglected.

About 26 percent and 6 percent of the children admitted to Professional Parenting and People Places were formally labeled status offenders. PRYDE counts about half of its population to be youngsters with histories of status offenses, and 89 percent of the admissions in PRYDE are children adjudicated dependent/neglected (refer to table 7). About one-third of Professional Parenting children had been formally adjudicated for delinquent offenses, and 11 percent and 10 percent, respectively, for PRYDE and People Places children. Thus, Professional Parenting had a majority of children who were formally entering the juvenile justice system. This situation was less often the case for People Places and PRYDE, due to either client or systems differences.

## Length of Stay

Do the three programs represent another residential effort that failed or are they providing stabilizing environments that produce enduring placements for the children? In addition to data on client characteristics, each program submitted data on the number of re-placements in different treatment homes while under the supervision of the program, and the length of stay with the program. Criteria for inclusion of the data were as described at the beginning of the chapter. For purposes of determining frequency of re-placements with program families and length of stay in the program, however, a 15-month follow-up period was established. Children who were still in the program at the end of the specified 12-month interval were tracked for an additional 15 months.

All three programs aspire to have the first treatment home endure for the child while in the program. Nevertheless, for a variety of reasons, a child must at times be placed in another home. Some of the reasons include *(1)* problem behavior of a child that prompts a request by a treatment family for that child's removal; *(2)* discovery by a family that they no longer want to be treatment parents (when this instance happens,

TABLE 7
*Legal Status*

| | %<br>PRYDE<br>($n=76$) | %<br>People<br>Places<br>($n=73$) | %<br>Professional<br>Parenting<br>($n=35$) |
|---|---|---|---|
| Formal Adjudication<br>Status offense★ | N/A | 6 | 26 |
| Formal Adjudication<br>Delinquent | 11 | 10 | 31 |

★Status Offense: Age-related offense, such as running away or truancy

*Note:* These data include cases only where a child was formally adjudicated as a status offender or delinquent child. Not included are cases where a diversion was used or no formal finding was established. N/A for PRYDE is due to Pennsylvania lacking formal adjudication of status offenses.

it is usually by a newly licensed family; *(3)* marital discord, separation, or divorce within the treatment family; and *(4)* a serious or sustained request for re-placement by the child. Approximately half of the children during this period in all three programs had no re-placements. Approximately 25 percent of the children in all three programs were relocated one or two times. Only one child had more than three re-placements: an extremely difficult child was placed in eight different homes over a period of 11 years, but he has been sustained for over four years in his last treatment home (refer to table 8).

## Summary

The questions that were posed at the beginning of this chapter were: What kinds of children do the programs serve and how well are they

TABLE 8
*Moves from One Treatment Family to Another Within Program*

| | Program Families | | | | |
|---|---|---|---|---|---|
| | 1st | 2nd | 3rd | 4th | 8th |
| % PRYDE children | 60 | 26 | 11 | 3 | |
| % People Places children | 47 | 32 | 11 | 10 | 1 |
| % Professional parenting children | 57 | 17 | 12 | 14 | |

sustained in placement? The data demonstrate that children entering the three programs are difficult and come from problematic families, where both the parents and the children exhibit a variety of problems. On the average, the children are first placed out-of-home for about four years, in a number of different residential programs, and enter a TFC program near the onset of their adolescence. Clearly, the need for placement outside the home is well documented, and the need for therapeutic care is substantiated. The potential for becoming part of the revolving door of child care is significant, yet these three programs appear to be able to stabilize children within a small and limited number of foster families.

# 3

# Recruiting and Selecting Treatment Parents

NANCY GROSS

AND

PAT CAMPBELL

RECRUITING AND SELECTING PARENTS to provide therapeutic foster care (TFC) is an extremely important and difficult task in creating and sustaining a workable program. Traditional foster care programs as well as those following the foster family treatment model invariably face recruitment difficulties. Though standard strategies for recruiting traditional foster parents are widely available, these strategies are often unable to produce parents for treatment-oriented programs. Treatment parents are not traditional foster parents; since the treatment function includes substantially more than custodial care, recruitment must address this difference. Strategies for successfully recruiting and selecting parents, based on the experiences reported by People Places, Professional Parenting, and PRYDE, are the focus of this chapter.

Planning, preparation, and plain hard work are the fundamental requirements for successful treatment parent recruitment. The care and re-education experiences required to help a troubled and troubling child demand an enormous commitment from a family. Recruiting homes for adolescents presents a special difficulty. Families tend to be less confident that they can deal with adolescent problems than with those of younger children, and they often fear that adolescents will adversely affect their own children. Pessimism abounds among recruiters of homes for adolescents:

> Adolescence is a tough development stage no matter how you cut it. Even in the "ideal" adolescent home there can be a high placement failure rate. This is not to say that homes for adolescents cannot or should not be recruited. It is simply that to my knowledge no one has discovered a foolproof or clearly successful way to do it. Results I have received from recruitment programs are clearly less dramatic in relation to recruiting adolescent homes. [Meltzner 1984]

Although recruitment may be difficult, it is not impossible. People Places, Professional Parenting, and PRYDE have all mounted successful, albeit sometimes problematic, recruitment campaigns. Common strategies are described first. Subsequent discussion considers differences or innovations unique to each program. Finally, the results in terms of families recruited by the shared and program-specific strategies are presented.

## Common Recruitment Components

### *Planning a Recruitment Campaign*

As with any difficult and multifaceted task, thoughtful preparation is essential. Whenever possible, a group should be involved; two heads really are better than one. Planning begins with questions. Who is the client population? What kinds of families might best serve this population? How can such families be reached? Planning should proceed from the answers to these questions. For example, if staff members think that working-class families would best suit the needs of their children, an article in an industrial plant newspaper or a presentation by program staff members at a plant staff meeting might be in order. Recruitment details, such as what to say when people make phone inquiries and what to do after the telephone conversations, must be carefully considered.

## Scheduling Recruitment Campaigns

Recruitment generally must be continual, for program growth and for replacing parents who leave. Sporadic recruiting is not productive. There can, however, be periods of increased campaign activities at certain times during the year. In between, the program staff should remain available to respond to all community inquiries and to take advantage of recruitment opportunities that arise spontaneously, such as an invitation to address a PTA or a local meeting of church leaders who may serve as resources for recruits. Summertime and holidays are unproductive times to recruit, for obvious reasons. Intensive recruitment activities should take place during the spring and fall months.

## Recruiting Media and Campaign Duration

Recruitment campaigns should span at least a week and take advantage of as many media resources as possible, so that potential applicants see or hear an agency's name more than once and in more than one place. Recruitment resources include posters, billboards, word of mouth, radio spots, display ads, presentations, newspapers, TV, and so on, within the limits, of course, of the amount of money, staff time, and other resources an agency has available.

## Stressing the Challenge of Professional Parenting

Traditional foster care or adoptive parent recruitment campaigns often appeal to the public's love of children and natural sympathies for homeless children. If the sympathy approach is used, perhaps by telling tragic stories or showing sad pictures, people tend to apply for well-intended but inappropriate reasons, such as "saving" a poor, neglected, abused child. This approach may, unfortunately, distract prospective candidates from the more important considerations of the added stress inherent in treatment parenting, the inevitable time and energy commitment required, and the discouragements that can happen. Couples entering a program with admirable but naive motivations are often quickly disillusioned and withdraw.

Recruitment information should, therefore, stress the professional challenges of the job, with predictable problems and pitfalls, thereby establishing more realistic expectations among potential recruits. Emphasis on the potential of treatment parenting as a career, on earning a second income, and on opportunities to grow personally and professionally through pre-service and in-service training creates a highly professional image of the role of treatment parents. This image is important in countering the traditionally negative reputation of foster parents as nonprofessionals at the bottom rung of the social services ladder.

## Responding to Program Inquiries from the Community

Recruitment must be a continuing priority for a program to remain in existence. All inquiries from the community must receive serious attention and enthusiasm even when the caller is not a potential applicant but is simply interested in learning about the services. Staff members can enlist all callers as recruiters by asking them to share program information with others who may be interested. First impressions are important; obviously, when an interested caller is treated casually, unenthusiastically, or unprofessionally, the recruitment potential drops dramatically.

All persons expected to respond to phone inquiries, especially secretaries or others not directly involved in service delivery, must have all the necessary information and understand the importance of the manner and style with which calls should be handled. Initial training in responding to inquiries works well with the staff at all levels.

## Following Up on Program Inquiries from the Community

After an initial inquiry, staff members must follow up promptly to keep the applicant's motivation level high. When candidates are not contacted for several weeks, they tend to lose interest. If a training/ orientation session has been scheduled, follow-up calls or letters should be used to arrange interviews or request additional information. When several weeks or even months will elapse between an initial inquiry and training, periodic (e.g., biweekly) contact can be used to complete required paperwork and to sustain the applicant's interest. Potential applicants often require several phone contacts before they feel sufficiently confident and informed to apply.

## Meaningful Compensation of Treatment Parents

A major adventitious difference between TFC and regular foster care is the substantially higher payment offered to treatment parents. Traditionally, foster parent compensation has been insufficient even to meet expenses. Through meaningful compensation, TFC is able to distinguish itself as a specialized program, which, in turn, supports the emphasis on the parents as professionals. Higher levels of compensation also allow the agency to represent the therapeutic foster care enterprise honestly in terms of having a job at home, a concept that appears to enjoy broad appeal. Higher rates of compensation will also result in larger numbers of interested and available families.

# Program-Specific Recruitment Strategies

## People Places

The evolution of People Places' recruitment strategy has followed a pattern similar to that of the Alberta program, a specialized foster care agency that conducted a comprehensive evaluation of recruitment methods [Larson et al. 1978]. This evaluation compared three general tactics: *(1)* informal contacts with potential applicants and sporadic radio and newspaper advertisements; *(2)* formal identification of potential applicants by addressing community organizations, in addition to radio and newspaper advertisements; and *(3)* formalized sharing of information through radio and television ads, news releases, talk shows, and newspaper articles and advertisements that emphasized specialized foster care as a career opportunity, especially for women, with a reasonable salary and professional support. All inquiries were followed up promptly with additional information and an invitation to attend an orientation session. Not surprisingly, the third approach yielded substantially more initial inquiries about the program.

Similarly, People Places initially relied upon classified advertisements and followed up on all referrals that came from other, less formal sources (e.g., word of mouth); from the start, treatment parenting as a career opportunity with good income was emphasized. As the responses diminished over several years, recruitment continued to emphasize treatment parenting as a career opportunity that could provide a good second income, but other considerations were added. One, which continues today, is the point that treatment parenting is a professional enterprise offering opportunities to work with a team of professionals who are available 24 hours a day for support and consultation. Second, recruitment targets families in which the mother is not employed outside the home and sees her parenting role as an important and primary activity. A third strategy derives from the agency's experience that the most effective parents have been those recruited by current treatment families. A bonus payment—a kind of finder's fee—is offered for help in recruiting a family who later completes training. Before each recruitment campaign, the agency invites the support of its "recruiting" families and supplies them with brochures to distribute to friends and acquaintances.

People Places also coordinates its recruitment efforts among several different media that prospective treatment parents will encounter, such as classified ads, public service announcements on local television and radio stations, and brochures distributed around the community to family-style restaurants and other businesses frequented by their treatment parent population. Recruitment campaigns are begun in fall, winter, and spring, several weeks in advance of training sessions so that ads can run for two or three weeks. Essentially, the campaign saturates all media resources for the two- to three-week recruiting period.

People Places constructs ads and brochures in ways important for effective use of the media: *(1)* the ads are appealing and catch readers' attention; *(2)* they emphasize therapeutic foster care as a career at home; *(3)* they accent certain personal qualities essential to do an effective job, such as enjoying the challenge of solving problems and the ability to keep commitments; and *(4)* they include a composite description of a typical youth's referral problems, needs, and family situation. Figure 1 represents two examples of ads.

## Professional Parenting

Initially, Professional Parenting experienced a great deal of difficulty in recruiting families. Reviewing its mistakes may prove beneficial to emerging programs or programs considering different recruitment strategies. Its first recruitment campaign relied on direct mail, consisting of information about the program and a questionnaire directed at respondent interest in becoming a special foster parent. Of 950 mailings to professionals such as social workers, teachers, and court counselors, 187 questionnaires were returned and, ultimately, four families were trained. All of these families withdrew from the program within a year.

The next campaign involved public advertising. Once a week for three consecutive weeks a classified ad was placed in five different county newspapers. This approach yielded no families who completed the pre-service training. During this time, a few families learned of the program

---

## FOR THOSE WHO WANT
## A DIFFERENT DEFINITION OF
## SUCCESS

As a teaching Foster Parent with People Places, success will be defined by the work you do and how you do it. You'll know you are doing a job for which high standards have been set. You'll face situations that challenge your parenting ability. You'll work with a team of professionals. And you'll know the satisfaction of completing demanding tasks successfully. Orientation sessions begin March 6 at 7:30 P.M. Call 555-8841. People Places is a private, nonprofit special foster care agency.

---

## WE FIND WINNERS!

Winners are families that can make and keep commitments. They are families that can share themselves and their lives with children in need. If your family has the time and commitment to work with young people like Connie, a black 16-year-old who has been abused, runs away, and has a low self-image, call People Places, 555-8841. We are looking for people interested in training to become Teaching Foster Parents. Professional support provided. Orientation sessions begin March 6. People Places is a private, nonprofit special foster care agency.

---

*Figure 1. People Places ads.*

through word of mouth, but these recruiting efforts did not produce enough successfully trained families to sustain the program.

Aiming primarily at the professional community, in the agency's particular setting, did not yield many interested applicants, and the academic language purposely used in the mailed recruitment materials failed to attract nonprofessional, working-class applicants. In addition, advertising was done sporadically, and only one medium was used at a time.

Following these early failures, Professional Parenting adopted many of the strategies employed by People Places that are now common to successful recruitment campaigns. Recruitment is presently continual, with intensive campaigns of two to three weeks' duration occurring four or five times a year. Before each campaign, staff members discuss new recruiting methods and improvements in current procedures. Specific staff members are designated for each recruitment activity. Recruitment messages are designed to appeal to working-class families and consist of eye-catching, easy-to-read promotional literature and advertisements in the classified or sports section of local newspapers. In addition, personal invitations to apply to the program are extended via speaking engagements at churches, PTAs, and other community, family-oriented organizations. The emphasis of all recruitment messages is on the potential of foster family treatment as a career at home that requires special, personal qualities, instead of a particular occupational or educational background.

## PRYDE

PRYDE Pittsburgh approaches recruitment somewhat differently from either of the other two programs. First, PRYDE staff members direct recruitment to middle-class, fairly well-educated people; the other programs focus on nonprofessional families in the lower and middle classes. This choice depends on several factors: *(1)* the community in which the program is located (urban vs. rural), thus determining to a large extent the pool of potential applicants; *(2)* the design of the program in terms of extent of training requirements and on-the-job responsibilities such as documentation of treatment; *(3)* pressures toward growth, which may create a strong dependence on those who initially call and apply; and *(4)* a program's history of effectiveness with different types of people (e.g., PRYDE finds middle-class parents to be effective treatment agents while Professional Parenting has experienced success with working-class parents).

This history or track record, based on different kinds of families as treatment families, determines the population of core families in that the initial families largely determine a program's future pool of families. Subsequent recruits' interest in the program is often influenced by the degree to which they can identify with parents already in the program, and subsequent applicants are often recruited through current certified parents, who recruit families like themselves. New programs must therefore recruit their first group of treatment parents with extreme care.

PRYDE's first recruitment efforts, like the other programs' efforts, were difficult and frustrating. Public presentations at PTA meetings or meetings of teachers at school (a targeted audience) did not produce much interest. Better results emerged from repeated mailings to their targeted audiences (middle-class individuals who have a long-term commitment to helping others, such as school and church personnel) and networking with community leaders. Campaigns that initially produced only one recruit after two months gradually evolved so that now there are five to 15 families routinely available for each training workshop and about two calls per week from interested families.

Unlike Professional Parenting and People Places, PRYDE Pittsburgh uses personal networking by both staff members and PRYDE parents as its principal recruitment strategy now that it has a well-established core of PRYDE parents. It has found that face-to-face or person-to-person recruitment produces excellent results in terms of both the number and quality of parents recruited. Since nearly all PRYDE parents have had no experience as foster parents, their entry into this program is foreign to them and requires a personal touch to dispel uncertainties regarding the nature of the job. PRYDE Pittsburgh reports that 62 percent of its parents were recruited during its first five years through networking. Staff members and current treatment parents talk with friends, co-workers, relatives, or community contacts about the program. Treatment parents learn during in-service training workshops how to tell about their PRYDE experiences in a way that will inspire others to consider applying to the program. Home recruitment meetings, in which friends of treatment parents meet at a PRYDE home with one or two central PRYDE staff members, show particular promise. Refreshments are served, and potential applicants can have their questions about the program answered by an experienced staff person. Those who show interest are given an application to complete during the meeting. Meetings resemble Tupperware parties—friends know that the purpose of the evening party is to consider become a PRYDE parent.

A second commonly used recruitment method at PRYDE is mailing campaigns. Letters describe the program and highlight treatment parenting as a home-based job opportunity for youth-oriented couples. Brochures and attractive flyers showing pictures of children and parents in different activities are sent to dozens or, on occasion, hundreds of individuals in local schools, colleges, universities, and churches. When possible, individuals' names are used instead of "Dear Colleague" in order to personalize the communication. If a staff member knows the individual, a personal note may be written on the letter. The recipient is asked to post the information where interested persons will see it. All letters state that someone from the PRYDE office will call the recipient of the letter within two weeks to discuss the results of the posted information, a tactic that increases the likelihood that the recipient will, in fact, post the brochure. Schools, colleges, universities, and churches are targeted, since these institutions have proven to be productive sources of good applicants, and since individuals with some education and possibly career commitment to children are considered important prospects for PRYDE parenting. One mailing to a secondary school caught the attention of a teacher whose sister eventually became an outstanding PRYDE parent. Another mailing was seen by a student in a social work master's program, and he and his wife eventually became PRYDE's "Treatment Parents of the Year." He has recruited his parents, his wife's parents, his sister, and his college fraternity brother, who in turn recruited his parents, who in turn recruited all of their sisters and brothers.

During PRYDE's first year, staff members discovered what they believe is an important ingredient to successful recruitment: every program presentation, whether by mail or in person, must end with a request for public commitment on the part of audience members. A description of TFC is nothing more than education for the audience, as opposed to strong recruitment, if there is no request for a show of hands of those interested in becoming treatment parents or those who may know of someone else who might be interested. Recruitment must use effective selling strategies such as the "close" to every sale presentation, which normally involves a commitment to purchase the product. Letters that request posting of brochures also can incorporate something similar to a close by informing the recipient of the letter that a PRYDE staff member will be calling to see if anyone has expressed an interest in the posted brochure. Public commitment and follow-through on presentations or mailings are key procedures for maximizing the effectiveness of foster family treatment recruitment.

Word of mouth can be considered yet another recruitment strategy, which occurs when incidental conversation about the program generates interest and a phone inquiry follows. It differs from personal networking in that the latter is a planned effort and word of mouth is not. It is also considered word of mouth when a family responds to the application question "Where did you hear about this program?" with the answer "From a friend." PRYDE reports that 33 percent of their treatment families in Pittsburgh were recruited through word of mouth in the first five years of the program. It works when treatment parents and personnel in other agencies are enthusiastic about the program, which means that PRYDE's contacts with treatment parents, other agencies, and the public in general must be positive, cheerful, and enthusiastic, so that people want to be a part of something special.

PRYDE historically limited its use of personal appearances on television talk shows, newspaper articles, and block advertisements mainly because these media do not allow for any public commitment from an audience. PRYDE was reluctant to use classified ads for several reasons: *(1)* to avoid recruiting traditional foster parents, who often come with incorrect expectations of this job; *(2)* to avoid the time-consuming task of screening many inappropriate applications (an advantage of face-to-face recruitment is that appropriate applicants are more likely); and *(3)* current treatment parents reported that they would not have responded to a typical foster care classified ad because they did not want foster care, they wanted a professional growth opportunity with reasonable pay. PRYDE Pittsburgh early in its history used a block ad that was attractive, emphasized a professional growth opportunity, and appeared next to the largest readership column (Ann Landers) on Mother's Day; yet only five couples inquired and none completed an application. The failure to produce more inquiries, however, may have happened because the ad did not include information on parent payment. After the program had been operating for five years, and most notably in PRYDE Maryland, newspaper advertising was used more successfully. Over 30 percent of the treatment families in West Virginia and nearly all of the foster families in Maryland were recruited from classified advertising.

And finally, PRYDE requires its staff members to target certain numbers of recruits by certain dates in order to produce a programwide commitment to specific recruitment results. During the planning phases of each recruitment campaign, staff members agree on the number of applicants that they will produce, and at the same time agree on the goal number of graduates from the next training. The weekly status of goals is displayed on a chart or reviewed in staff meetings. Thus the staff has week-by-week feedback on the progress of recruitment and can intensify the drive if the interim goal is not achieved.

## Selection

Although treatment parent recruitment and selection are, in many respects, different processes, recruitment serves an important selection function. Recruitment efforts focused on civic groups and school-related organizations, for example, will produce a different pool of potential candidates from those focused exclusively on church congregations. Hence, decisions about desirable versus undesirable applicant characteristics must be made before the first recruitment efforts.

When a pool of interested and available candidates has been recruited, the formal selection process begins. Three categories of selection variables should be considered during the screening of applicants for pre-service training: *(1)* the agency's licensing criteria; *(2)* the applicant's parenting skills; and *(3)* the applicant's character or reputation. The following paragraphs describe each of these categories, how each is assessed, and whether strict adherence to certain standards is necessary within each category.

### Licensing Criteria

Licensing criteria refer to the minimal requirements established by each state concerning the prospective foster family's home, health status, ages, and other state-mandated standards. TFC agencies licensed under foster care regulations will become thoroughly familiar with the rules and standards for selecting foster parents in their states. Whether prospective treatment families and their homes meet these standards is usually evaluated during phone conversations, review of applications, fire and health inspections, a home inspection by program staff, and from results of physical examinations. If a family is lacking in some of these respects, adjustments in the deficiency may be possible. For example, if a very promising couple has five children of their own and state foster care regulations prohibit more than five children (foster children plus biological children), then a waiver through state procedures for this regulation may be possible. Adaptations in other areas, however, often are difficult or impossible to make. If the bedrooms in a family's home are smaller than the regulations require, for instance, that family would have to be dropped, and any further consideration of their suitability on other grounds could not be justified.

### Parenting Skills

The second set of criteria, parenting skills, is probably the most critical and also the most difficult to evaluate. All three core agencies, through experience and close observation of successful and unsuccessful couples, have derived a set of parenting qualities they search for in applicants. The presence or absence of these qualities is assessed during an interview and/or during pre-service training by evaluating the applicants' participation in discussions, behavior rehearsals, and responses to orally presented youth-treatment parent vignettes. The following qualities normally are evaluated.

First, treatment parents sometimes expect disturbed and disturbing children to be able to function in the same manner, academically and socially, as their biological children. The treatment parent's ability to set realistic expectations, or to modify unrealistic ones when warranted, is important.

Second, whether it is the consistent use of natural consequences (e.g., the opportunity to watch television is a privilege) or a complex point system, treatment parents must accept the importance of and be willing to use systematically proven behavior management skills such as positive praise, contingent use of rewards, and other purposive reinforcement strategies for behavior change. Scolding and threatening (the unfulfilled promise of consequences) are not adequate substitutes for tangible behavior consequences or contingent use of praise.

Third, applicants must show a desire to learn, and not be offended by having their parenting skills supervised and, in many instances, altered through training and supervision.

Fourth, children with behavior problems need families who will help them work through their difficulties without quitting at the first sign of trouble. Therefore, applicants are evaluated on their estimated level of commitment and their tenacity in the face of frustrating circumstances.

When a parenting skill deficiency in any of these area is identified during an interview or pre-service training, the family's response to further instruction and rehearsal is likely to indicate whether the family is amenable to change. If so, the combination of on-the-job training and supervision may prove sufficient to remedy any difficulties.

## Character or Reputation

Finally, effective selection includes the assessment of a couple's personal, marital, family, legal, and career (financial) adjustment. Reference information and staff impressions serve as the principal sources of character information. References are requested from individuals such as neighbors, teachers, family physicians, ministers, and employers.

Applicant records are also checked through local court and welfare systems as well as the statewide protective service bureaus. Information from these sources is essential to ensure that the family is free of any previous experience that would potentially undermine their ability or suitability to work with special-needs children. When a negative reference is received or record of some personal problem found, consideration is given to its nature, severity, and recency. Decisions regarding problems in this category are necessarily conservative, because the option for changing any of the couple's current marital, career, or legal histories is generally limited or impossible.

In addition to these staff-determined selection variables, treatment parent candidates tend to assess spontaneously their own suitability to serve the program and often will, at various stages of the process, withdraw from further consideration. Applicants must be encouraged to assess themselves through each step of the application and certification process. In initial contacts, families decide whether they are possibly interested in becoming treatment parents. Next, they need the opportunity to learn more about the program so they can make an educated decision as to whether their family is suited for the responsibilities. This learning occurs when, during interviews and especially during the pre-service training, families receive candid information about the children, program expectations, and stresses involved. Only then can a family make an informed appraisal of their personal suitability for the job. Encouraging self-selection is a comfortable way to identify and discourage families who are unlikely to persist through problems and, therefore, increases the likelihood that families who remain in the program will provide stable, quality care and treatment for troubled children.

Staff members must be wary of personal feelings in judging families.

A particular staff member might not feel comfortable with a particular family, but the family might, nevertheless, be an excellent match for a troubled youth. Decisions regarding the acceptability of a family for treatment parenting should involve several staff members who compare their impressions of the couple and sort through the gathered information on the family.

## Recruiting and Selection Effectiveness

The three core programs have encountered varying levels of success with the recruiting and selection strategies described above. PRYDE Pittsburgh, owing in part to its location in a densely populated metropolitan area, reports that it enjoys a steady stream of qualified parent applicants, although it always seems to need more or different or stronger treatment families. The PRYDE staff points, in particular, to the success of the personal networking by staff members and especially active PRYDE parents, and in recent years to successful use of advertising.

People Places and Professional Parenting, conversely, continue to struggle to maintain pools of qualified and licensed families in their more rural and thus much less densely populated service areas. PRYDE's experience in rural West Virginia seems to reflect similar difficulties in recruiting sufficient numbers of highly qualified, well-educated treatment couples to maintain its population of 50 children.

The most significant loss of prospective candidates across all three programs occurs at the level of actual application; that is, when couples call in but fail to return the application materials subsequently sent to them. A substantial percentage, though a much smaller absolute number, of couples are lost at the level of training and, later, licensure. For example, over a six-month period PRYDE Pittsburgh received 198 calls from prospective parents but received only 57 applications (28 percent). From these applications, only 20 couples completed the training (10 percent), and 12 served children (6 percent of the initial pool of inquiries). The programs all continue to experiment with various refinements and adjustments aimed at minimizing attrition at all levels of their recruiting and selection process. Regardless of the efforts, however, TFC programs must be prepared to produce large numbers of inquiring couples since the selection, screening, and training process will reduce the initial pool substantially.

People Places has concentrated on reducing the attrition from the point of inquiry to certified treatment families. In three consecutive recruitment campaigns, the program was able to maintain 28 percent of its initial inquiries through the selection and training process. Despite this improvement, People Places continues to experience wide variation in the number of couples who initially inquire about the program, eventually complete the training, and then serve a child. One technique that the program has used to increase the percentage of couples who complete the screening and training process is relying more on strategies of personal networking by staff members and treatment parents, much like those employed by PRYDE. Direct person-to-person recruitment should reduce the number of inappropriate inquiries and the resulting need for screening out so many families.

Ideally, a TFC program will use potent recruitment strategies that produce high numbers of inquiring couples who are appropriate candidates for the job. Through the screening process, many of even these appropriate candidates will be eliminated as they learn of the required commitment and energy and inherent risks in treating troubled children within their homes.

The treatment parents who remain at the end of this vigorous, time-consuming screening show some fairly consistent demographics within each of the core programs. Approximately two-thirds of the PRYDE Pittsburgh parents have had educational training beyond high school, whereas in the other programs nearly the reverse is true—two-thirds of the parents have not had educational training beyond high school. There are several possible explanations for this difference. First, Professional Parenting and People Places both aim their recruitment at populations without college experience, with whom they have had most success. PRYDE initially targeted a better-educated population because of its training requirements and level of treatment parent responsibilities. Because it was successful with this population of treatment parents, it continues its recruitment efforts for couples with education or training beyond high school. Second, PRYDE Pittsburgh's urban location provides a larger number of educated parents from whom to recruit. Finally, PRYDE pays a higher monthly stipend, which may attract more highly educated parents.

The average age for treatment parents working for People Places is in the middle forties whereas both Professioal Parenting and PRYDE treatment parents' ages are around 37 years old. Most of the families in the three core programs have biological children. The average number per family is three at Professional Parenting, twice the average for People Places. PRYDE's figure is in between, 2.2 children.

Professional Parenting had couples with the largest number of years married, an average of 18 years. People Places and PRYDE showed close averages of 12 years and 11 years, respectively. One finding across all programs is that most couples are married for a substantial period of time before entering the therapeutic foster care program.

By mid-1984, People Places, with over 12 years of operating experience, had treatment families averaging 47.59 months of service; Professional Parenting, four years in operation, had treatment families averaging 20.69 months of service; and PRYDE, with three years of operating experience, had treatment parents averaging 17.42 months of service.

As for the ethnic distribution of the foster parents, percentages for People Places and Professional Parenting roughly correspond to the ethnic percentages in their localities. For instance, 27 percent of People Places' treatment parents are black compared to 20 percent of the population. Professional Parenting is located in rural North Carolina where 7 percent of the population is black; 6.7 percent of their foster parents are black. PRYDE Pittsburgh with 57 percent black foster parents, however, is located in a county where only about 12 percent of the population is black and where the city population is about 20 percent black. PRYDE attributes its large population of talented black treatment parents to early, vigorous recruitment of strong black families. These families, in turn, have since recruited their relatives, and so on.

The task of recruiting, selecting, and maintaining treatment foster parents is increasingly becoming a priority among the growing TFC programs. It is also likely to become increasingly difficult as the demographics of families in this country change, and insufficient pay to treatment parents persists. Evidence of the increasing need for treatment parents appears everywhere, from federally funded programs for improvements in recruitment, selection, and retention of foster parents to the results of recent surveys that indicate recruitment of treatment parents, especially for troubled teens, is the greatest barrier to the development of this model of care [Child Welfare League of America 1987]. The experience of the three programs represented in this book, however, indicates that even in the face of historic and current difficulties, families can be found for troubled children and adolescents. It takes commitment, energy, creativity, and a strong belief that many families want to make a difference in children's lives; they need only to learn how that can be possible by becoming treatment parents.

## REFERENCES

Child Welfare League of America The Shortage of Foster Family Homes: A National Dilemma. Washington, D.C.: CWLA, 1987.

Larson, G.; Allison, J.; and Johnston, E. Alberta parent counselors: A community treatment program for disturbed youth. Child Welfare LVII: 47–52, 1978.

Meltzner, S.R. The Road to Quality Foster Care: A Comprehensive Recruitment Manual. King George, VA: American Foster Care Resources, Inc., 1984.

# 4

# Referring to, and Placing Children in, Treatment Homes

EILEEN MARY GREALISH
AND
PAMELA MEADOWCROFT

CHILDREN ENTER A THERAPEUTIC foster care (TFC) program through a referral process that begins when a referring agency sends documentation of a child's troublesome behavior to the placement agency. The process ends after the child is placed in a treatment home. The time from receipt of referral to placement may vary from a day to several months.

The referring agency has several objectives in making such a referral. First, the referring agency must secure an appropriate, effective placement for the child in the least restrictive setting. Trends within the mental health field and recent legislation necessitate placement in a setting as close to normal as possible while still being able to meet the child's educational and treatment needs. In most cases, the least restrictive residential setting is a home. Consequently, TFC programs, because they are home-based yet serve children who require special services, are fairly nonrestrictive placements. The second objective of the referring agency is to give the child the best available placement without regard to the child's race, age, or religious preferences. Third, the referring agency, as public custodian of the child, must conserve public funds by choosing a cost-effective setting.

The goals of the referral process differ for the agency providing the residential services. First, the provider agency must identify those children who can best be served in its particular type of setting. Second, the information obtained in the referral process allows the provider agency to begin developing appropriate educational and treatment plans. And third, when the provider agency is a TFC program, the referral information is essential to choosing an appropriate family. Proper matching of a child with a family maximizes the chances for a successful placement, and is therefore considered a key element in the referral process.

## Referral

Referrals for TFC come from those agencies responsible for placement of children away from home. Thus the large majority of children referred for placement in TFC come through the local or state child welfare agency or juvenile court that has custody. Typically, if the youth is an adjudicated delinquent, then the referral source is juvenile court; if the child is a status offender or otherwise termed dependent, then the referral source is the public child welfare agency, although both the court and the agency may be involved with other educational and mental health agencies. None of the children placed in treatment homes of the three programs in this volume was directly referred by their biological parents, although TFC programs do exist where parents maintain custody and voluntarily place their children through mental health agencies (for example, Parent Therapist Program, Akron, Ohio). Table 1 illustrates the percentage of referrals that come from the two major sources for the three core programs.

To determine if a child is appropriate for TFC, several kinds of referral information are necessary. First, a family history of the child enables the receiving agency to determine if return home is a realistic goal and points to the likely length of stay. This history should portray the current quality of relationships among family members, the level of involvement of the family, recent and historic problems the child has had within the family, any additional stresses the family has experienced or is now experiencing, and the reasons why the child requires services outside the home. TFC programs also require recent psychological and/or psychiatric evaluations of the child. These diagnostic summaries provide information on the extent and nature of the child's troublesome behavior and can also include recommendations concerning the appropriate setting and educational placement of the child. School records help the staff in considering educational plans and possible foster families. The great majority of children in the programs have had significant levels of school failure. A medical history is necessary to determine whether the available treatment parents can meet particular medical needs the child may have. Some handicapped or medicated children may need to be placed with foster parents who have or are willing to learn special medical skills. And, finally, referral information must include a thorough description of the child's recent problematic behavior—including reasons why the most recent placement is no longer feasible and why the child's situation requires a treatment foster home rather than regular foster care.

Appropriate, individualized treatment planning, including steps necessary for preventing a particular child's misbehaviors, depends on full, accurate information, including the frequency and severity of the behavior problems. Treatment parents must have full access to (or be fully informed of) the child's record. Full information on a child in need of out-of-home treatment is often difficult to get. The staff must be prepared to follow up each written referral by discussions about the child with the referring agency staff and anyone else who knows the child well.

Children who enter TFC homes have a variety of problems— behavioral, emotional, and, in some instances, physical difficulties. The population is generally characterized by truancy; disruptive behavior in school or the community; running away; verbal and physical aggression toward adults, peers, or younger children; depression; suicidal thoughts or actions; physical abuse of animals; theft; substance abuse;

TABLE 1
*Sources of Referrals for the Three TFC Programs*

| Program | % Public Child Welfare | % Juvenile Court |
|---|---|---|
| PRYDE | 93 | 7 |
| People Places | 87 | 13 |
| Professional Parenting | 100 | 0 |

property destruction; sexual promiscuity; or failure to thrive. Although the three programs report having children with borderline intelligence (IQs 69–79), none of the three is specifically designed to work with mentally handicapped children; similar programs have, however, been developed for this group.

Some problems may deter acceptance of a child into a treatment parenting program. A recent history of arson, which poses an obvious possible danger to the family, could potentially exclude a child, although PRYDE has served several children for whom fire-setting was a major problem, and People Places is treating children with this problem. Serious, uncontrollable aggressive behavior on the part of a large child can be another barrier to acceptance, but because of the degree of individualization possible in a treatment home, some highly assaultive children can be placed if foster parents are available who possess the skills and family composition to handle them. In all cases, the final acceptance standard appears to be the ability of the TFC program to locate a family with the appropriate skills and family composition.

Other criteria for accepting a referred child include the child's age, commitment of funds from the referring agency, and prospects for an appropriate educational placement. All three programs mainly serve children between the ages of eight and 18; few programs state firm age restrictions. Acceptance of children who are younger does occur, but only if the referring agency can make a compelling case that the child could not be served well in regular foster care or some other available program.

Appropriate educational placement is often difficult. In some areas, school districts are reluctant to accept foster children who are placed within their districts. In other areas, appropriate educational services are simply not available. People Places, for this reason, often uses its Pygmalion School, an approved private school for emotionally disturbed children that is one of its services. PRYDE makes use of Pressley Ridge Day School, also an approved private school for emotionally disturbed children, when a child demonstrates consistent failure to benefit from public schools. Though it is a major goal to place children in the least restrictive educational setting, 15 percent to 20 percent of all PRYDE children usually require the stronger structure and individualized instruction available in the private setting.

TFC programs normally interview children during the referral process, using an interview form of their own design. Interviews help the staff learn children's attitudes toward treatment home placement, their foster family preferences, and their descriptions of their current problems. Interviews help the staff to develop a relationship with the child, observe the child's interaction style, and orient the child to treatment home placement. Interview information is also used in matching the child with foster parents, describing the child's physical appearance to potential families, partially verifying the written referral problems, and beginning to plan a program for the child in the event of placement.

## Matching

Matching a child with an available family is understandably the most important step in the referral/pre-placement process. Matching is defined as the selection of a family with the strengths and skills that can best assist a particular child in making behavior changes, while also taking into account the preferences of the family. Although all foster parents in the three core programs receive extensive training and supervision, some have certain strengths and skills that make them more appropriate for certain children than for others. To compromise the "skills match" is potentially to compromise the likelihood of successful treatment. A program may not be able to accept for placement any child for whom an appropriate family is not available at a given time.

Foster parent characteristics to be considered include capacity for nurturance, availability for supervision, communication style, level of perseverance, ability to be consistent and patient, and readiness to praise a child. Lifestyle variables often play a major role in matching. The kind of leisure activities the family enjoys, the kind of home in which they live, the neighborhood, the foods they like, and their level of religious involvement all can influence the nature of a placement. Geographic location can also affect the matching process: living near biological parents, living in a rural setting, living far from the old environment to minimize engaging in delinquent activities or running away from the treatment home.

Socioeconomic status (including educational level, lifestyle, achievement orientation, and income) and cultural similarities are also matching variables that can conflict with each other. If the child's biological family functions fairly well, then TFC programs recommend placing the child in a treatment home of comparable socioeconomic status. If the child's family is extremely dysfunctional, however, the TFC program is less likely to use characteristics of the biological family as matching variables.

Professional Parenting finds that placing children from lower-class backgrounds in the homes of middle-class foster parents rarely produces a successful placement, but PRYDE experiences considerable success placing severely deprived children in homes of middle-class foster parents because cultural similarities predominate. In PRYDE's largest site, Pittsburgh, children and treatment parents share a common urban culture. In contrast, Professional Parenting serves primarily rural youths who have little in common with well-educated, middle-class parents in the community where the program is located.

Family composition and interaction style can be determining factors in matching. A youth with a recent history of abusing younger children should not be in a family with infants and toddlers. A youth who expresses a strong dislike of older parents should be with youthful treatment parents. A youth who becomes agitated with highly verbal adults should not be matched with chatty treatment parents. And treatment parents whose parenting style tends to be somewhat stern or bossy may not do well with a youth whose most serious referral problem is the inability to follow adult instructions.

When parents enter the treatment parenting program, they often indicate strong preferences for a child of a certain age, sex, or race. These preferences, though they can be modified through staff consultation and counsel, should be considered in matching. Many foster parents would prefer younger children. Since TFC programs rarely serve young children, a match with the treatment family needs to be done on factors other than age. The three programs find that treatment parents generally are willing to work with a child of an age different from their preferences, especially when other preferences are met.

Even physical characteristics of the child and of the treatment parents can influence a matching decision. If the child bears even a slight resemblance to a treatment parent, the likelihood that the child and parent will hit it off is increased. Some youths have strong preferences for being placed with parents who "look a certain way."

A systematic method of matching makes the process easier. Staff members at People Places have been experimenting with rating each treatment parent's skills for handling common problem behaviors for children within their program (e.g., noncompliance, aggression, stealing, lying, hyperactivity, cursing, peer-interaction problems, running away, enuresis, tantrums), and on lifestyle variables such as leisure activities and socioeconomic status. Those treatment parents whose ratings most closely match the child's characteristics are considered the best match.

Once a TFC program identifies a potential treatment family, they are given complete information on the child. Often they meet with the staff in the office to read through referral material or have the staff interpret the materials for them. A written summary of the child's more seriously troubling behaviors helps treatment parents remember critical information. Treatment parents serve as an extension of the professional staff; they must have the opportunity to make an informed decision about the children to be placed in their home. They have the right to refuse to accept a particular child and still be considered for other children.

## Pre-Placement

Pre-placement visits between a child and a TFC family provide an opportunity for staff and treatment parents to see if the intended placement meets the needs of the child. The treatment parents can check the accuracy of the referral information and provide additional input for treatment planning. The staff can determine if a foster parent has sufficient skill for the treatment of a particular child's problem behavior. The pre-placement process provides the child with an experience, rather than a mere description, of this placement option. The child not only sees the home and the community in which he or she may live, but also experiences routine family activities, the usual daily schedule of the home, and the customs of that family.

The three programs generally require at least two pre-placement visits before coming to a decision. In most instances, the first visit involves some support from the agency staff and may occur in the offices of the receiving or referring agency. The second visit takes place in the treatment home and is normally a longer overnight or weekend visit with the entire family. Practices may vary according to the needs of the child.

The pre-placement process really begins with the referral information given to the prospective family. Staff members who have interviewed the child add their own observations to the body of information sent by the referring agency, including a physical description of the child, a description of any relevant behaviors noticed during the interview, and the child's positive attributes. After reviewing this information, the treatment family can then request a meeting.

A staff member introduces the child to the family, including the treatment parents and all other members of the household, helps them get acquainted, and leaves when the family and child begin to talk comfortably. When the treatment parents are hesitant about meeting the child, the arrangements may change. Videotapes of the child (or seeing the child through an observation window) permit the family to decide against working with a particular child without the child experiencing this rejection. Taking the treatment parents on the initial interview of the child, before telling the child about the family placement as an option, may avoid disappointing the child.

Families are encouraged to keep pre-placement visits as natural as possible, even though there is a strong inclination for families to treat the prospective foster child as a special guest. The child should learn something of household rules and values as well as common family activities on each pre-placement visit.

The pre-placement process for treatment family and child ends after the first meeting, if either does not wish to pursue placement. Another treatment family would then be considered for the child, and another child for the treatment family. If the child seems reluctant to pre-place again with a particular treatment family, the staff must determine if the hesitation is due to general fears of living with any family or if it can be better explained as a lack of the right chemistry.

After a good first pre-placement meeting, a second meeting takes place overnight or during a weekend. Holiday weekends, while providing a special event for a child, do not usually represent normal family activities, and placement decisions should not be based entirely on holiday visits. After the second visit, both the treatment family and the child are asked again if the placement should be pursued. If either party decides against placement, the process stops; if both parties agree to placement, a date is set with the referral agency.

A child's location may vary the pre-placement process. For example, psychiatric hospitals do not normally allow a child to leave the hospital for weekend or overnight visits; several day-long visits at the hospital help the treatment family and the child to make the placement decision. Geographic distance between the treatment home and the child's current residence may impede pre-placement visits at the treatment home; the use of videotaped interviews of the child has proved to be an efficient first "meeting."

The duration of the pre-placement process varies greatly. For some children, a slow transition over several months from their current residence to the treatment home will improve the chances for a successful placement; other children may need to be placed within four or five days. Often, referring agencies and families want to have a child in placement before major holidays or before the beginning of the school year, requiring a rapid placement. The three programs are able to accommodate individual circumstances. A thorough pre-placement process, however, increases the likelihood of a good match betwen the treatment family and the troubled and troubling child. And it goes without saying that having a pool of available homes, offering choices, is a big step toward thoroughness.

## Special Issues

TFC programs must frequently deal with resistance on the part of a child and sometimes of a child's family. Programs may also experience resistance in the procurement of referrals, especially when a program is new and lacks a track record of success with difficult children.

### Resistant Children

Placement or a change in placement can be extremely threatening to children. Placement in a foster family setting may be frightening or somehow aversive to the children, particularly when their own families have failed to meet their needs. Some children view the family structure as inviting more failure, since failure characterized their own family experience. If children have found through experience that parents are dangerous persons, then a new family is something to fear. Children may also fear losing the affection of their own family as a consequence of joining a treatment family. Staff members encounter these fears throughout the referral/placement stages and must vigorously use relationship-building strategies during all their contacts with a child. This process begins during the interview, which is cheerful in style and enjoyable by intent, often in the face of unresponsiveness from the youngster. A dialogue about the child's preferences and goals is initiated at this point and continued throughout the process.

The degree to which the child participates in placement decision making goes far to mitigate resistance. PRYDE staff members use the motto, "If you want cooperation, get participation," to guide their involvement of a resistant child. An actively involved child, whose input is heard and acted on, is far more likely to cooperate with the process. Negotiation may be employed to increase the child's participation as well, particularly when issues such as entry date and type of treatment delivery system must be decided. Often, however, placement options may be or should be limited. The TFC program may have little or no choice in an available treatment home. The referring agency may want the child to be placed only in a treatment family and not in any residential program. As helpful as a youth's participation in placement decision making can be, the costs may outweigh the benefits—troubled and troubling youths have historically shown that they are poor decision makers. When options are limited, the staff must actively encourage and, at times, insist that the child live with the available treatment family, pointing out that no other options are available. In the few cases where staff members have asked outside caseworkers, probation officers, and other professionals to help a resistant youth in reaching a placement decision, the results have generally been disappointing. They may be ill-informed about how treatment-parenting programs serve children and unfamiliar with the prospective treatment families. All too often they portray this treatment service as "foster family care."

Initial screening of the referral and a careful child-family match will prevent some resistance. Sometimes a child's lack of certainty stems from his or her observations of the treatment family's habits and expectations. A meeting between the child and the prospective family may be necessary to explore any conflicts about family rules and expectations. Again, negotiated compromise will allow each participant input into the plan, and conflicts can be resolved in advance. Expectations about church attendance, bedtimes, chores, smoking, and any other unclear issue are best resolved before placement.


### Resistant Biological Families

Placement in a treatment home requires either the child's removal from his or her own family or from a residential facility. The parents may have negative feelings about having their child placed in another family's home. This reaction is true even in cases when the parents request placement of the child or have in some way clearly endangered the health or welfare of the child. Parents' inability or unwillingness to care for their child may be acutely embarrassing to them. When a child is removed, the parents may feel that the whole world is suddenly watching their performance. The selection of a TFC program may further aggravate the parents' feelings of shame and failure. Parents whose children are placed in traditional residential settings often receive sympathy from their community; the removal of the child, followed by institutional placement, indicate to some that the child is at fault. When a child is placed with other parents, however, regardless of their special qualifications as treatment professionals, the biological parents may find that they are more likely to be judged inadequate by the people in their lives. If a child's problem can be solved in the community, or in another person's home, the parents may well be confronted by questions as to why they did not solve the problem themselves and so prevent the removal. These strong feelings and others, including guilt and grief, may well cause the child's own family to regard the treatment home placement as negative and shameful.

Staff members reduce or prevent strong parental resistance by educating the child's parents about the service. Describing the training and salary received by the treatment parents is particularly effective, because this information illustrates the professional qualifications of treatment parents. A description of the supervision and consultation format enables the biological parents to see that even professional parents must receive additional guidance on tough issues. The provision of services to the biological parents and the stated goal of return home for a child indicate to the parents the program's investment in the return of their child.

The most powerful factor in reducing parental resistance is the relationship between the parents and the program staff. Staff members approach the parents in a non-threatening, positive manner. Unless geographical distance precludes it, contact is frequent and instructive, starting during the referral process and continuing throughout the placement. When the treatment parents are introduced to the biological parents, the treatment parents reinforce their therapeutic role by offering to support the parent–child relationship. Even the simple acknowledgment that the parent–child relationship is important can go a long way toward reducing the parents' resistance.

Enlisting the support, however minimal, of the biological family gives the child a clear message about the placement. Children are more likely to cooperate when they see that their families have agreed to placement in a TFC program. Children and parents then can discover that treatment will enhance, rather than terminate, their relationship. This discovery results in greater motivation for success on the part of all concerned.

*Resistance from Referral Sources*

The degree to which TFC programs must actively solicit referrals depends on several factors: the referral sources' knowledge about the TFC model, the quality of the services, the interpersonal relationships between TFC staff members and referral agents, and the age of the program.

Due to common misconceptions about the nature of TFC, program staff members must educate referring agencies about their services. Continuing education minimizes incorrect assumptions about the types of children best served in these programs. Because TFC looks similar to foster care, and because foster care is historically quite well understood and defined, referring agents may assume that there is no, or little, difference between the two services. The major differences between treatment parenting and foster parenting account for their different costs. A referral agent who is not reminded of these differences may well choose the cheaper placement.

TFC programs have used several ways to increase knowledge of their services. People Places has great success with monthly informational mailings, which are included in billing statements; it also sends promotional materials to local public welfare departments and notifies referring agents at the end of each training class for new treatment parents. The three TFC programs featured here all make occasional presentations to referring agencies and invite staff members from referral sources to participate in their training programs. Frequent communication about the progress of individual children also serves an educational function. Finally, as variations of this model of care and treatment proliferate, professionals are becoming increasingly aware of the model's characteristics.

The quality of any program's services will affect referrals, although good programming alone is rarely sufficient to maintain an adequate referral rate. Professionals in the social service/juvenile justice community have to be told about these services and the results they produce. If a TFC program places children who would otherwise be placed in a residential facility, then referral sources will be inclined to refer these children to TFC. If even very disturbed youths are able to make some progress while in a treatment home, then referral sources will use this service as an important youth care resource.

A third, often pivotal, factor affecting referrals is the relationship that TFC staff members have with staff members of referral agencies. An open, cooperative relationship allows the referral agent to hear about successful aspects of the program. It provides opportunities for education about the model. A positive working relationship maintains program viability.

The age of a program or the length of time it has been providing TFC services also determines the rate of referrals. Only with time can a newly established program educate referral sources sufficiently, develop positive relationships with referral sources, and demonstrate quality service. In the emerging phase of any new TFC program, a special amount of time and effort should be devoted to promotional and educational activities.

The three programs represented in this volume receive a large number of referrals as a result of their success with troubled and troubling children and their general good reputation. Usually 70 percent to 85 percent of the children discharged each year in PRYDE depart for less restrictive settings: own home, independent living, adoption, or regular foster care. Follow-up on all discharged children (successful and unsuccessful) indicate that one and two years later, 73 percent are living in less restrictive settings and are employed or attending school. Because of this level of success with a seriously difficult population of children and with ongoing interagency communication, PRYDE receives two to five referrals a week. In a typical year, PRYDE Pittsburgh receives 180–220 referrals or about 25 percent of all children from that county requiring out-of-home placement that year. These results show that TFC can effectively decrease referral resources' resistance to placing seriously disturbed children in private homes.

# 5

# Training and Supporting Treatment Parents

PAMELA MEADOWCROFT
AND
EILEEN MARY GREALISH

PERHAPS THE SINGLE MOST IMPORTANT characteristic of treating seriously troubled children in foster homes is the package of comprehensive staff support services that treatment parents receive. Without support services, even a substantial increase in treatment parent per diem payments will fail to prevent burnout.

The intrinsic necessity of pre-service and ongoing training distinguishes the various forms of TFC from traditional foster care. Treatment parents are professionalized to serve as the primary agents of change for a child. Other forms of support, such as in-home consultation, pay, evaluation, professional opportunities, crisis intervention, and social events, all serve to maintain high levels of treatment parent performance. Giving special, frequent, sincere, and highly personalized praise for their performance or accomplishment is a major feature. Foster parents who begin to falter in their commitment to the foster child often have not received sufficiently frequent and varied training and acknowledgment for the contribution they make to the child, staff, and program.

## Parent Training

The parent training in all these programs uses a behavioral or social learning approach based on the programs' theoretical orientations: children's problems develop from years of learning their behavioral patterns within a variety of social environments. Learning results from direct teaching by peers or adults, from indirectly observing problem behavior of others (modeling), and from experiencing gratifying consequences of their behavior. To counteract years of learning, treatment parents need to become highly skilled, daily teachers of new interactions and coping behaviors.

The content and method of training differ from other approaches to parent training such as rational emotive therapy, systematic training for effective parenting (STEP), and so forth [Bernal 1984]. Treatment parents learn how to analyze a child's behavior in terms of the contingencies that produce the behavior and how to perform specific strategies for changing the child's behavior. As the primary treatment agents for the child, these foster parents must be able to use good communication and behavior management techniques effectively and systematically. They must also be able to analyze misbehavior, plan effective interventions, and prevent escalating aggression or other troublesome actions.

Consequently, the three programs teach the following parent behaviors: *(1)* consistently discussing and enforcing rules; *(2)* frequently using reinforcers or rewards for good behavior and rarely using punishment for bad behavior; *(3)* nurturing and accepting a child as he or she is; *(4)* giving the child age-appropriate responsibilities; and *(5)* modeling good behavior [Martin 1972]. The power of such practices is demonstrated by studies showing that delinquency has been kept to a minimum when parents set and implement consistent rules and use interactional skills that encourage trust [Cooper 1977]. The core programs emphasize these parenting skills and the daily teaching of acceptable behaviors.

The training tracks include pre-service training that prospective treatment parents must complete before acceptance into the program, in-service training workshops and/or advanced training classes, and, most important, in-home consultation.

## Pre-Service Training

Although the number and length of sessions and specific content of each may vary, a range of at least ten to 25 hours indicates the importance of training prospective treatment parents before permitting them to serve a troubled child in their home.

*Purpose*     The general purposes of pre-service training illustrate why TFC emphasizes it so strongly. First, the staff has the opportunity to assess the appropriateness, the strengths, and the weaknesses of individuals in relation to the staff's future decisions regarding matching a child with a particular family.

Second, training classes also provide the prospective treatment parents with the opportunity to ask themselves whether they have the time, energy, and commitment to work with a troubled child. There are many indicators in the training structure. If parents cannot find time to attend classes regularly and punctually; if they find that the homework or other class requirements are too tiring, or that they have little energy by the end of the class; if they find the task of managing the class paperwork difficult and understand that the job includes record-keeping requirements, they can withdraw from the program during training and forestall future failure with a troubled child.

Third, pre-service training provides a common form of communication between staff members and treatment parent candidates. All the staff members have professional training and perspectives on child behavior that are accompanied by a special vocabulary and problem-solving orientation. To increase the likelihood that candidates will be able to follow through on treatment recommendations once a child is placed, they must have at least a subset of this special vocabulary and view of behavior.

Fourth, as one treatment parent said, the training provides a "place to go from" with a newly placed child. Grounding in good communication skills and behavior management reduces having to fall back later on trial-and-error learning.

Fifth, when all candidates receive the same training, a program can begin to evaluate the effectiveness of different training strategies. Moreover, common training provides the basis for standardized day-to-day evaluations of treatment parent performance.

Sixth, the training serves an important networking purpose. By the end of each training class, participants know each other, share their phone numbers, and look forward to seeing each other at future in-service meetings.

Finally, the training provides an opportunity for the staff to model program values such as enthusiasm and commitment. It functions as a rite of passage for the trainees, familiarizing them with program stories and legends.

*Scheduling*    Scheduling of training classes is set for the convenience of working couples or the working spouse and therefore sessions take place in the evening or on weekends. PRYDE schedules ten 2½ hour classes over a six-week period, which includes one night a week for six consecutive weeks plus four Saturday sessions. PRYDE has tried various schedules, including all ten sessions over two weekends, Friday evenings and Saturdays over four weeks, and one session a week over ten weeks. Generally, given the amount of homework between sessions and the skills/concepts to be learned, trainees and staff members prefer the six-week scheduling. Training classes for PRYDE begin every two to three months regardless of the size of each class, to keep the momentum of recruiting and training going; however, experience indicates that the best class size is from five to eight couples. Professional Parenting schedules its 16-hour-training over two weekends and is thus able to bring candidates quickly into service. People Places schedules its six three-hour sessions in a fashion comparable to PRYDE. All programs agree that staff members must interact with prospective treatment parents over at least three sessions to begin to determine their skills and commitment.

*Content*    The content of each program's pre-service training reflects the amount of time allocated to the training; the availability of qualified staff members to teach and their commitment to particular topics; state requirements for training; experience with strategies that work best with the population of children served; and material that is teachable, usable, and acceptable to candidates in each of the three programs. Although TFC programs emphasize performance training ("how to") in pre-service workshops, they also include information about systems issues such as program expectations, state regulations, the experience of foster children, and so forth. The degree of emphasis placed on information versus performance training varies across the three programs. People Places provides training on treatment skills in all six of their training sessions, and PRYDE emphasizes performance training in 80 percent, or eight, of its training sessions.

Even with some variations in training content, the three programs show remarkable similarity in the parenting skills and information they teach. The following topics can be found to a greater or lesser extent in each program's training and therefore should be considered essential for pre-service training of candidates: general overview and context of TFC; analyzing behavior in terms of antecedent events, behaviors, and consequent events (A-B-Cs); using positive reinforcement; teaching through direct instruction, modeling, feedback, praise, and discipline; promoting a positive relationship with children; and a review of common behavioral, social, or emotional problems exhibited by the children served.

An *introduction* or *overview* typically presents:

> The history of the agency and the program
> How TFC differs from institutional or traditional foster care
> Descriptions of children served (including stories concerning the most serious case failures)
> Reasons applicants should not become treatment parents and reasons they should
> A detailed review of the policies for treatment parents (preferably in written form) and state laws governing foster care
> A description of treatment parent services and expectations of treatment parents while in training and once certified
> A description of children's families and their involvement with their children
> The program philosophy on treatment and discipline, with emphasis on the social learning approach (behavior analysis) to analyzing and changing behavior

Generally, this overview not only gives prospective treatment parents the information they need to make an educated decision in regard to becoming treatment parents, it also serves to discourage them if they lack the necessary time, energy, and commitment to work with children with problems.

When candidates learn to *analyze behavior* and *target behaviors* in need of remediation, they acquire the beginning tools for becoming professional treatment parents. They learn:

How to define a behavior problem (and a positive behavior) in specific, operational terms

How to identify antecedent conditions that may have contributed to the behavior

How to identify consequences of the behavior that may influence the behavior

How to change antecedent and consequent conditions so that the behavior will change

Precision in communicating about a behavior and its contextual circumstances assists treatment parents in several ways. First, it allows them to maintain more objectivity and thus avoid escalating emotionalism on their own part and the resultant less effective parenting. Second, it provides them with a means for more accurate communication with staff members regarding a problem (or a success). Third, precisely identifying a behavior problem or success for a child removes any ambiguity regarding exactly what the child did that was wrong (or right).

All three programs emphasize *positive reinforcement*. Eliminating inappropriate behavior (including attitudes, feelings, and thoughts) through positive means is more effective than using punitive methods. Reinforcing positive behaviors, such as sharing emotions orally in a calm tone of voice will result in a natural decline in the opposite, negative behaviors, such as demonstrating emotions with physical aggression. The programs teach constructive behavior change in which new behaviors are added to a child's repertoire to replace those that were not as socially productive.

One reinforcement technique that candidates learn is that of giving a complete social reward (descriptive praise and/or contingent praise). They learn to show genuine appreciation of a child's positive behavior, identify the behavior for the child, and provide the child with a rationale as to why that behavior was positive. For example, when a child offers to help the treatment parent cook dinner, the latter would say warmly with a smile or hug, "Billy, thank you for offering to help me. I so appreciate it when you volunteer to help me because it makes me think you care about me and maybe even want to learn to cook!" A complete social reward must immediately follow the good behavior for it to have maximum effect. An emphasis on social rewards requires treatment parents to shift from the typical focus of catching children misbehaving to "catching them when they are good." Not only do children learn from social rewards, but social rewards also build a positive relationship between the child and the treatment parents.

A second reinforcement technique is the contingent use of material or activity reinforcers. In addition to social rewards, treatment parents learn to provide the child with privileges, allowances, outings with friends, and so forth, dependent upon the child demonstrating some specific positive behaviors (or making some progress toward a positive behavioral goal). Again, if parents consistently and contingently use reinforcers such as these for positive behavior, then the incidents of misbehavior will begin to decrease as long as the usual satisfying outcomes to the child for his or her misbehavior are prevented or minimized.

Since all the core programs view maladjustment as the result of poor learning experiences, all expect treatment parents to re-educate children on a daily basis. Treatment parents learn that when they experience some inappropriate, distressing, or bothersome behavior, they must first assume the child has never learned the proper way of behaving in this particular situation and, therefore, they need to *teach*.

Treatment parents learn that teaching requires several steps. First, they learn how to determine what to teach. The skill to be taught must be clearly defined, including all the subskills that may be part of the larger skill. For example, in teaching a child to apologize, the child must learn several components such as culturally appropriate eye contact, neutral tone of voice, saying "I'm sorry," describing the misbehavior, and describing what he or she will do differently in the future.

Treatment parents then learn how to teach, which includes explaining why the teaching is necessary, modeling and describing the behavior being taught, having the child rehearse or practice the skill, praising for good performance (or sincere attempts), and correcting where necessary.

The prospective treatment parents learn to use teaching as a method to prevent problem behavior. For example, they use their teaching skills to establish the behaviors the child will need on a family outing, in church, in meeting new people, in enrolling in school, or in explaining tardiness to the teacher. Professional Parenting includes a section in its training entitled "Preventative Teaching," in which treatment parents learn to state reasonable behavior expectations of the child in advance. They first view a videotape of a treatment parent talking with a child before going to a picnic. The tape portrays both an incorrect and a recommended way to approach the problem. In the first part, the treatment parent is unreasonably harsh in her demands; in the second part, she is specific and pleasant in describing her expectations. After viewing and discussing the tape, the trainees read a behavior rehearsal script, then practice the situation with a staff member playing the role of the child. The script for this particular example follows:

> *Preventative Teaching: Before leaving on a family outing to go bowling, you engage the child (a boy, in this instance) in a conversation on what behaviors you expect from him. Your main concern is that you would like to have the family spend the evening together, but you realize a lot of his friends may be there and could want him to spend his time with them. The boy gets upset because he will have to spend the evening with the family. Be sure to:*
> 1. *State what you expect and a rationale for that expectation.*
> 2. *Deal with the child's immediate resistant behavior:*
>    *a.  Ask the child to stop the behavior*
>    *b.  Ask the child to look at you*
> 3. *Describe possible problems—the child may not know what to say if friends ask him to come with them.*
> 4. *Describe some things he could say to his friends.*
> 5. *Provide practice on how to respond to friends.*

At the conclusion of the rehearsal, the staff member provides feedback to the trainee on both strong and weak areas of the interaction.

Because troubled and troubling children and adolescents will misbehave while in a therapeutic foster home, prospective treatment parents must be taught effective and appropriate *discipline techniques*. By state laws and program ethics, they learn that they cannot use any methods of physical punishment or methods that demean the child. The strategies prospective treatment parents learn include response cost (or loss of privileges or points), time-out (brief removal from positive activity), and overcorrection (practice of the behavior that corrects a misbehavior). For example, PRYDE trainees spend one workshop learning how to give and take points on a child's motivation system. This response-cost strategy along with remedial teaching of the correct behavior produces the most positive behavior gains and reduction of misbehavior.

These strategies prove to be most effective when the child has a positive relationship with the treatment parents. Therefore, the three programs all teach prospective treatment parents ways to *promote positive relationships*. These methods include, for example, spending some positive time with the child daily, communicating negative feelings to the child in a non-defensive way, soliciting suggestions from the child in the daily operation of the household, encouraging the child to share his or her feelings through a communication technique called "active listening," ensuring that the child receives praise every day for some positive behavior, and including the child in all family activities. Treatment parents learn how to listen to the child and how to describe their feelings in a calm, non-hostile way whenever the child does misbehave. Good communication not only promotes positive relations with a child, but it also keeps the child open to learning new ways of interacting.

Throughout the training the candidates learn to apply parenting skills to the special problems of these children. They learn to use teaching skills to prevent or correct behaviors such as sexual promiscuity, acting out in school, or fighting with peers. They learn to use a token economy, such as a point system, to shape more adaptive behaviors and reduce aggression, refusal to follow instructions, or talking back.

In addition to these common topics among the three programs, PRYDE and People Places train candidates to *record behaviors and maintain other records* for clinical use. As described in detail later in this volume, PRYDE parents make use of a daily point system for each child and keep a daily log on their interactions with the child and on the child's activities in the community. These records enable continual assessment of progress and parenting skills. The pre-service training teaches candidates how to use these records by practicing at home with their own children. Similarly, People Places teaches trainees how to keep records on parenting skills (e.g., use of descriptive praise, nagging comments) and on children's progress on treatment goals.

The remaining variations in training content can be attributed to state regulations, the need of the particular trainee group, or staff commitment to a particular topic.

PRYDE teaches additional information/skill topics including *restraint, avoiding confrontations, negotiation or problem solving, and making friends. Passive physical restraint* is taught because some state regulations require this skill of foster parents. TFC, however, does not endorse its use since to do it properly and safely requires the presence of more than one adult. Thus the skill is often taught within the context of avoiding confrontations through good communication skills, planned prevention, and negotiation/problem solving. PRYDE and People Places treatment parents learn a multi-step problem-solving method called *negotiation*. More generally, negotiation is a structured method for achieving compromise with an adolescent on certain rules or expectations that he or she wishes to change. This eight-step procedure helps to de-escalate power struggles and increases the likelihood that the adolescent will follow through on the agreed-upon resolution to a conflict. The steps used in the PRYDE program include engaging the adolescent in a negotiation interaction, defining the problem from both the treatment parents' and the child's perspective, generating solutions, choosing the best solution (based on all parties' judgments as to acceptability), describing implementation procedures, and following up to evaluate the solution. Shortened versions of the full negotiation process are used to gain the youth's input into daily decisions such as choices of meals, television programs, or time for lights-out. Negotiation also teaches children an effective way of compromising in relationships. A final suggested topic to be presented in pre-service is *helping children to make friends*. If a child has friends who are delinquents, the likelihood that he or she will engage in delinquent behaviors increases; thus the need exists to ensure that each child has both the skills and the opportunities to make prosocial friends.

*Style and Format of Training Session*    Usually, pre-service training follows a fairly structured, academic format. Sessions have objectives and/or outlines of material to be covered; trainers function as lecturers and discussion leaders; the training room is arranged like a classroom with the trainers in the front and the trainees sitting at tables where they can take notes and read the handouts for each session. Even though there is a degree of structure and formality, the trainers' style requires high energy, is cheerful, humorous, and casual, and demonstrates commitment. A friendly casualness is made possible through the use of first names (everyone wears a large name tag on which the first name is printed in letters large enough to be seen from the front of a classroom), the serving of beverages and snacks at each session, the encouragement of informal interactions before and after a session, and the use of personal experiences on the part of trainers to illustrate certain training points. The structure and formality help to reinforce the view that the training is important, the trainers are the experts, and the trainees should work at mastering the content. The friendliness of staff trainers and the genuine interest in the well-being of the trainees conveys to the latter that the program will be supportive.

Using various instructional media enhances the lecture/discussion format. Transparencies highlight the critical aspects of each workshop. Films or videotapes of treatment parent-child interactions give candidates opportunities to practice analyzing behavior and predicting future behavior. For example, PRYDE and People Places use videotape examples of each of the parenting skills that trainees must learn to perform. They observe good examples and poor examples of other treatment parents using the skills (e.g., teaching, implementing a point system, using descriptive praise, using active listening or direct expression of feelings). From these observations, they learn to make additional discriminations that are important in performing the skills.

All three programs require trainees to practice the skills that they teach. The candidates receive role-playing situations typical of interactions that occur in a treatment home. They then use these behavior rehearsal situations to practice the various parenting skills. Upon completion of the practice, they then perform the skill, receive critical feedback from staff trainers, and eventually show mastery of the skill.

*Trainers*     Each of the three treatment parenting programs developed, uses, and teaches its own training materials. In this way the training is tailored to the program, the children served, and the recruited applicants. In-house development ensures a high level of commitment on the part of the program to the skills being taught. An in-house training manual reflects the expertise of the staff; thus the staff and candidates share a common perspective. By serving as trainers, staff members keep their own treatment skills sharp, and they can model commitment to the program's ideals. Staff are also able to make better treatment parent-child matching judgments after getting to know the treatment parents well in the training. A subtle but equally important reason for staff members to serve as trainers involves the relationships that develop in the training between staff members and candidates. After the latter complete a training class and a child is placed in their home, one of the staff members who served as a trainer in their class may become their supervisor. Having had this staff person as a teacher supports their cooperation with later supervisory recommendations. Finally, those staff members who serve as treatment parent supervisors and as trainers are in an excellent position to evaluate training effects (e.g., whether the treatment parents actually use the skills correctly after the training), and they can make experience-based suggestions for training changes.

The number of staff trainers for any class size should be no fewer than two. Two trainers can exchange reactions after training, demonstrate the skills in role-playing situations, and maintain audience attention better by shifting from one trainer to another in a fast-paced fashion. In addition, utilizing at least one active treatment parent to assist and share his or her experiences in using the treatment strategies strengthens the commitment of trainees to the training information.

*Passing the Training Class*    The pre-service training of treatment parent candidates serves as a powerful screening mechanism. Throughout the sessions, the trainers encourage prospective treatment parents to drop out when they show a persistent lack of skill or commitment to working with an emotionally disturbed child in their homes.

Preset standards for passing the training should be sufficiently rigorous so that poorly skilled, improperly motivated, or uncooperative applicants do not pass, yet the standards must be flexible enough to allow a diversity of candidates to pass. The many types of troubled children served in TFC require many types of treatment parents for successful matching of a child and a family.

The standards for passing the pre-service training differ slightly among the three programs, although all have set criteria concerning attendance, completion of homework, performance of treatment-parenting skills, subjective evaluations by the staff, and adherence to state regulatory requirements.

All programs require the satisfactory completion of the state foster care requirements either before entry in the pre-service course, or at least before completion of the training. The standards include such matters as adequate space and furnishings in the home for a child, a realistic view of a foster child's role in the family, good physical and mental health of the foster parents, good references from community leaders who know the family, and so forth. In some states, certification as a foster parent precedes entry into TFC; in such instances the pre-service training and other requirements come second to state approval.

Candidates must attend all training sessions, complete any make-up sessions, and satisfactorily complete all homework assignments to be eligible for certification as a treatment parent in any of the three programs. Unexcused absences and chronic tardiness prevent certification—these couples would be encouraged to drop out even before the training ended. Early in PRYDE's development only the primary treatment parent needed to attend all ten training classes. The secondary treatment parent had to attend only four of these sessions but complete all homework. Over the course of time, PRYDE learned that those couples in which both attended all ten sessions showed higher involvement and usually succeeded more easily with seriously troubled children. PRYDE accordingly modified its requirements so all candidates must complete all sessions.

Trainers' subjective evaluations of a trainee provide an essential basis for certification, as, for example, in such negative impressions as a couple too easily manipulated by adolescents, a candidate who was un-cooperative with a staff member or resisted learning the training material, or a candidate with an overly authoritarian style in the training sessions. Other evaluation criteria include the degree to which a trainee shows commitment to program strategies; willingness to stick with a tough, troubled child; professionalism; and flexibility and tolerance.

Another criterion for passing the training, with more potential for objectivity, involves a trainee's performance of treatment-related skills. Skills can be subjectively evaluated by the trainers or written criteria can be used to assist them in achieving consistent, fair evaluations. For each parenting skill, such as teaching or negotiation, the PRYDE staff uses a checklist of component skills. Candidates perform the skill during role-playing tests. Trainees who demonstrate components of the skill in a natural, smooth fashion pass the performance test. Even if candidates attend all sessions, they must still pass all performance tests before they can pass pre-service training.

### In-Service Training

Pre-service training cannot establish mastery of critical parenting skills—nor can it address all the intervention strategies useful for the problems of emotionally disturbed children and adolescents. For true competence building, treatment parents must receive training after a foster child moves into their home. In-service training takes two forms: in-service training workshops and home consultation.

*In-Service Training Workshop*     In-service workshops resemble the pre-service training—groups of treatment parents meet with a trainer in a classroom setting for instruction or practice of new treatment skills. These meetings serve numerous purposes: to disseminate new information about treatment and parenting; to promote group identity and the sense of being part of an exclusive group; to maintain involvement; to promote supportive relationships among participants so that they can see each other as resources; to provide feedback to all staff members regarding the effectiveness of recommended intervention strategies; to meet any new state training requirements; to discuss new or changing administrative practices; to train participants in additional treatment-parenting skills; to professionalize the treatment parents further; and to reinforce the use of the pre-service training skills.

Topics for in-service training are determined by participants' requests; by staff identification of a need for training or information in some area, including topics not covered sufficiently during the pre-service training; by a change in policies, procedures, or state requirements; and by indications for a particular topic resulting from evaluations of treatment parents' skills and the progress of children. Topics may include sex education, sexual misconduct, mental illness, substance abuse, and the effects on treatment families of having a troubled child in the home, to name only a few.

The frequency and attendance requirements of the workshop programs differ among the three agencies, from a minimum of four hours to a maximum of 20 hours per year. PRYDE requires attendance at eight of the ten two-hour sessions each year; compliance contributes to annual evaluations and commensurate per diem increases. All the programs use at least one in-service meeting as a social event each year.

*Home Consultation* Only after placement of a child in a therapeutic foster home can highly individualized, case-specific training begin. If a youngster has substance abuse problems, the treatment parents receive educational materials on substance abuse and strategies for working with a substance abuser. If a child has a past history of fire-setting, the treatment parents receive special training in managing fire-setting behavior. The pre-service training establishes program expectations, provides trainees with a vocabulary for discussing children's problems with the staff, and begins parenting skill development. Home consultation develops these skills through the experience of helping the foster child progress. The pre-service training introduces the trainees to the program; home consultation maintains treatment parents in the program. It is, perhaps, the single most important support component of TFC.

Home consultation teaches treatment parents new skills or provides them with necessary information for interacting with and teaching their particular foster child more effectively. To determine their training needs, the supervisor may require them to demonstrate in the home their current skills in role-playing situations or *in vivo* situations with the foster child. The daily records that treatment parents keep on their own and the child's behavior provide yet another source of information for the supervisor to determine home training needs.

At the beginning of a placement, in all three core programs, staff members who work most closely with a treatment family (e.g., case consultants, parent supervisors, or program managers), visit homes at least weekly for, usually, a three-hour meeting. The frequency and duration of these meetings may be greater if the treatment parents' skill level is low and/or if the problems of the child require extra in-home preparation of the foster family. In subsequent months, the frequency of visits may gradually decline. Only after a child has been with a treatment family for over six months and is showing good adjustment may home visits decrease to twice a month.

Though in-home consultations may decline after a period of stability and growing parent skill, TFC programs must be prepared to increase the supervision intensity as soon as signs of increasing difficulties arise. Review of treatment parents' daily records and continued frequent phone contacts enable the staff to determine if and when supervision should increase. After serving over 250 troubled children, PRYDE perceived a frequent cycle of honeymoon (up to six months), deteriorating behavior (six to nine months), and restrengthening of appropriate behavior (nine months or more).

Home visits with treatment parents give them general support and an opportunity to review a variety of child-related issues such as school problems, relations with the child's own family, or administrative concerns. The sympathetic ear of a supervisor helps to maintain commitment; however, listening to treatment parents' concerns or complaints without active home training will not lead to a successful placement. Parents need the technology that these three programs teach to be able to work with a difficult, acting-out child.

Phone contact with the treatment parents is another form of home consultation. At least weekly and often daily, staff members and treatment parents talk on the phone. Each program provides parents with a 24-hour answering service so that staff are available to treatment parents after work hours. An answering service is used frequently; for example, at PRYDE, with a population of 70 children in its Pittsburgh site, 50 to 75 calls each month commonly come through the PRYDE emergency number.

TFC does not expect total independence of treatment parents. They must be able to discuss possible decisions with their supervisor before taking action on any one of them. The average number of regular phone contacts with treatment parents for each supervising staff member in the three core programs is about two calls a week per case.

## Treatment Parent Pay

Although TFC programs' rates vary, all pay significantly more than regular foster family care in the community in which the TFC program is located. Adequate compensation is essential to attracting and keeping foster parents who can tolerate the demands of parenting and treating a troubled child. Professional Parenting has a pay range of $400 to $900 a month, depending on the severity of the child's violent, aggressive behavior, with $500 being typical. People Places pays between $500–$600 a month per child, plus additional monthly payments for incentive purposes. Treatment parents can earn $20 a month for completing paperwork in a timely fashion, plus another $20 for completing dental and medical appointments for the child. Travel expenses for the child are covered, and treatment parents are also reimbursed for property damage caused by a placed child, as well as phone expenses related to the child.

PRYDE in Pennsylvania pays a beginning per diem of $22 (this amount is greater in Maryland—$32) or about $650 a month as compared to a local foster care per diem of $13.50 for adolescents. Treatment parents can receive up to a maximum of $27 per day (or about $810 per month). All increases are based on a formal, semiannual PRYDE treatment parent evaluation (described below). Thus the payment can be used as a form of support in that it reinforces a job well done, gives parents something to work toward, and makes the skills that are taught in the pre-service training, in-service training, home training, and advanced training more salient. Most expenses must be met from the per diem, including minimal medical costs not covered by medical assistance, all transportation, vacations with the PRYDE family, clothing (except for an initial clothing allotment of $100 to $300, depending on the child's needs), the child's allowance, special events and special rewards for the child, and respite care. During times of special intervention, in which a great deal more parenting time and training is necessary, PRYDE may increase the per diem for a short time. Thus the per diem can be used for motivation. In its more rural sites, PRYDE West Virginia pays treatment parents additional for out-of-county transportation costs. Reimbursements for damages by the PRYDE child are normally reviewed on a case-by-case basis.

## Treatment Parent Evaluation

Training gives skills; the training relationship between staff member and treatment parent adds incentive to use the skills; good pay helps keep parents using the skills even though the child fails to make hoped-for progress; and performance evaluations keep parents working to improve their skills. Evaluation of treatment parents' performance rewards those who do a good job and gives corrective feedback to those who need to change or improve. Evaluation influences parenting behavior through accurate, specific, written feedback and therefore serves an educational function.

In TFC both the physical environment and behavioral environment of the child are closely and continually evaluated. Caseloads remain small to enable the staff person to provide the variety of aforementioned support services and to evaluate the level of treatment services each child receives. Evaluating treatment parents in these three programs varies in the degree of detail, objectivity, and consequential power. Nonetheless, all such treatment programs must be prepared to provide accountable treatment through regular client assessments and evaluations of treatment parents' performance.

At the informal end of the parent evaluation continuum, staff members' observation and consultation reveal any inadequate practices. Remediation is supplied, and, if the treatment parents fail to change, termination would be considered. PRYDE, People Places, and Professional Parenting all use this staff process for evaluating the quality of foster parenting.

PRYDE and People Places use formal methods of evaluation as well. These evaluations, regularly scheduled for all parents, primarily serve a training function; areas of weakness normally are treated with extra in-home training and staff assistance. People Places completes a rating scale on 12 critical behaviors every six months; treatment parents receive remediation help and a report on their rating that emphasizes improvement.

PRYDE uses an evaulation system that takes into account many sources of program data, giving treatment parents a plan for improvement and the agency a means of overall program evaluation. Each evaluation follows a specific format and deals with five evaluation categories: *(1)* the child's performance; *(2)* direct treatment and parenting; *(3)* treatment family environment; *(4)* indirect treatment; and *(5)* administration. Treatment parents receive a separate rating in each category, an overall score based on an average of the five category ratings, and a written report describing strengths and weaknesses in each category. Completion of a treatment parents' evaluation requires about 15 hours of records reviews and staff/child interviews. The comprehensiveness is important to maintain quality care and to serve as a useful learning device. Evaluations are scheduled after treatment parents have served a child for six months, 12 months, and annually thereafter. Depending on the overall evaluation rating, they will receive a per diem increase of up to $2.00. Those whose overall rating indicates marginal performance are placed on probationary status and risk being terminated if they fail to show improvement within three months.

## Additional Support Services

It might seem that excellent training, good pay, and frequent, detailed evaluations would be sufficient to maintain good treatment parents in a TFC program. Nonetheless, the three core programs all experience the need to provide additional support services, including respite care (emergency and planned), crisis intervention, professional opportunities for treatment parents, and special recognition.

### Respite Care

Respite care provides treatment parents with a break from parenting. A prearranged "vacation time from the child" allows treatment parents to have time alone or time with their own children. The placed child leaves the home for a day to a week and stays with another treatment family held in reserve for respite only, or an active treatment family for whom the respite child is a good match. Respite care can be an important deterrent to burnout; unlike front-line professionals in an institution for troubled children, treatment parents are on the job 24 hours a day, seven days a week. In those instances where children have regularly scheduled home visits with their own families, respite services may not be necessary. Treatment parents may be reluctant to use respite care for a variety of reasons, such as loss of pay (if this procedure is not an additional benefit), feelings of guilt over wanting to get away from the child for a while, and concern about the continuation of proper treatment in the respite placement. Respite arrangements produce the best results when the respite parents continue the same approach to the child that the treatment parents have maintained.

Two negative outcomes of respite care can be expected if it is used at the wrong time or in the wrong way. First, the child may feel rejected and refuse to go to a respite home. A careful match with the respite family will help the child enjoy the respite experience. Also, careful explanations of the purpose of respite early in the placement will increase the likelihood of cooperation on the part of the child. Second, respite care should be avoided, if possible, during a crisis. Only after the resolution of a problem would respite care be advisable. If a problem situation is usually handled by removal of the child, then the child may well feel rejected and the treatment parents and the staff may inadvertently lapse into this passive form of problem resolution—removal of a child becomes easier for treatment parents than changing treatment strategies. Of if the child finds the respite experience more reinforcing than the treatment home, misbehavior in the original home might increase.

Some TFC programs reserve some families to serve only as respite providers; others use active treatment parents. In the latter instances, families can trade respite weekends and the children placed with other troubled children can share the common experiences of being in treatment homes. (Obviously, the treatment parents involved must feel sure that the children will get along well with each other.) The use of respite-only parents, however, has certain advantages, including being able to recruit individuals who may be unwilling to commit themselves to long-term placements. Still another way of providing this service is to hire respite babysitters who could be well-trained, semiprofessional staff members who go to the treatment home and stay while the treatment parents are away.

### Team Interventions

Ideally, any crisis would be resolved with the child remaining in the original treatment home. At times, however, retaining the treatment home for the child may require a temporary removal to another treatment or respite home. Another method, when the crisis does not appear absolutely to require removing the child, is to use a team of staff members for intervention in the original home. A crisis team may include the particular child's family supervisor, plus at least one other staff person, usually a senior staff member or psychologist consultant, the composition of the team depending greatly on the nature of the situation. For example, if the child's crisis has to do with substance abuse, the other team member would be a staff member with expertise in this area. In this way, a team can increase the skills available for training treatment parents in this particular situation, as well as bring in more objective, professional viewpoints and thus give the treatment parents and the supervisor renewed hope or vision of improvement. The team and the treatment parents design an intervention plan that might include counseling services for the child, a psychiatric evaluation, additional training, and/or extra pay for the treatment parents who would then implement special skill teaching or motivators for behavior change. Intense team support continues through the initial stages of the special intervention.

## Professional Opportunities

When treatment parents receive special recognition or have opportunities to increase their professional skills and contribute to program development, they demonstrate increased levels of commitment. The three core programs invite treatment parents to participate in many aspects of the program both for program improvement and their motivation. Treatment parents serve as training assistants during each pre-service class. PRYDE has hired outstanding treatment parents as supervisors and evaluators of other treatment parents. Treatment parents in the PRYDE programs have received college credit for completing the pre-service training and serving children. Each year, the program staff elects one outstanding foster family during foster family week. PRYDE uses an advisory board, composed of highly regarded treatment parents, to obtain their input into program development. The three agencies also encourage treatment parents to present their experiences at program in-service meetings and at local and national meetings concerned with youth care. A program newsletter that solicits articles and news items from treatment parents and children helps maintain a high level of enthusiasm for program participation among the treatment parents.

## Special Recognition

Some forms of recognition for treatment parents may seem gimmicky or hokey, but the effect of such rewards can often do more for morale than a per diem increase. Staff t-shirts for treatment parents who have worked closely with the staff on special interventions let the treatment parents know that they too are staff. A dinner or lunch with the director for completing a year with a very difficult child can be the extra pat on the back that treatment parents need to maintain their excellence. Special letters from the director for a job well done, or a pre-placement well executed, or a fine performance in court reinforces each of these contributions from treatment parents. Greeting cards for birthdays, illnesses, births, anniversaries, and holidays let treatment parents know that they are part of a program that cares for them as persons and as families. Conferring on some outstanding treatment parents the status of Master Treatment Parents increases the likelihood that they will be emulated by other parents. If this status is based on specified criteria and requires recognizable indices of success, then a certificate of master status can be a meaningful reinforcer for treatment parents. And, finally, relaxing parties for treatment parents and the staff strengthen the former's identification with the program, increase opportunities for networking among the treatment parents, and give them a chance to socialize with all of the staff members.

## Results of Support Services to Treatment Parents

If training and support services are successful, a program should receive satisfactory reports from treatment parents, they should remain in the program for an extended period, and children should not need to be transferred to different treatment homes frequently or completely removed from the program for unsatisfactory behavior.

Maintaining the commitment of treatment parents to a troubled child can be measured in three ways: attrition, tenure, and satisfaction. Turnover rates of foster parents to handicapped children are quite high. The loss of a treatment parent from a program entails an enormous loss of invested staff time in training and supervision, the loss of a valuable resource for a child in instances where the parents were skilled, and, often, removal of the child from the program. Losing more than 20 percent of a program's trained treatment parents over time seems to be too high, given the implications for losing one treatment parent. Yet turnover rates in treatment parenting programs, even with the intensive support, tend to be higher than 20 percent the longer the program is in operation. The percentage of treatment parents who leave the program as compared to those who remain or are recruited increases over time. For example, PRYDE lost only 15 percent of its treatment parents between 1981 (beginning of the program) and 1983. Yet from 1983 to 1986 the loss rate increased to 20 percent. PRYDE parents left for one of three reasons: 6 percent moved out of the service area; 10 percent were terminated for failure to cooperate with staff supervision; and 12 percent burned out—they no longer wanted to work with a troubled child in their own homes. Based on the parent attrition experienced by Professional Parenting and People Places, TFC programs should expect a loss of at least 30 percent of the treatment parents over a five-year period.

Rarely do treatment parents remain active as long as regular foster parents. Although all three programs have treatment parents with tenures as long as the program itself, these families are few. From its inception in June 1981 until January 1987, PRYDE Pittsburgh trained and certified 113 PRYDE families. Of those who dropped out during this period, the average length of service was 18 months. Of the remaining active parents, the tenure range was as long as 66 months for three couples from one of the original training periods in June 1981. The shortest tenure among the active parents in January 1987 was three months for the 12 couples who were trained in the fall of 1986. The average length of service among the active parents was 23 months—a representative average to be expected among TFC programs.

Another measure of the success of support services is treatment parent satisfaction. Professional Parenting disseminated a support services evaluation questionnaire to 19 treatment parents, most of whom were active at the time, that measured the level of satisfaction they felt for many of the program's support services. One item on the questionnaire, for example, under the general category of "Program Orientation and Licensure," asked the treatment parents to indicate, on a seven-point scale, "How satisfied were you with the orientation information received about the program before you decided to become a professional parent?" with seven being most satisfied. On this item, and on all but two of the remaining 32 items, their average rating was at least 6.0. The two items in which the average rating was below 6.0 were above 5.5. Thus, this group of treatment parents report high levels of satisfaction with the program support services. (More details on this survey appear elsewhere in this volume.)

The PRYDE program regularly uses pre-service and in-service training evaluations after each class or meeting, asking for responses on the degree of usefulness of the information, its clarity, and the respondents' belief it will be used. Participants rate the meetings highly. Their suggestions for improvement and for things to continue to do help guide the program's development of support services.

A final way of evaluating support services is through treatment parents' reports and stories. Those who served in regular foster care programs before becoming treatment parents report in all the programs a great difference between treatment parenting and foster parenting. They report that the training is critical to their day-to-day interactions with the children. Treatment parents are able to reach a staff person, even in the middle of the night, for assistance. They have a genuine experience of support—of not being alone in their treatment of a troubled child. They report pleasure with the clarity of the expectations of treatment parenting and the high level of professionalism expected of treatment parents.

## REFERENCES

Bernal, M. Consumer issues. In Dangel, R. F., and Polster, R. A. (eds.), Parent Training. New York: Guilford Press, 1984.

Cooper, J. J. Adolescents and Youth: Psychological Development in a Changing World. New York: Harper and Row, 1977.

Martin, B. Parent-child relation. In Thompson, I., and Dackens, W. S. (eds.), Application of Behavior Modification. New York: Academic Press, 1972.

# 6

# Organizing and Staffing Therapeutic Foster Care Programs

PAMELA MEADOWCROFT
WM. CLARK LUSTER
AND
BERNIE FABRY

OF THE SEVERAL REQUISITE COMPONENTS for the therapeutic foster care (TFC) programs described in this volume, an obvious key ingredient is the selection, training, and supervision of the professional staff. Treatment parent recruitment and training, sufficient fiscal resources, an accepting professional and lay community, appropriate referrals of children, and matching treatment parents and child all interact to become the fabric of a program. As critical an issue as funding can be, a much more pivotal component of an effective delivery system is a technically competent, highly motivated, and creative group of professional problem solvers. With an appropriate staff, child referrals will come. Creative staff members can locate and train the families who will treat the youngsters. Assuming the need is strong enough and that financial resources are available to a sufficient degree, an aggressive, competent professional staff can educate the decision makers to meet the need and use those funds to develop professional parenting programs.

The organizational structure within which the program must operate also plays a critical role in the eventual success of the program. Needless to say, the administrative structure is the life blood of the organization. Too loose an organizational structure will cause the program to flounder because of lack of direction, financial problems, and communication disagreements. Little or nothing is accomplished because staff energy is drained by funding crises, mission confusion, or personnel hassles.

Too tight or conservative a structure will sap the momentum of the most highly motivated professional. Staff creativity is stifled because decisions can be made only at the highest levels of the bureaucracy. Every untoward incident, every runaway, every disgruntled placement resource becomes a major crisis. When the organization structure says, "We've never done it like that here," or worse, "We can't do that here," new problems, new issues, and new events will not be handled well. One major weakness of highly structured, bureaucratic programs is the tendency to require referred youngsters to fit the program. Rigid selection criteria (IQ, age, sex, specific behavior exclusion) can dilute one of the major advantages of the TFC model—the ability to deal successfully with a wide range of needy youngsters.

## Staff Selection

The obvious starting point for this program component, the professional staff, begins with the initial selection and training of people. In PRYDE, the staff members who directly supervise treatment parents are called Parent Supervisors/Community Liaisons (PS/CL). Within People Places the title is Program Managers; Professional Parenting refers to their front-line professional staff members as Program Managers as well. Selection of these staff members is based on academic preparation, previous job experience, and the requirements of the particular agency.

Limitations would be the available pool of otherwise qualified applicants and the urgency of filling the position.

The three core programs require as a minimum academic credential for professional staff a baccalaureate degree for entry level positions, with preference for advanced degrees. Pay scales reflect the various levels of preparation, but are generally low, as is typical of nonprofit, social services. All three programs subsidize further professional growth by providing educational benefits to their staff members and time off as compensation for 24-hour on-call responsibilities.

The areas of preparation for staff members vary from program to program, although each emphasizes hiring those with training in behavior analysis and experience with troubled children. Among other TFC programs, the most common rationale for professional staff members to have credentials in social work, psychology, special education, or some other area of preparation appears to be the history of the particular organization. If, for example, the executive director of the organization has a background in social work, it is quite likely that the administrative staff members will have or would aspire to an M.S.W. degree. The executives of the three core programs have degrees in behavioral psychology, hence the emphasis on this training among staff members.

State or local licensing requirements or regulations may specify academic backgrounds such as "The program director will have at least an M.S.W." or "There must be one state-certified psychologist for each 60 residents." More recently, requirements have been broadened to include statements such as "Direct child care staff will possess a degree from an accredited college or university in psychology, social work, child development, education, or some related area." For administrative and supervisory positions, years of experience in a related area have also become an acceptable substitute for graduate training and degree.

Athough the three programs encourage further educational attainment among staff members, specific skills rather than professional credentials are of utmost importance. The skills for staff members who work directly with treatment parents would include *(1)* the ability to develop creative intervention strategies and programs that would reverse the failure cycle in which most of the youngsters and their families find themselves; *(2)* the ability to communicate appropriately in oral and written form with a wide range of audiences; *(3)* a solid background in the profession, with particular emphasis on behavior analysis, behavior change techniques, and training for parenting; *(4)* the ability to function as a contributing member of a treatment team; *(5)* the physical energy and personal security to deal with the responsibility of six to 16 youngsters, their families, and their treatment parents; and *(6)* the ability to supervise, train, and motivate the adults providing treatment.

In addition to these skills of the front-line professional staff, the program directors bring special skills to the job, such as leadership, planning, financial management, research, personnel administration, community relations, and board communication.

As with all successful organizations, supervisory staff members must have a wealth of energy, a bias toward direct intervention and problem solving, and the ability to choose, train, and lead a staff of caring, competent professionals. Finally, the administration and supervisory staff must be able to deal with the day-to-day pressures of responsibility for a wide range of events over which they have little direct control.

## Organizational Structure

### Caseloads and Staff Roles

To provide the necessary in-home training of, and consultation with, treatment parents, supervisors must be available to visit the treatment homes weekly, consult with treatment parents on the phone, represent the child in court, with other social services, and with schools, and visit the biological family. Consequently, TFC requires small caseloads. Among the three programs represented here, caseloads range from an average of as few as six cases to as many as 12. When treatment parent supervisors have caseloads as low as six, they are able—in fact, expected—to perform many other program functions as well, including working with the child's own family, providing the child and treatment family with community and school liaison services, assisting with treatment parent recruitment and training, and program development activities. When they have a higher caseload, such as 12, their functions are not as multifaceted.

Nonetheless, these TFC programs generally do not separate the functions of recruitment, selection, and training of treatment parents from treatment parent support services. By combining these functions, establishing relationships with treatment parents begins at their entry into the program. Staff members who consult with treatment parents and work directly with the children are well equipped to explain realistically the services and expectations to prospective treatment parents. These staff members also know from firsthand observations the weaknesses of particular treatment parents that may be a barrier to providing good service to a child. Thus, involvement of staff members in all aspects of the program increases the effectiveness of program services.

Services provided to the children tend not to be provided by a variety of specialized professionals; the child is not assigned to a mental health worker for his or her therapeutic needs, a caseworker for management of public services, a family worker for liaison with the child's family, or an educational specialist for assistance with educational planning and placement. Instead, one person—the PS/CL or Program Manager—performs most of these functions for the child. One professional, then, is available to the child and the family on a 24-hour basis; he or she assesses the child's needs, evaluates the biological family, and supervises the child's treatment home. One professional develops the treatment plan in concert with the child and the treatment parents; develops any other special motivation systems or intervention plans for behavior change; counsels the child's biological family in programs where that is possible; and works with the schools, public agencies, court, and other community resources to create the context for the child's success. One professional providing all services to the child prevents mistakes and failures in communication and obviates the tendency for weighty bureaucratic structures to grow.

The frontline professional staff members, then, have complete responsibility for the children and families under their supervision. They have the authority to intervene when necessary, change treatment plans, and make other case decisions. This level of responsibility and autonomy is a significant departure from that of the caseworker-supervisor hierarchy or from the various multiple-member teams that are common in many agencies.

### Program Size

An organizational structure is influenced not only by the staff roles, caseloads, and general program philosophy, but also by program size. Based on the survival difficulties that small therapeutic foster care programs have demonstrated, we conclude that program viability requires at least a program size of 20 children, and two staff members, clinical consultants, and a secretary. Without this critical size, recruitment of talented foster parents is more difficult, since the most powerful recruit-ment method, word of mouth, is limited by the small number of treat-ment parents. Also, matching a child with a treatment home is limited by fewer available families. Re-placements within a program are not possible when the program has too few families. Most important, without at least two staff members, and preferably three, staff enthusiasm diminishes and teamwork is not possible.

With larger program size come issues of organizational structure. How should a 20-child program be staffed to provide necessary supervi-sion? How would this staffing pattern differ if the program had 50 children in homes within two hours from the program office? What would a large program's structure require to serve 200 or more children? The following brief descriptions of two of the three programs featured in this volume illustrate an organizational structure that has worked for a relatively small program and one that is effective for a large program.

Until 1985, Professional Parenting had a typical population of 20 children staffed with two full-time and two part-time professionals. The program director and the assistant program director also functioned as the case consultants, or treatment parent supervisors. Each had major case management responsibilities for ten children. The director of re-search and evaluation for the Study Center (the larger organization of which Professional Parenting is a part) served as a consultant to the program with direct responsibility for research and program evaluation. The Study Center director had overall responsibility for the program, shared administrative responsibility for the program with the program director, had responsibility for budgeting, and served as a program consultant for admission, recruitment, training, and family consultation. After 1985, Professional Parenting expanded into Asheville and Winston, North Carolina, resulting in a census of about 40 children. With this moderate program size, the program director no longer carries individual cases and has assumed the responsibilities of supervising program man-agers, each of whom carries a caseload of about eight to ten children.

PRYDE is a large, growth-oriented TFC program with a capacity of about 200 children in three states, served from several offices. PRYDE's growth is an example of how individual program units stay small while the entire program grows large. The benefits of a small program include generating and maintaining a family feeling among staff members and treatment parents, permitting the manager of the program to know all the treatment parents and each child fairly well, thus keeping the expert decision makers close to the clients and direct services. The benefits of a larger program, however, may provoke many programs to expand: larger numbers of treatment families allow for better matching; expansion allows for upward mobility of talented staff members and therefore can lead to greater staff morale; overhead costs can be reduced, keeping costs low while being able to add more highly skilled, specialized staff members or consultants. Although all three of the core programs provide technical assistance to social service/mental health programs in developing TFC services, the implementation is prolonged when new staff members are responsible; PRYDE has answered the demand, therefore, and expands each year by seeding new offices with experienced staff members or allowing current offices to expand to a maximum size of about 50 children.

PRYDE has five program sites, each serving about 50 children. Each site is managed by a site director, who reports to the PRYDE program director. The site directors, the program director, and the director of model implementation form the core executive management team responsible for program development, consultation, fiscal matters, and quality of services. Large program sites, such as PRYDE Pittsburgh, with 60 children, are divided into teams of 30 children, with each team supervised by an assistant director or a program supervisor. In addition to a team supervisor, teams comprise approximately five PS/CLs, each responsible for all of the supervision and treatment of as many as seven children. In each site, all staff members share responsibilities for the recruitment and training of treatment parents, while within each team (or smaller sites) all staff members share case information and on-call responsibilities.

Because PRYDE West Virginia is rural and treatment families are therefore geographically spread out, (as is the Professional Parenting program in North Carolina), it serves 60 children from two offices each with its own site director.

From these two program examples, certain organizational principles seem evident. A reasonable management size is 20 to 30 children. The manager of a program this size would carry some cases. Staff members at all levels need to be connected to the program and its development. Consultants or part-time staff members for clinical services, research, and fiscal management are also necessary for program components of this size. Expansion programs can form building blocks of 20 to 30 children, adding additional layers of management personnel as each block achieves a size of 20 to 30 children. Based on all three programs' experience, it is unlikely that a TFC program can be managed at a high level of quality if it exceeds about 50 children, unless additional management layers are in place, as exemplified in PRYDE.

## The Unique Role of a Treatment Parent Supervisor

The role of treatment parent supervisor or treatment parent consultant is unique to TFC, although it includes such typical foster care functions as maintaining up-to-date case records, representing the child in court, and ensuring that the child receives health services and that each child's welfare is protected. In addition to case management activities, treatment parent supervisors function as teachers, counselors or mental health specialists, residential supervisors, and consultants. They assist with all training services provided to treatment parents. They develop and modify treatment plans, and they supervise the treatment parents' implementation of treatment procedures. They provide treatment parents and children with around-the-clock consultation or assistance by phone, in the home, the school, or the community. They may advise treatment parents in handling the child during a crisis or actually give the treatment parents physical assistance (e.g., chasing after a runaway). They may consult with the child's teachers and give them effective strategies for classroom intervention. They often talk with the children directly to assist them with particular problems or help them to acquire new perspectives. The job requires many talents and a willingness to work evenings and weekends—whenever the treatment parents need them. Consequently, parent supervisors can be overwhelmed, especially since no prior training or education prepares them for all facets of the job. Therefore, on-the-job staff training and supervision become important aspects of TFC to prevent staff burnout and ensure the development of job-relevant skills.

## Staff Supervision and Training

To those staff members who work directly with treatment parents, TFC must offer frequent, accessible supervision and training. The three programs considered in this volume encourage informal staff interactions through small program size (or management components), creating partners, sharing offices, or even placing the coffee pot in the director's office. Formal supervision takes place regularly, usually weekly, although supervision and case consultation are available to all treatment parent supervisors at any time of the day or night. Since caseloads are small, in-depth analysis of problems, successes, and continuing treatment of the child are possible.

Because treatment parent supervisors must perform most of their job functions some distance from the office, direct observation of their skills is difficult. Therefore, most supervision activities include reviewing case data and discussing the cases. The three programs can provide good clinical supervision because of the records that treatment parents and staff members keep on the child's daily performance and on the treatment family's interactions with the child. Records maintained by the treatment parents include documentation of point system performance if the child is on a point system, of any other behavior change strategy, of the child's activities, and observations of critical events (e.g., phone contact with the biological family or a school problem). Daily records maintained by staff members include a brief written description of every contact regarding a case; thus, each consultation call to the treatment parents, each treatment home consultation, a call from the child's public agency caseworker or teacher are all recorded in a case contact notebook. Case contacts and treatment parents' daily records are routinely summarized for case supervision purposes and give staff members the immediate and long-term information they need to decide upon indicated interventions or needed treatment parent training. The records also ensure that staff members are doing a good job of training and consultation in the home. The staff members at People Places code each of their contacts as serving one of 15 purposes. During supervision meetings, they can readily see if they are spending too much time handling case logistics instead of training the treatment parents, for example. Supervision need not always be crisis-oriented when daily, specific, and comprehensive records are kept.

Data-based, frequent, and constructive case supervision enables TFC to provide quality treatment. Supervision alone, however, is not sufficient to establish the necessary skills among staff members who work directly with the treatment parents. TFC programs must be prepared to provide frequent staff training. The low pay scale for treatment parent supervisors, evident in all three programs, prevents the programs from hiring individuals who come with all the necessary skills. Rather, the emphasis must be on hiring enthusiastic, high-energy, skillful communicators who have an openness to being trained. Ideally, individuals who are hired have some background in behaviorally oriented problem

solving. Much of this technology can be taught by the program, however, as long as the individual clearly subscribes to the general view that
troubled and troubling behavior results from troubled and troubling
environments.

Staff training within the programs takes several forms: orientation
or entry training, in-service training, graduate school classes, other professional development activities, and the treatment parent pre-service
classes. Within PRYDE, much of the staff training has had to be formalized because of the program's expansion and frequent need to add
new staff members. Thus, the program provides a standard orientation
program to new staff members and has a staff training manual that
describes all aspects of the job. Smaller non-expansion programs would
not require such formalized training materials. Although People Places is
not oriented toward expansion, it does provide frequent technical assistance to other program developers and thus has developed training
materials for this purpose.

All three programs do provide formal training in at least the content
of the treatment parent pre-service training. Staff members achieve mastery of this material by participating in the training as "students," reading
the training materials and conducting the training sessions. All three
programs also use skilled behavior analysts for teaching staff. Each
program has at least one administrator who is a psychologist with
professional experience in behavior therapy.

Each program provides its staff members with an educational benefit
so that they can receive relevant job training by attending professional
conferences, workshops, or graduate school classes that deal with such
topics as family therapy, sex abuse, or delinquency. Some programs
assign certain available graduate school classes to staff members where
formal staff training can be given by the local university or college. At
PRYDE, a master's degree can be obtained in three years while working
in the program. This individualized graduate training program is
arranged through the special education department of a local university
but taught at the PRYDE offices by university faculty. The graduate
school program creates a strong incentive for staff members to stay for at
least three years—a secondary benefit.

Finally, the three programs use all of the staff members to teach each
other. During weekly staff meetings, in addition to case reviews for
supervision purposes, staff members have opportunities to present information that benefits service delivery. The staff assists new members by
showing them how to keep their case records current and by taking them

on home supervision meetings, to court, or to the child's school, where the new members learns through observing. Experienced staff members serve as daily teachers to new staff members by being available for questions and sharing case information informally.

## Cost

The TFC model provides a least restrictive setting and highly accountable treatment for children who might otherwise be institutionalized. The cost comparison, treatment service, and naturalness of the setting make TFC a particularly attractive alternative to institutionalization. All three programs represented here are lower in cost than local youth care institutions but are higher than local foster family care costs. In general, the greater the intensity of treatment, the higher the per diem cost of TFC. Thus, if children receive, daily, planned, documented, and staff-intensive remediation activities, treatment is considered more intensive than if a child receives intervention services when problems arise.

The 1988 per diem costs of the three programs to referring agencies ranged from $36 to $55. The PRYDE Pittsburgh per diem of $55 included all costs related to youth care, medical costs (except those covered by medical assistance by a state-funded medical benefits program for disadvantaged children), clothing, transportation, counseling, other special services, services to biological parents, and follow-up services after a child is discharged. The per diem cost of about $36 for children in Professional Parenting homes is typical of most referrals except those youngsters designated as "Willy M" children, a term used in North Carolina for children who, as a result of a class action suit, receive special funding for placement resources; these children are characteristically extremely disturbed and disturbing. People Places' per diem of about $36 is supplemented by additional reimbursable expenses, including transportation of children, counseling, and special services such as independent-living skills, so that the actual per diem cost may be as high as $45. Since institutional costs range from $55 to $600 per day, the costs of treatment parenting are clearly competitive.

Initial start-up costs cannot be absorbed by per diem income alone. Newly developing TFC programs must have additional sources of income or have funded contracts. Professional Parenting has relied on federal, state, and private foundation grants to reach a cost-effective, break-even point. PRYDE had a one-year start-up grant from the Pennsylvania Commission on Crime and Delinquency to cover the initial high per diem costs. Size of a program has serious fiscal implications: if a program remains too small, under 15 children, cost effectiveness and competitive fee structures are difficult to achieve. Treatment parents are paid at least 40 percent of the received per diem income; this high percentage is not typical in foster family care.

## Creating Excellence in Therapeutic Foster Care Programs

In most instances the pay scale for staff in TFC programs is slightly below that found in the public sector. How, then, can highly talented, eagerly committed staff be recruited and maintained? It is the context of management that makes these programs work [Peters and Waterman 1982]. Even if a program adopted all of the technology indicated in this volume, it would not produce a successful TFC program unless it created a context in which rapid, creative problem solving and adaptations of procedures could be carried out.

The level of staff autonomy and encouragement for creative contributions common to the core programs provide the right context for creative individuals. Although there are standard procedures and parameters of treatment planning to be followed, each child's treatment plan is highly individualized; thus, each staff member has a hand in developing novel, tailor-made programs for the children on his or her caseload. Progress by treatment parents is a success of the staff members who supervise them—and staff members receive highly visible recognition for their successes. Accomplishment is applauded by all the staff members at group meetings. Outstanding performance during a month may merit some special recognition. Public recognition and personal satisfaction foster enthusiasm for one's job.

The supportive, cooperative management style common to these programs provides another contextual variable for good staff morale. Staff members at all levels are treated as partners, with dignity and respect. There is an insistence that all staff members excel, that each be a "hero" in some area. Staff members who have autonomy in responsible positions have a great deal of control over their own schedules, areas of excellence, and their own job destiny. Burnout tends to be high only in those professions and positions where the individual has little control over job-related outcomes.

The three programs are characterized by a family feeling. Administrators are available and visible to the staff; they model program values to the entire staff. They too work long hours and are available to staff members on a 24-hour basis. In other words, the management style must reflect the same supervision support as that provided to treatment parents.

Excellence in TFC programs also results from basing decisions on data, analyzing the data, and solving problems with them. A commitment to program evaluation, accountable treatment, and data-based supervision allows the three programs considered in this volume to know whom they are serving, what they are doing, what appears to be working, and what needs to change. Data on all aspects of a program infuse the staff with excitement. The staff can see where the program has come from and where it is going; they are a part of creating the program each day.

To achieve excellence requires a bias toward action, a sufficiently loose organization so that different staff members can jump to special projects when needed, and an emphasis on experimentation—allowing staff members to make mistakes. Since the children can create unpredictable situations, a program must be willing to act swiftly, try new interventions, and accept mistakes. For the new interventions that work, the staff should receive cheers; for those that do not work, little should be said. The emphasis is on praising individuals and, when necessary, criticizing groups.

An empowering administration cannot operate out of a complex structure. Thus another contextual variable for maintaining staff morale and high achievement is to keep the program simple. PRYDE's use of small teams and sites is an effort to act small within a large program. Organizational goals must be simple and few in number. Program growth, high levels of successful discharges of children, and high levels of skilled treatment parents are all simply stated directions behind which all staff members can align themselves.

Finally, the context for high staff morale is an obsession with comitment to service. With service to the treatment parents, the children, and the children's own families as the preeminent goals, growth will occur naturally.

## REFERENCES

Peters, T. J., and Waterman, R. H. In Search of Excellence: Lessons from America's Best-Run Companies. New York: Warner Books, 1982.

# 7

# Providing Services to Children in Therapeutic Foster Care

PAMELA MEADOWCROFT
ROBERT P. HAWKINS
EILEEN MARY GREALISH
AND
PAMELA WEAVER

A MAJOR GOAL OF THERAPEUTIC foster care (TFC) is to bring about changes in socially and personally significant behaviors of troubled and troubling children, and to expand existing and develop new adaptive behaviors. Treatment—viewed as re-education of the child to behave effectively and responsibly in society [Hobbs 1982; Phillips et al. 1974]— occurs in the private homes of mature adults who function both as foster parents and as the primary treatment agents. In light of the belief that the troubled and troubling behaviors that the youngsters exhibit result from troubled and troubling environments, the logical first step is to change those environments. The primary strategy for doing this, in the three programs described in this volume, is to move the child to a home where the foster parents are skilled and active "teachers" and have the motivation and support to effect re-education, or treatment.

That placement is in a family within the mainstream community provides significant possibilities for incidental treatment. Children have daily opportunities to observe and imitate the treatment parents' social skills. The children are also exposed to most, if not all, of the normal everyday tasks that make up adult life. A child who is removed from a family to an institution tends to have a fragmented view of daily life, learning that when something must be purchased, he or she must get a purchase order from the accounting department; when a light bulb burns out, the maintenance department must be contacted. Children in TFC observe healthy marriages and parenting role models within their treatment families. These opportunities for incidental learning are a key to successful foster family-based treatment. They provide children with experiences that may well be very different from those in their biological families (and certainly different from those in institutions).

Although incidental learning is important in all TFC programs, planned interventions for troublesome behavior are also characteristic of this model, though the frequency and methods of particular strategies vary across programs. All three programs in this volume use professional counseling for their clients, but the main source of counseling and behavior change is in the daily interactions between the treatment parents and the youngsters. Clinical research shows that traditional talk therapy often fails to produce any significant effect among troubled and troubling adolescents [Glaser 1980]; behavior contracting, token economies, and other highly structured behavior change strategies demonstrate more effectiveness for this population of children. Implementation of these behavior change plans is the responsibility of the treatment parents. To assist them, staff members from the three programs are frequently available to establish behavioral contracts and assist with problem solving; the treatment parent supervisor or program manager is always present in, or approves of, treatment plan negotiations. Yet moment-by-moment interactions, providing consequences for the child's behavior and structured teaching, are the responsibilities of the treatment parents. In this way, the intensiveness of the treatment that TFC can provide depends on the degree to which a child is involved in activities that are arranged for behavioral remediation.

The three core programs share the general view of treatment as re-education and, therefore, have several characteristics in common: active teaching, the selection of target behaviors, an emphasis on the positive social consequences for adaptive behaviors, an emphasis on liaison services, and common behavioral treatment strategies.

## Active Teaching

Although the treatment parents do an excellent job of teaching passively through the models they set (e.g., regarding home organization, respect for the law, interpersonal courtesies), through their teaching of their own children, through their facilitation of constructive activity, this situation is true of any good home, and this situation would be true in any special foster care program that recruits foster parents effectively and selects them carefully. What is unique to the three core programs is their emphasis on active, planned, frequent teaching. The foster parents are viewed as filling a professional role and are expected to teach the child whatever he or she needs to learn in order to be effective and responsible. Inappropriate behavior on the child's part is not viewed as his or her fault, but the fault of past learning, which can only be remedied through new learning. The child's problem behaviors are not viewed as a sign of inner emotional disturbance, but rather as evidence of what the child needs to learn.

Obviously, this view places a heavy burden of responsibility on the treatment parents. They cannot leave the "real" treatment solely in the hands of a mental health professional who sees a client weekly, as is normally done in special foster care [Barnes 1980]. The learning experiences the treatment parents provide the child *are* the treatment. Therefore, the quality of pre-service training, in-service training, and support services for treatment parents are of critical importance. Staff members communicate their high expectations of and support for the treatment parents with such implicit or explicit messages as the following: "Stick with this youngster; it took him or her years to learn this misbehavior, it will take at least months to learn the new behavior." "We know it's a miserable pain and embarrassment (remember, we told you it would be), and we admire your 'guts' in enduring it." "Remember the skills we taught you; let's apply them consistently to this problem behavior." "None of us is a perfect teacher (therapist); all we can do is our best, and that's what we're doing now."

In solving problems, the three programs expect the treatment parents to work with staff members in planning interventions that involve the direct teaching and motivation of desirable performance. This teaching may require routines that are carried out several times a day on a planned schedule, or may require only responding in a certain way when certain behaviors occur. The programs also expect the treatment parents to work with others (e.g., teachers, community leaders, neighbors, or relatives) to get their support or assistance in promoting the child's learning.

Finally, the programs expect treatment parents to be involved with any group or individual that the programs provide to meet the special needs of the client or to correct for the particular weaknesses of the treatment parents (and staff). Most individual counseling provided by program staff members (or outside mental health resources/consultants) is normally short-term and problem-specific. Typically it is used to assess the problem, discover what may work best for the child, and then teach the treatment parents how to manage this problem or teach the child objectively in the home and community. Counseling the child in these three programs serves as another training opportunity for the treatment parents (and staff).

## Selection of Specific Target Behaviors

The behavioral view shared by the three programs suggests that teaching (treatment) is most effective when it is directed at relatively specific observable behaviors rather than at general characteristics, traits, or hypothesized inner variables [Hawkins 1986; Mager 1975; Martin and Pear 1978]. Thus, in attempting to remedy any serious problem, the objectives that are likely to be selected are such specific behaviors as the following: "says something positive about him/herself," "looks directly at the person speaking when being given an instruction," "uses an 'I-feel message' to express feelings orally using appropriate language and voice tone," and "does not use obscene language around family members or friends." As this last objective illustrates, the direct focus is sometimes upon eliminating some maladaptive behavior, such as when a treatment parent stopped talking with a 15-year-old boy whenever he described talking to his dead grandmother. By ignoring such delusional talk, its frequency should decrease. Often, however, the direct focus is on "constructing" behavior [Schwartz and Goldiamond 1975] that is more adaptive than some existing performance, such as when a youth who behaved in various rude ways was taught to ask for things courteously, to thank people, to answer the phone with pleasant words and tone.

## Planning of Specific Consequences

It has been widely documented that the events that immediately follow a behavior determine the future frequency of that behavior. Although there is much more to teaching than assuring appropriate consequences, without such consequences the desired learning is unlikely. Thus, all three programs teach and motivate treatment parents to use or arrange for consequences that will *(1)* strengthen desired behaviors; *(2)* weaken undesired behaviors; *(3)* avoid strengthening undesired behaviors; and *(4)* avoid weakening desired behaviors. That is, all the programs make frequent, planned use of the basic behavioral principles of reinforcement, punishment, and extinction.

For reasons of ethics as well as effectiveness, the programs emphasize use of consequences that strengthen desired behaviors, particularly the "six A's" known as "social reinforcers": attention, acknowledgment, appreciation, approval, admiration, and affection. Treatment parents are taught and motivated to provide such social reinforcers routinely. This reaction is particularly important when the child exhibits a behavior that has been targeted as a desirable objective, but it is also important to give these reinforcers non-contingently in the sense that, although the child has not done anything especially correct, he or she is at least not misbehaving at the moment.

The use of non-contingent affection and attention is probably important for several reasons. First, these social events seem to be important for making the child care what the treatment parents (and perhaps others) think of him or her, and thus, for establishing approval as a reinforcer and disapproval as a punisher. Certainly disapproval would be a much larger stimulus change in a pleasant, supportive environment (which includes frequent non-contingent reinforcement) than it would in a relatively neutral environment, and thus it might function as a more powerful negative consequence because of the general ambience of positive social events. Second, non-contingent social reinforcers probably do much to promote calm, relaxed, assertive performance—in effect, the qualitative dimensions that lead others to say that the child is more "confident," less "defensive," or has gained in "self-esteem." Finally, the modeling of positive social behavior by a treatment parent is likely to bring out a positive reciprocation (imitation) from the child, which the treatment parent is likely then to reinforce through an even more positive response. Good relationships are built on such exchanges and are the foundation for much of what treatment parents accomplish with children.

## Emphasis on Liaison Services

The programs described in this volume are also characterized by a high degree of staff involvement in liaison services, which facilitates significant and productive cooperation between agencies. The ecological, "whole child" approach espoused by these programs necessitates such cooperation [Wahler 1969]. Since treatment addresses each environment in which the child spends appreciable time, including school, visits with relatives, community recreational activities, a consistent and balanced treatment approach requires continual communication regarding the child's behaviors and interactions in each environment.

### School Liaison

The majority of the children served by TFC programs experience some degree of difficulty in educational settings. Many children require special educational services, primarily due to diagnoses of learning disability, social and emotional disturbance, behavior disorder, or educable mental handicap. In some cases, mainstreamed students are informally labeled by their reputations for truancy, lack of achievement, or a tendency to be generally difficult to manage. School issues are therefore part of most children's treatment, and the appropriate school placement is a high priority.

Planning for educational placement must begin early, during the referral process. Options for a child may include mainstreamed education, minimal special education support through a resource room, a full-time (or nearly full-time) special education classroom with some mainstreaming potential (physical education, lunch, art, and so on), or full-time private or public special education without any mainstreaming. Staff members determine options for school placement through the initial referral and other assessment information. The staff must choose the least restrictive alternative available that will meet the learning needs of the child, in keeping with the requirements of Public Law 94-142, the Education for All Handicapped Children Act.

The three core programs have encountered occasional reluctance on the part of local school systems to accept the children they serve. School personnel may view the child as a potential troublemaker because of the child's status as "in treatment." In addition, financial constraints seem to cause resistance in some cases, particularly if the child needs expensive special education services and the state (or school districts) have no mechanism to transfer the extra funds from the child's original home school district to the current district. The staff, therefore, must try to involve the school staff in planning for the child and respond to school requests for support or intervention as rapidly and effectively as possible.

People Places invites school staff members to attend the selection interview, which involves them in the placement process from the outset. Schools are informed in advance of the arrival of new children, so that the school staff can plan for class assignment and materials.

Professional Parenting staff members accompany treatment parents and children to the school to assist in setting up new placements. The treatment parents are taught to support the school placement by following up on teacher reports, keeping track of a child's progress, and maintaining communication with teachers and other involved personnel.

PRYDE treatment parents are also trained to perform these functions, although they share responsibility with the treatment parent supervisor. The latter usually initiates the education placement, since the staff is knowledgeable about education laws, the different school district requirements, and the child's particular educational needs. The PRYDE treatment parents gradually learn to advocate effectively for their children as the placement progresses.

Written daily communication with teachers may be necessary to ensure accurate reporting of the school day by the child, to detect and then intervene or assist in academic and conduct problems, to provide the child with special praise for good school performance, and to reinforce effective teacher behavior quickly. TFC often uses school notes or daily school reports on which teachers report critical positive and negative incidents, evaluate a child's performance on selected objectives, and inform the treatment parent of assigned homework. This information enables the treatment parent to reward specific behaviors during the school day or see more general trends that may require early intervention. A note may also be used by the treatment parent to inform the teacher of the child's progress at home or to describe any events occurring in the home that may affect the child's school day. In an extensive review of research on the use of school notes, Atkeson and Foreland [1979] found that they effectively improve children's school behavior.

People Places and PRYDE have access to private, special education schools run by their agencies. Pygmalian Day School and Pressley Ridge Day School serve children who require a highly structured learning experience where academic and behavioral remediation can be accomplished. Children must be referred to these schools by the public school in the child's district and be approved by the state for this most restrictive educational setting. Children attend these schools only when a less restrictive placement is not adequate or available. About 15 percent to 20 percent of the children in these programs attend the agencies' schools.

### Community Liaison

The main purpose of community liaison is to maximize the child's opportunities for positive social experiences in the community. Unlike institutional programs where group recreation is planned and implemented by the recreational staff, TFC emphasizes community activities for each child with opportunities to interact with well-adjusted peers. Institutional identification of children is avoided; organized community activities (e.g., camping, ball playing, Christmas caroling) for groups of children from within the program are discouraged.

All three programs' staff members and treatment parents involve children in community activities such as Scouts, the local Parks and Recreation Department, Elks, Big Brothers/Sisters, YWCA/YMCA, Boys' Clubs of America, and so forth. People Places includes treatment goals related to participation in community activities, so children are rewarded for their efforts in this area. Professional Parenting families are frequently active in a variety of community activities and are strongly encouraged to assist their children in participating. When treatment parents or another member of the family are involved, they can introduce children and help them begin to fit into the organization. PRYDE treatment parents are hospitable to the prosocial friends of their children and open their homes to sleepovers, dinner visits, and hanging out. During pre-service training, they learn how to teach children to select positive friends and maintain relationships with peers, thus increasing the possibility that the children will form satisfying relationships. Performance evaluations on PRYDE treatment parents and children's progress evaluations include the number of prosocial friends the child has and the types of activities the child pursues outside the home so that this important area of development is seriously addressed.

TFC programs also require treatment parents to ensure that adult neighbors and community members accept the child. In introducing the child to community friends, the treatment parents express their pleasure with having the child in their home and their confidence that the child will be a contributing community member. Because information about children is confidential, treatment parents must be sensitive to questions about why the child does not live with his or her own family. A general response, such as "Joe needs a little time away from his own family and we were glad to provide it," will probably answer most questions. Persistent questioning may require a more definite response, for example, "I agreed not to discuss Joe's history." Treatment parents and children often seem happy to think and speak of themselves as foster parents and foster children.

When community problems arise, TFC programs must be prepared to react in a way that will prevent discrimination against a child. Irate neighbors and community officials may accuse the child of misbehavior. Treatment parents learn to approach these situations by listening carefully to the report, expressing confidence that the problem can be solved, offering to explore the problem immediately with the child, thanking the person involved for delivering the report, and following up with the person to describe measures taken to resolve the situation. Treatment parents learn to maintain a calm, confident communication style in these situations, which lets the others know that the situation is well in hand and will be resolved.

Any property destruction in the community or treatment home by a child creates liaison needs. Professional Parenting maintains a contingency fund to reimburse families for destruction of property in the community by a child placed in their home, so immediate restitution can be part of the solution. Usually, when restitution is necessary, treatment parents arrange for the child to earn whatever amount of money is necessary to pay for damages. If the child cannot make timely payments, then program funds are used in different ways (e.g., matching each dollar the child pays, paying the victim of the destruction and having the child repay the program).

Job finding for older children requires yet additional liaison support. A TFC program may contact job services programs, such as those provided through the federal Job Training Partnership Act, to arrange employment. Treatment parents and staff members may also use their personal or professional community contacts for employment opportunities and need to provide the older adolescent with frequent, extensive training in job hunting and interviewing skills.

### Public Agency and Court Liaison

The referring agency and juvenile court must be regularly informed about a child's progress. Representatives of the public agency or the court are generally charged with the responsibility of supervising the overall progress of treatment and formulating recommendations on whether the placement should continue. These recommendations are formalized, in many cases, during review hearings before the child's judge. Caseworkers and probation officers are consulted when a treatment plan is initially developed and throughout the placement. Critical incidents, such as runaways and delinquent acts, must be reported by the staff so that the allied professionals can contribute to possible modifications of treatment or inform the child's judge, if this action is necessary.

Methods for maintaining consistent communication vary across the three core programs. People Places uses letters to report significant events to referring agents. Some PRYDE staff members host monthly lunches with public agency caseworkers to ensure regular communication, with specific reports or phone calls filling in as needed between in-person contacts. Judicial reviews and quarterly progress reports provide additional opportunities for sharing information. When these contacts are conscientiously maintained, referring agencies are able to justify the child's placement within a treatment home and to support each child's treatment and discharge plan.

## Variations in Treatment Services of Each Program

All three programs use a variety of individualized behavior change or re-education procedures because these procedures work well for a troubled and troubling child. Behavior change procedures are also well defined and therefore, in many instances, treatment parents can be trained to implement these strategies with a high level of skill. A final advantage of behavior change procedures is their focus on producing an observable, reliable change in a child's adjustment. Although the three core programs adhere to similar behavior change strategies, they differ in terms of how consistently and formally the procedures are used for all children. Treatment parents in all three programs are expected to assess the child's behavior and to use, to varying degrees, contingent consequences, intensive management systems (token economies, point systems), behavior contracting, and skill teaching.

### Professional Parenting

Children referred to the Professional Parenting program typically present two core problems that have shaped that program's philosophy of child services and treatment. First, they have either been abandoned by or legally removed from their biological parents and are usually referred for indefinite placement, that is, with no plan or intent that they be returned to the biological family. Second, as is the case in all TFC programs, most children have moved among various care and treatment facilities for several years before being referred to Professional Parenting. This desultory circuit of failed placements has often left these children with the attitude that "Nobody really cares about me," or "I can do as I choose because nobody can control me."

This characteristic referral scenario, combined with an increasingly better understanding of the strengths and limitations of the treatment families that the Professional Parenting program is able to attract, has led its staff to the following choices and priorities concerning child services and attendant treatment strategies: *(1)* An overriding initial goal for each child entering placement is the successful integration of that child into the family unit of his or her treatment parents. *(2)* When that initial integration has been accomplished and the placement appears to have stabilized, a second goal is to ensure or maximize the durability of the placement. *(3)* The best tools for accomplishing these two goals are the natural strengths and parenting skills (which the program selects for) of the treatment parents and the application of specific behavior interventions, as required, which exceed the presenting skills of program families and must, thus, be trained and monitored. *(4)* These behavior interventions are assignable along a continuum of structure or "naturalness" with simple praise and ignoring at one end of the range, easily implemented behavior contracts and daily school notes somewhere in the middle, and more highly structured or intensive management methods (e.g., direct staff counseling, individualized point motivation regimens) at the other extreme. *(5)* Finally, the program emphasizes the use of the least restrictive intervention necessary to meet the treatment needs of the child, and the flexibility to alter readily the level of treatment structure as a child's needs and behaviors change.

With these goals in mind, Professional Parenting provides the following treatment services for all children: pre-placement preparation; individual written treatment plans; child progress reports; meetings with children; and individual and group counseling. This set of services also is common to People Places and PRYDE, with some minor variations.

Pre-placement preparation occurs when a decision has been made to place a specific child with a specific family. This preparation takes place in the context of a meeting of the treatment parents with the program staff to *(1)* examine all salient aspects of the child's social history; *(2)* anticipate what problems or behaviors are likely to present themselves and how soon they should be expected; and *(3)* review and rehearse specific strategies and interventions that are to be applied, either from the outset of placement or when expected child problems or behaviors do occur. These pre-placement preparation sessions do not constitute formalized or long-term treatment planning (see below) but do produce a kind of miniplan during the first month.

After a child has been placed with a program family for one month, the program manager develops a written individual treatment plan for that child. The plan considers the child's pre-program social history, all observations and data reflecting the child's first month in placement, and long-term goals suggested by the child's treatment parents, teachers, and referral agent. Treatment plans specify the reasons for the child's placement in the program, special services to be provided to the child or to the program family, in-home and at-school performance goals (and independent-living goals for children within a year of high school graduation or legal majority), and include a "permanent plan," that is, a long-term plan that remains relatively unaffected by the child's interim progress. Treatment plans are perused and signed by the treatment parents before being submitted to the child's referral agency caseworker, at which time they become part of the child's permanent file.

Revisions and adjustments to individual treatment plans take the form of child progress reports, which are attached as addenda to the child's original treatment plan and also submitted to the child's referral agency. Progress reports document the child's academic and behavioral performance in school, progress and problems within the professional parenting home, contacts (if any) with the biological family, and any medical or health-related events occurring during the reporting interval.

Suggestions, recommendations, and revisions of long-term goals are summarized at the end of each report. The progress report interval is six months for most children and three months for children in certain diagnostic categories.

In addition to the incidental contact they have with placed children in connection with routine treatment home visits, program managers also schedule private visits on an as-needed, but at least quarterly, basis. These one-to-one interactions occur away from the Professional Parenting family and are intended to *(1)* promote a trusting relationship between the child and the program manager; *(2)* aid in the prevention (or detection) of any form of abuse or neglect; and *(3)* assess the child's level of progress in, and satisfaction with, the current placement. The private visits also afford an opportunity to identify any special needs a child might have, such as adjustments in allowance, frequency of contact with the biological family, medical or dental needs, special counseling, and so forth. Private visits most often involve taking the child out for pizza or ice cream but have also successfully centered on going roller skating, taking long walks, attending a basketball game or other school function, and the like. Pertinent substance of private child visits is documented in case notes and later summarized in child progress reports.

Finally, in addition to arranging for special outside medical or psychological services for children with special needs, the Professional Parenting staff provides in-house group and individual counseling as required. Most such counseling is problem-specific and is usually short-term. Individual counseling—offered by regular program staff who are also licensed practicing psychologists—has been addressed to a broad range of emotional and behavioral child problems judged to be beyond the skill of program parents to address directly. Group counseling is also provided by staff members with specialized training and experience.

## PRYDE

Similar to the Professional Parenting program, PRYDE develops a general treatment plan for each child in placement. Pennsylvania law requires that children in placement have formal treatment plans that describe the placement goal (e.g., return home), general treatment goals for the child (e.g., improving peer interactions), the education and vocational services to be provided, the visitation plan for the child's biological family, and the latter's goals (e.g., will attend PRYDE biological parent group.) Each plan requires the signature of the child, the child's parents, the PRYDE treatment parents, and staff members of PRYDE and the referring agency.

PRYDE also provides each child with a daily written plan that lists specific behavioral goals the child needs to achieve with the treatment parents that day. These daily plans most often take the form of a point system or some highly individualized token economy.

Each PRYDE child has a daily list of objectives (a point system) because the program believes that the plans help prevent problem behaviors from growing. The program considers this structured intervention necessary for the children it serves. If training foster parents in effective parenting skills alone were sufficient, then further intervention in family functioning would be unnecessary (although routinely developed, written treatment plans maintain a high level of service accountability, which is increasingly important in all children's services). Given the severity of the problems most children display upon entering the program, however, more formal interventions are necessary; in PRYDE, the daily structure provided by these point systems is considered basic to the child's treatment, just as an individualized education plan and the attendant activities are basic to a special educational program.

To construct individually sensitive, daily point systems, PRYDE uses referral materials and other assessment tools and information sources to guide the development of behavioral objectives. The child's caseworker, own family, and/or counselor from a previous placement provide descriptions of the severity and form of the child's problem behaviors. Observations during the intake interview and subsequent pre-placement visits in a treatment home provide current information on the child's behavior. Treatment parents keep a Log of Daily Events during pre-placement visits, which includes their observations of the child's behavior in their home. (After formal placement, treatment parents complete the log daily.) PRYDE also uses standardized instruments such as the Child Behavior Checklist [Achenbach and Edelbrock 1979] to help define behavioral objectives in the point system. The child, treatment parents, and teachers may also complete the checklist within the first 30 days of placement. The profile derived from this checklist serves as a baseline of behavior problems against which annual or discharge evaluations using the checklist can be compared.

All treatment goals and objectives are clearly defined in precise and objective language [Mager 1975; Martin and Pear 1978]. Role-playing and spoken or written examples of each objective may be used to clarify expectations of the child and make certain that the treatment parents will be able to recognize consistently the occurrence or non-occurrence of a treatment behavior. This precision in defining a treatment behavior facilitates consistency on the part of treatment parents, permits objective evaluation of the child's progress, and thus serves as the means by which treatment goals can be reached and systematically eliminated from a treatment plan.

The staff, treatment parents, and the child develop the daily point system by the end of the child's first day in placement. When a treatment system reflects a child's own personal goals and addresses issues that he or she selects as important, the child is more likely to comply with the plan, which specifies behavioral objectives and determines the number of points to be assigned to each behavior. Each child's list of objectives differs from each other child's, but some objectives are common for many children, such as "follows adult instructions within 30 seconds and without backtalk," or "lets foster parents know of whereabouts at all times."

The point system is part of a token economy in which tokens or points are exchanged for each occurrence or non-occurrence of a particular treatment objective. Points or tokens are exchangeable for activities, allowance, snacks, and even material goods such as special clothing items, sports equipment, or an album.

Motivating a child to do well in treatment areas through a point system has many advantages. It allows the program to *(1)* reinforce good behavior of a child who really may not care about adult approval, disapproval, praise, or respect; *(2)* reward behavior immediately (with points that can be exchanged later for major or minor privileges or goods); *(3)* increase the likelihood that the treatment parents, who dispense praise along with the points, will become a meaningful source of approval for the child; *(4)* punish inappropriate behavior in a non-emotional way by simply subtracting points, which is less likely to produce an emotional counterreaction on the part of the child; *(5)* break down larger rewards such as a special activity into smaller pieces so that the child can clearly see the accumulation of good behavior as eventually paying off; *(6)* always have an effective reinforcer for a particular behavior, since points or tokens can be exchanged for a wide variety of things the child may want; *(7)* have a quantitative record of the child's performance for measuring progress and thus an accountability method for assuring treatment services; and *(8)* keep the child and treatment parent focused upon the critical goals for the child. A major advantage for requiring all children to begin with point systems is that this structure can be gradually eliminated as good performance persists rather than be instituted when poor performacne begins to emerge.

Based on research in motivating children to learn and change [Kazdin and Bootzin 1972] and on PRYDE's experience with using point systems, this form of a treatment plan works well. Instances in which inappropriate behavior escalates in a PRYDE home usually can be traced to the incorrect design or implementation of a point system. Children frequently express a high degree of comfort in the consistency of consequences and explicit expectations that their point systems provide.

Each child's point system targets three types of behavior: treatment, maintenance, and social/emotional development behaviors. Treatment behaviors are those that have to be strengthened or weakened if the child is to be viewed as making an adequate adjustment in his or her community. Treatment objectives on a child's point system describe the desired behavior that normally is expected to replace annoying, undesired behavior. For example, if a child demonstrates anger through episodes of frequent, intense verbal aggression, a treatment objective would be "uses an I-feel message to express anger in a calm voice." Each point system has approximately four to 20 behaviors, with points gained for each occurrence of the behavior (e.g., "tells foster parent calmly that s/he feels frustrated and upset over something"), or points lost for each occurrence of the misbehavior (e.g., "verbal aggression"). Special problems with academic or school behavior are also included as part of the treatment objectives.

Maintenance behaviors are chore-related responsibilities that are often more oriented toward the convenience of all family members than toward the child's adjustment. Maintenance objectives, however, do target important skills related to independent living and home care.

Social/emotional development behaviors enhance the child's interaction skills, adjustment in the community, or school performance, but are not considered sufficiently problematic to be regarded as treatment behaviors. Examples include "watches one-half hour of educational television each night" or "reads book of his choice for 45 minutes each day."

To assure that the point system maintains a treatment emphasis, as opposed to a staff convenience emphasis found in many institutional programs [Holland 1978], treatment behaviors must constitute at least 60 percent of the total objectives, and, normally, no more than 20 percent of the objectives may be chore-related behaviors. Thus, PRYDE point systems include few chores and many subtle, positive emotional and social treatment behaviors.

Each behavior listed on a child's point system is "worth" a specified number of points for loss or gain. Older children work for point totals in the thousands since large point consequences better sustain their interest [Phillips et al. 1974]. Children who are unable to understand extremely large numbers are given smaller numbers of points (10 to 100 per behavior) on their point systems. Small point consequences may be insufficiently concrete to have a reinforcing effect for some children; for these youngsters, physical tokens, such as checkers, poker chips, or stars on a chart, help the child to see the accumulation of consequences for good behavior and effectively maintain the child's interest.

Children actively work toward the accumulation of points to earn the activities or material goods that the points can "purchase" (i.e., "back-up" reinforcers), sometimes simply to achieve the maximum number of points possible, or perhaps to please others. The total number of points or tokens achieved determines a child's "privilege level," on which only certain activities, allowance, or other rewards are available [Phillips et al. 1974]. As with the behavioral objectives, each child's choice of privileges is determined in consultation with the child and the treatment parent to assure that the activities and other rewards are reinforcing to the child and will be reliably awarded by the parents.

Most children's point systems consist of three levels of privilege. Level I is set for the lowest range of point earnings and indicates poor performance: privileges are fairly meager and restrictive. The child may receive no allowance, be allowed only one call to a friend, and have an early bedtime. A child receives Level II privileges for an average range of point earnings (and thus an overall average performance); the child can choose more interesting activities and tangible rewards than on Level I. For excellent (Level III) performance, demonstrated by the accumulation of many points, a child has the most meaningful rewards available, which motivates the child to perform well.

In implementing a point system, treatment parents use one of the three main types of delivery: a daily point system, a physical token system, or a merit system. The most common is the daily point system, in which accumulated points determine a daily point total that, in turn, determines the next day's privilege level. Therefore, on Monday the child who successfully achieves a high percentage on the day's required objectives for Level III performance has available Level III privileges on Tuesday. Although each behavior can immediately result in point gain or loss, the concrete, back-up reinforcers for the accumulated good behaviors are not available until the next day. Obviously, the daily point system is used only for those children whose behavior responds to delayed tangible rewards.

Treatment parents learn to implement the daily point system in such a way that the child has increasing responsibility in its implementation. Initially the treatment parent must immediately provide a consequence for each occurrence or non-occurrence of a treatment behavior by telling the child that the behavior will gain or cost the agreed-upon points, praising the child for the positive behavior, and recording the points on the point chart. At any time during the day the child can refer to the point sheet and know how many points he or she needs to reach the top level of privileges by the end of the day. As this immediacy and consistency of point consequences (along with other procedures) produces increases in prosocial behavior, and as the child and treatment parent learn the point gains and costs for treatment behaviors, the treatment parent can begin to record point gains and losses less immediately. Instead, the treatment parent and child can review the whole morning's behaviors at the end of the morning and the afternoon and evening behaviors at the end of the evening, awarding points at those two times. Eventually the parent and child review the behavior only at the end of each day and record points once.

For young children, or others for whom delayed rewards are less effective, the treatment parents use manipulable tokens or small numbers of points as immediate consequences for each target behavior as it occurs. As points are gained or lost, privileges are gained or lost immediately. For example, a child who expressed a strong interest in auto racing was given a concrete, immediate-payoff, token system involving a large race track and a small car. The child started each day with his car on the starting line, indicating that he currently had Level II privileges, and was therefore permitted to play outside, play with video games, or listen to the stereo. Each success the child experienced allowed him to move the car ahead one notch (equivalent to one point) on the track. A failure required the car to be moved backward an agreed-upon number of notches. Levels were indicated on the race track itself through the use of chekered flags. If the car moved from Level II to Level I, the child immediately lost the Level II privileges, was required to remain inside, and given opportunities to engage in positive behaviors that would allow the child and the treatment parent to move the car back up the track until the child regained Level II privileges. When the car passed the flag at Level III, the child was permitted to play in a special area, serve favorite treats to his or her friends, and go to the neighborhood candy store unsupervised. The amount of the child's daily allowance was contingent upon the position of the car at bedtime.

A merit system is used for children who have shown consistent, long-term progress on a daily point system, or children who are nearing discharge and thus should be weaned from the high degree of structure provided by the daily point system. Merit systems allow for a necessary increase in the delay of a consequence for treatment-related behaviors, starting with a one-day delay and building to as much as a week's delay of back-up reinforcers (such as allowance) for overall weekly performance.

The process of moving from an immediate consequence for a particular behavior to a merit system in which overall performance is rewarded at the end of a week is gradual. As the child makes progress on the point system (e.g., shows no point losses for a particular behavior over three months), behaviors are dropped from the system or combined into more global goals. Treatment objectives such as "does not call other children in the home a creep" and "does not hit or otherwise interrupt other children in the home during evening homework" may become "gets along with other children." At the same time that treatment behaviors are collapsed into larger goals, the child takes on more responsibility for completing his or her own point system. Initially the treatment parent fills in each point loss and gain and totals all points for a daily review of performance. Then the child assumes responsibility for recording most point losses and gains with adult prompts and supervision. Eventually the child completes the daily point chart and treatment parents check for accuracy. The final merit system is a short list of treatment goals that the child and treatment parents monitor independently and review weekly. This final system may be much like the rules and expectations required of a typical adolescent to have certain weekend privileges. Though a shift to merit should take place as rapidly as possible for each child, the children and families often report that the point motivation system helps maintain a more trouble-free adjustment because expectations are so clearly defined. Nonetheless, as discharge planning progresses, the daily structure in the PRYDE home begins to lessen for each child.

In addition to the formalized point systems for all children, PRYDE requires all treatment parents to use certain skills on a daily or nearly daily basis. These skills include common communication strategies (active listening and direct expression of feelings); problem solving; relationship-building techniques (e.g., uses child's idea, gives social reward/ praise); and skill teaching. Treatment parents must complete the daily log of events, which asks them to report on their use of each of the skills. Because PRYDE views its treatment parents as teachers of everyday family behavior, the report requires them to provide daily skill teaching opportunities. They are trained in analyzing a task and systematically teaching a child to perform it. Teaching occurs daily, in many different situations, both formally (using all components of the skill-teaching interaction), and informally (using, for example, just a description of a desired behavior and praise for it). Teachable tasks range from everyday skills such as sewing and driving a car to complex social skills like apologizing, accepting feedback, and entering a conversation.

Like Professional Parenting and People Places, PRYDE uses other special interventions as needed for particular children. One special intervention strategy includes standard behavior therapy practices. For example, a program of graduated exposure to darkness was developed for a child afraid of the dark (systematic desensitization for fading-in of previous escape cues [Martin and Pear 1978]). The intervention, implemented by staff members and treatment parents, used relaxation techniques and a child diary. Successive goal achievements earned the child trips to a video game arcade (a highly preferred activity). Once the child could tolerate darkness, natural consequences (ability to sleep at night, freedom from fear) began to maintain the behavior effectively, and the arcade trips were gradually decreased and finally eliminated. Special interventions such as this one have been used for fire-setting, bed-wetting, sexual deviance, special school problems, and so forth.

A second category of intervention somewhat distinct from each child's point system is behavioral contracting. The written contract signed by the treatment parent, child, and staff members specifies in detail the child's performance criteria and rewards to be earned, the responsibilities of the staff member and treatment parent, and the length of time (usually relatively short—two weeks or less) covered by the contract. Contracts are often used when a target behavior on the child's point system continues to show point loss or is unresponsive to point loss.

Despite the emphasis on the behavioral approach, traditional talk therapy also has a place in PRYDE. Treatment parent supervisors may do counseling themselves, ask another supervisor to do so, or refer the child to a consulting clincial psychologist or psychiatrist within the Pressley Ridge agency who serves as a "therapist consultant." Approximately 25 percent of all PRYDE children receive one or more therapeutic services from an in-house psychologist or psychiatrist. The therapist consultant seeks the issues that are not being adequately addressed in the child's daily home treatment plan and provides the treatment parents and supervisors with alternative methods of remediation. Thus, professional therapy is integrated into the treatment home, with the treatment parents being responsible for follow-through.

*People Places*

People Places recognizes that spontaneous family interactions and activities provide powerful learning experiences for troubled youths. Planned interventions support and extend these experiences in a systematic, proactive manner. Individualized "A-B-C" Teaching Plans are developed for each new youngster to remediate problem behavior or interpersonal skill deficits by training and reinforcing prosocial skills. Children participate in the negotiation of teaching plans, which normally target severe problem behaviors early in placement, then shift focus toward independent-living and self-management skill development once the children have achieved stability in the teaching parent home and community.

Before designing any teaching plan, People Places collects baseline data on the child's problem behaviors as described in referral materials by having treatment parents take frequency and intensity data on these behaviors. Although many children may show their best behavior during this early period, these baseline data add to the referral information and help in selectioning appropriate treatment objectives, in determining the level of existing skills, and in making decisions related to delivery systems or motivational strategies.

Those behaviors most likely to jeopardize a child's continued placement in a family and community setting, such as vandalism, running away, or aggression, are given first priority for structured interventions. Contingencies and reinforcement schedules for each problem behavior are developed with the participation of the child. Although all children in People Places' homes begin with behavior change programs targeting referral behaviors, treatment parents vigorously train no more than three or four goal behaviors at any one time. It has been the agency's experience that treatment parents are able to focus best on a few significant treatment areas at a time and that success tends to breed success, often resulting in improvements in non-targeted behavior as well. During the focus on the three or four target behaviors, some treatment parents may use a point-gain system, others may use behavior contracts, others a great deal of structured teaching, and still others a combination of these methods. All such interventions use common "A-B-C" teaching format with data collected daily on progress toward teaching goals specified in each plan.

Treatment plans in the form of point systems are not developed for all People Places children and PRYDE and People Places consequently differ on the response to inappropriate behaviors. Whenever a PRYDE child displays an inappropriate behavior that appears on his or her point system, a predetermined number of points are deducted; thus the "punisher" or negative consequence is a mild "response cost" [Martin and Pear 1978]. If point loss is insufficient, then a behavior contract supplements the punisher. Treatment parents use extinction (planned ignoring) only for less troublesome behaviors. In contrast, People Places targets prosocial alternative behaviors for systematic reinforcement through separate, individualized "A-B-C" plans, focusing on three or four goal areas at a time. Other problem behaviors are dealt with informally through extinction and frequent reinforcement by positive, alternative behavior.

Once remediation of specific deficit areas has been accomplished through the application of planned interventions, treatment procedures are extended to include skills not ordinarily taught systematically in families, such as independent-living and pre-vocational skills. Goals and objectives, however, continue to be operationally defined, and progress is tracked daily to ensure that intentions are translated into practice.

People Places also uses other treatment procedures to maximize behavior change in children. To promote and maintain the reinforcing nature of the adult-child relationship, treatment parents spend at least ten minutes each day in fully positive, non-contingent time with the youngster. This positive time strategy is consistent with the program's focus on de-emphasizing punishment or negative consequences for misbehavior while maximizing the power of the treatment parents' approval and attention.

Group or individual counseling also are available from licensed counselors and psychologists. Cognitive behavior modification and social skills training procedures are emphasized in contrast to more traditional talk therapies. Counseling interactions may be goal-based or may function as a means through which children can begin to understand the causes and context of their original problems. A "This is my life story" approach has been employed successfully, one which is characterized by the counselor helping children to write about and analyze the events of their lives to date.

Generally, People Places is committed to attaining behavior change through the least intrusive means possible. Where remediation of a problem behavior appears to be possible through informal means, a formal intervention is not undertaken. While remediation of presenting problems and the development of prosocial skills are the focus of specific structured intervention, this program believes that the broader, informal socialization experience of stable family living over time is likely to have the most profound influence on the child's overall learning and adjustment.

## Evaluation of Treatment

Progress in treatment must be evaluated frequently so that necessary changes can be made in the treatment parents' behavior (e.g., types of consequences used for treatment behaviors) to produce maximum progress. Frequent evaluation of treatment plans guides the adjustments needed as the program accumulates information on the child and as the treatment parents become more skilled. The three agencies explicitly invite treatment parents and children to request reviews of daily treatment plans, if in place, or any other aspect of treatment while in the program. Revisions in all programs are accomplished through a cooperative negotiation process involving staff members, treatment parents, and children.

### PRYDE

PRYDE's daily point system and the daily logs allow for continual data-based evaluation of treatment. Treatment parents send in or give the staff members on a home visit their accumulating daily point sheets, logs, and bimonthly data summaries, which are simple graphs of key data from their daily records showing the percentage of days on which the child gained or lost points for each treatment behavior, the quality of the day for the family members in their interactions with the child, and the percentage of use of the required daily parenting skills. This information can reveal positive or negative trends in the child's behavior and thus help prevent crises; it can assist the staff in evaluating parenting effectiveness; it can demonstrate to treatment parents the time-limited duration of a child's poor performance; and it can maintain treatment accountability to purchasers of this service.

## People Places

People Places staff members evaluate treatment plans primarily through examining daily point charts when these are in place. Program managers may also track the frequency of requests for help from the treatment parents or statements about "giving up." The staff draws information from the changing length of intervals between a child's outbursts or the changes in the duration of each episode. In addition, brief descriptions of daily positive experiences between treatment parent and child are recorded on a short form along with a rating of the general quality of interactions with the child throughout the day. Although alternative reporting methods are permitted, daily reports are required and linked to a portion of the treatment parents' monthly payment. Completion of the form normally requires no more than two or three minutes of a treatment parent's time each day. This information, along with data about the frequency of success on target behaviors, is used to fine tune treatment planning. These data are also used to motivate treatment parents to continue working with a difficult child during times when progress seems slow and laborious.

## Professional Parenting

Professional Parenting staff members use two main methods to evaluate behavior change. During weekly consultations, case consultants ask treatment parents and children about their progress in any areas of concern. When a family is implementing a structured intervention, behavior charts, stickers, and point cards may be available to review progress. In most cases "natural" consequences (i.e., those normally available for a behavior in a typical family) are used to motivate children to achieve their objectives, and the effectiveness of these is discussed with the treatment parents at frequent intervals throughout the placements.

# Discharge Planning and Follow-Up Services

To ensure the continued success of children after discharge, plans for discharge must be developed early in placement for those who are not likely to remain until emancipation (age 18). Professional Parenting has not had much experience with discharge planning due to the long-term

nature of their children's placements. Therefore, the following description is based primarily on the experience of People Places and PRYDE.

Sometimes the discharge of a child is out of a program's control
because of a court decision, time-limited placements, unsuccessful placements, economic reasons, or a change in the biological family's and the
child's interest in returning home. Because of this possibility, not all
children in these programs receive the benefit of a planned discharge, and
more intensive follow-up is indicated.

When discharges can be scheduled, the plan is developed in conjunc-
tion with the public agency representative, the biological parents (or
family to which the child will return), the child, the program worker, and
others who are involved in the child's treatment. In general, the discharge
process involves setting goals for the child and his or her family that must
be attained before discharge. (If the goal for discharge is independent
living, the child's own family may not be involved.) Biological parents
who are involved in the child's treatment receive training. In People
Places it consists of two or three days of training in effective parenting
skills by the program managers. In PRYDE, the intensity ranges from
participation in biweekly group meetings, weekly training sessions with
the supervisor, to both group and individual training. The content of the
individual training in both programs is tailored to the needs of the
parents and the child; individual training also occurs in the home or
community where the skills will be used.

Whatever the discharge plan, follow-up after discharge is important
to the plan's success. The structure of follow-up services varies among
the three programs. In Professional Parenting, follow-up is the responsibility of the local department of social services; however, due to the
long-term nature of the program, few children have been discharged to
date. Aftercare services for children discharged from People Places is
optionally purchased by public agencies in approximatley one out of ten
cases. PRYDE's follow-up service is considered part of the regular per
diem cost when the child is in placement. Treatment parents sometimes
share with the treatment parent supervisor the responsibility for follow-
up contacts with the child. Follow-up plans usually involve phone contacts (one per month), occasional home visits by the supervisor, continuation of biological parents in their group (twice per month),
supervisor's outings with the child, invitations to the child to in-services,
and availability of the supervisor for crisis intervention. The PRYDE
program's frequency of contact normally decreases significantly after the

first three months, although formal follow-up evaluation of each child is conducted annually for at least two years.

## REFERENCES

Achenbach, T. M., and Edelbrock, C. S. The child behavior profile: II. Boys aged 12–16 and girls aged 6–11 and 12–16. Journal of Consulting and Clinical Psychology 42: 223–233, 1979.

Atkeson, B. M., and Foreland, R. Home-based reinforcement programs designed to modify classroom behavior: A review and methodological evaluation. Psychological Bulletin 86: 1298–1308, 1979.

Barnes, K. Individualized Model for Specialized Foster Care for "Hard to Place" Juvenile Offenders. Washington, D.C. (1337 22nd Street, N.W., 20037): The National Center on Institutions and Alternatives, 1980.

Glaser, D. The interplay of theory, issues, policy and data in criminal justice evaluations. In Klein, M. W., and Teilman, K. S. (eds.), Handbook of Criminal Justice Evaluation. Beverly Hills, California: Sage, 1980.

Hawkins, R. P. Selection of target behaviors. In Nelson, R. O., and Hayes, S. C. (eds.), Conceptual Foundations of Behavioral Assessment. New York: Guilford, 1986.

Hobbs, N. The Troubled and Troubling Child: Reeducation in Mental Health, Education, and Human Service Programs for Children and Youth. San Francisco: Jossey-Bass, 1982.

Holland, J. G. Behaviorism: Part of the problem or part of the solution? Journal of Applied Behavior Analysis 11: 163–174, 1978.

Kazdin, A., and Bootzin, R. R. The token economy: An evaluative review. Journal of Applied Behavior Analysis 5: 343–372, 1972.

Mager, R. F. Preparing Instructional Objectives (2nd edition). Belmont, California: Fearon-Pitman, 1975.

Martin, G., and Pear, J. Behavior Modification: What It Is and How to Do It (2nd edition). Englewood Cliffs, New Jersey: Prentice-Hall, 1978.

Phillips, E. L.; Phillips, E. A.; Fixsen, D. L., and Wolf, M. M. The Teaching-Family Handbook. Lawrence, Kansas: University of Kansas Printing Service, 1974.

Schwartz, A., and Goldiamond, I. Social Casework: A Behavioral Approach. New York: Columbia University Press, 1975.

Snodgrass, R. D., and Bryant, B. Special Foster Care: Past and Present. (In preparation.)

Wahler, R. G. Setting generality: Some specific and general effects of child behavior therapy. Journal of Applied Behavior Analysis 2: 239–246, 1969.

# 8

# Serving Families of Children in Therapeutic Foster Care

EILEEN MARY GREALISH
ROBERT P. HAWKINS
PAMELA MEADOWCROFT
AND
PERCILLA LYNCH

THERAPEUTIC FOSTER CARE (TFC) serves children who have multiple previous placements and histories of serious family problems. The children and their families have experienced several years of separation or erratic patterns of living as a family unit. By the time the children are placed in TFC, their parents or other caretaking family members no longer want them, cannot manage them, and are often uninterested in even trying. Prevention of the repeated removals from the family may never have been tried by mental health/social services, or, if it had, it was repeatedly unsuccessful. Nevertheless, intensive in-home services for seriously troubled children and their families are increasing and may help prevent youngsters from entering the foster care system. For those seriously troubled children whose families have not benefited from in-home services, or who place their children at severe risk, removal of the children becomes the only option.

Once TFC is chosen as the placement option for children, how will the program involve their families in their treatment? How will the program support family reunification if that is the plan? And if the children will not return home, what will the program do with the strong family ties they and their parents may have that may impede continuing adjustment in the treatment home?

The services to the child's family described in this chapter are based on the experiences of PRYDE and People Places. The Professional Parenting program primarily serves children for whom reunification is not planned; rather, long-term foster care is viewed as necessary to meet their needs. There is a growing body of research [Kazdin 1987; Wolf et al. 1987] demonstrating that conduct-disordered, delinquent children have persistent problems or a chronic disorder not treatable with any current methods, and their families are unable to influence the children's behavior. Instead, this view concludes, these children need long-term, highly structured environments in which close supervision is possible. TFC can meet this need. The Professional Parenting program is an example of a long-term care model without provisions for family reunification, whereas PRYDE and People Places serve children for whom the placement plan most often includes return home. These programs must, therefore, assure involvement of the child's family if this goal is to be achieved successfully and if the child's return is to be permanent.

In both programs, planned contact between most of the children and their families occurs. In some cases, contact may be required by state regulations. In other cases, contact may not be part of the plan because parental rights are terminated or are in the process of termination. In most cases, however, planned contact is important for the child's social-emotional development; it can increase the likelihood of successfully returning the child home; and it promotes successful continuation of the child's placement in the treatment home.

Involving the parents of disturbing children in treatment can be difficult, though it is widely recognized that family intervention is important or even critical to successful treatment of the children themselves [Larson and Talley 1977]. These children's families frequently have multiple problems [Braukman 1979; Butehorn 1978; Schaefer et al. 1984]; may not share the same values as the "helping professional" [Kadushin 1977];

may not have the skills and financial resources to make some of the changes that seem needed [Aponte 1976; Patterson 1982]; and sometimes speak so differently from the professional that simple, mutual comprehension is difficult. Different approaches, including structured parent training, have been attempted, with variable success [Haapala 1983; Patterson et al. 1975; Stuart 1974].

The families of children placed in PRYDE and People Places homes have long histories of multiple problems. According to written referral material at PRYDE and estimates by the People Places staff, nearly all the parents show serious deficits. The majority of parents are alcoholic or have been adjudicated neglectful of the child. PRYDE referral information indicates that nearly half of the parents have been found to be physically abusive. Because the number of "founded" abuse cases typically underestimates actual occurrence, People Places estimates the occurrence of abuse by monitoring children's reports of past abuse after they have been in treatment for a while. This estimate is about 60 percent, and even that figure may be too low. Nearly a third of the child population under care has sexually abusive families. These data support the view that the families of children in TFC have serious problems that must be confronted if the children are to have successful contacts with them or eventually return home. How People Places and PRYDE work with these families is described below.

## People Places

People Places is required by state standards to enter into a written agreement with the referral agent regarding visiting and assignment of responsibility for tasks related to the parents. The degree of parent involvement is most generally affected by distance, since the program covers a broad geographic area. Program managers arrange for children to visit their families normally at the program office on a case-by-case basis, depending upon the relationship between the child and the family. Flexibility is an inherent part of the plan: some children see their parents weekly; other children never visit their families. In cases where the parents and the child visit, People Places offers parent training during the visit. Relationship issues that emerge during visits function as departure points for intervention and counseling. The occurrence of family visits is not earned by the children in People Places, since visiting is part of the treatment plan, but the length of the visit is contingent upon the children's behavior while in their treatment homes. The biological parents are asked to monitor progress informally on one or two of a child's goals during the visit. This information is used by the program manager to plan future visits and, in some cases, to initiate discharge planning.

People Places ultimately measures the success of its services to the biological families after discharge by determining whether a child has remained with the family during the follow-up evaluation. Interim service measures include successful, completed visits and keeping of other appointments with the staff. During a placement, program managers usually contact the child's family by phone once or twice per quarter, with an increase in contact around Christmas and other holidays, when youngsters as a rule have home visits. As discharge approaches, contact intensifies in some cases, with the program manager spending two to three days training the parents in positive child management techniques and communication and relationship skills. The Program manager is also available to arrange the new school placement for the child upon return home and to initiate contact between the family and the public agency. These and additional follow-through services are actually purchased by the public agency in approximately one of every ten cases of discharged children.

## PRYDE

The planning of services for parents of PRYDE children did not promise to be rewarding, since many professionals (including PRYDE's) had generally achieved little success with this population, and preexisting model programs for dysfunctional parents were not available. The population of families to be served was characterized by up to ten years of involvement in the child welfare judicial system and serious deficits in parenting skills.

The early plan required the treatment parent supervisors/community liaison (PS/CL) to work individually with each child's parents, develop a trusting relationship with them, gradually assist them in working with various systems (welfare, social security, housing), and teach them parenting and relationship-building skills important for improving or maintaining their youngster's adjustment to their family and society. This plan included a family assessment through a parent interview that obtained descriptions of rules and expectations used by parents, evaluated the clarity and consistency of these rules and expectations and the degree to which the consequences were consistent with them, assessed how much emphasis was given to positive versus negative consequences, and other such matters. At the interview and subsequent meetings with the treatment parent supervisor, the parents were encouraged to set goals for improvement of their parenting skills, which the supervisor then tried to teach them, usually in the family's home during a monthly visit. This individual work continues but because of the special problems PRYDE encountered with troubled families, a support group component was added that is described in some detail below.

Both the assessment and the teaching of parents are difficult tasks. Simply contacting parents, scheduling individual meetings, and following through on meetings are not easily achieved. The progress of the family, or goal completion, is often much slower than the child's progress. Discharge planning becomes difficult when children are ready to return to homes that are not yet prepared to receive them in a manner that would support continuance of their positive adjustment.

Pennsylvania state regulations give children the right to visit their families twice each month. In the absence of significant danger to the child, visits occur in the family home and frequently involve spending one or two nights. The differences in the two environments—treatment home and family home—are so pronounced that positive behaviors exhibited in the treatment home may not generalize to the child's own home. In fact, the child's behavior during and after a visit with his or her parents often becomes quite disruptive; the parents then express frustration and hopelessness regarding their child's progress.

Predictably, the PS/CL's initial efforts to assess and teach parents were infrequent and inconsistent. Other activities inevitably consumed nearly all of the PS/CL's time: developing children's treatment plans, assuring their success in school, representing them in court, working with the treatment parents, and so on. Agency records indicate that at least eight times as many telephone calls and four times as many home visits were made to treatment family homes as to family homes. Treatment parents were reliable and produced results; the children's parents did not and were not approached as regularly.

## Group Processes

When individual liaison with parents proved inadequate or insufficient, a group meeting of parents for parent training was tried. It provided more efficient use of staff time, and it would ensure that the liaison services were provided.

In addition to cost effectiveness, group processes can have several advantages. First, adaptive verbal behavior can be taught through modeling, prompting, and various forms of reinforcement. For example, parents who exhibit good problem-solving skills (generating several alternative courses of action, realistically predicting likely consequences of each course, and selecting the most responsible alternative) receive approval from the group leader, who in turn can prompt other group members to reinforce those behaviors also. Similarly, other parent behaviors can be taught, including realistic plans for carrying out a course of action, describing productive behaviors in positive terms, and even courteous listening.

A second, closely related advantage of groups is the magnitude of reinforcement available. Approval and interest from one or more professionals and several other persons are more powerful than one professional's praise. Social reinforcement in the group need not be limited to the obvious (but fleeting) praise, such as "That's a good plan" or "I like your analysis." It can take the form of excitedly elaborating on or extending an idea the parent offers, reiterating the idea in more eloquent terms that make the parent appear brilliant, bringing out what makes the idea good, telling a vignette that supports what the parent has said, or drawing out other parents who are also likely to add reinforcement. Of course it is important that the leader minimize the reinforcement of maladaptive verbal (and other) behavior, such as making excuses, acting helpless, not participating, demeaning others (especially those in the group), or blaming one's children for having problems. The leader can usually deal with this sort of difficulty by redirection to more adaptive behavior or by turning the group's attention to another member who is likely to model more positive adaptive responses. On occasion, a mild form of punishment may have to be given in the form of disagreeing with a parent's description or tuning one's attention away from a parent whose verbalizations are rude or otherwise persistently counterproductive, but clearly punishment is to be avoided if possible.

A third advantage of groups is the ease with which social situations can be simulated, so that parents can practice responses to various situations they may face. Furthermore, the presence of several parents makes it easy to get varied and multiple sources of feedback for those performing each simulation. This interactivity sharpens discriminations and skills in a natural, concrete way.

A fourth advantage of groups is that trust and truthful sharing can be established earlier than might otherwise happen with some of the parents, because they have the opportunity to observe others being honestly self-revealing and receiving leader acceptance and social rewards for it. Related to this is a fifth advantage: parents can sit silently, with few demands placed upon them, without disapproval, and some learning can take place even before a parent is ready to be an active participant.

The first parent group was a structured, skills-training class. Since the treatment parents were achieving positive gains with the children, the staff believed that the same training and structure the treatment parents received would help the parents with their children on home visits and when the children returned home.

Group meetings were held in classroom style, with one central staff member teaching, and another assisting in a group of some four to ten parents. Topics for each session were selected in advance, with each unit devoted to a particular parenting skill. The skills to be taught included social rewards, understanding and promoting positive relationships, positive discipline, motivation, communication, teaching, negotiation, and helping children make friends.

The format of the classes varied slightly, but it always included a lecture style of introduction, illustrative simulations, small group discussion, and role-playing practice, a question-and-answer period, and a task-based assignment that involved using the skill at home and reporting on the results. After the first four meetings, as a result of feedback from parent participants, a "special issues" component was added to each class—group problem solving of common issues, such as communicating with the treatment parents, telling your family and friends about your child's placement, handling your feelings of guilt, or having a successful home visit.

Most of the parents of the children in placement at PRYDE were invited to attend this first class. Only one parent whose location was known was excluded; she was acutely psychotic.

This first group was not successful. To succeed at all, it had to meet at least two first-level objectives: attendance at the group sessions and participation in the group [Hawkins et al. 1983]. To succeed more fully, some second-level objective had to be met: behavior (or other) changes in the home, and maintenance of those changes. Only 21 percent of the invited parents attended per session, on the average, with a range of 13 percent to 30 percent. Attendance was so inconsistent that a unit lesson approach was impossible. A different method was required.

The primary purpose of the new format intended the parent participants to identify and take the next small step in improving their relationship with their child. The ten components that follow were considered the important determinants of success.

### Family Attendance by Invitation Only

An examination of all the families revealed many similarities among them but also some significant differences. The most common similarity was a deficiency in parenting skills, particularly in the use of positive discipline and communication skills. For some families, their parenting deficits and their relationship with their child were the only issues seriously disrupting their lives. Other families were plagued by a wide variety of difficulties, including lack of decent housing, marital problems, financial difficulties, and deficient communication skills with their own families or superiors at work, all of which precluded families from attaching much importance to remediation of their parenting behaviors. Still other parents were characterized by one or more grave problems such as serious, active mental illness, continuing substance abuse including active alcoholism, participation in criminal activities, verbal assaults toward professionals, long-term unwillingness to participate in parenting or even seeing their child, and lack of any permanent address at which the parent could be reached. In the staff's opinion, this third group of parents showed very little progress regardless of the type of interventions used, and their presence was detrimental to the involvement and progress of the parents who were less dysfunctional.

To determine which parents were appropriate for group meetings, the PS/CL for each family's child visited the parent two to four times and called them frequently over a four- to eight-week period, in a process of soliciting their contribution toward an understanding of the history of the child. Those who appeared likely to benefit from and advance the purpose of the group were invited to participate. Group size was kept at less than 12 families. The parents knew that invitations were limited, and they were pleased at having been selected.

### Public, Realistic Written Commitment Regarding Attendance and Participation

When the parents were to be invited, the PS/CL contacted the family, extended the invitation, gave them a schedule of the next five meetings, and asked them for a verbal commitment to attend all five sessions. Upon arrival at the first session, parents were asked to sign a written agreement to attend the five meetings and keep the basic rules of the group: *(1)* attend all five sessions or, if unable to attend, let a staff member know as soon as possible; *(2)* arrive promptly, in adequate health, "straight" (i.e., no drugs or alcohol), and be with the group as fully as possible; *(3)* give full attention to whoever is speaking and offer useful comments; *(4)* keep everyone's comments completely confidential (except to one's partner or spouse). At a later date, two more ground rules were added to assist in managing the group and to increase participation: *(1)* smoking permitted only before the group meeting began and during a break; and *(2)* group members permitted to leave their seats for food and beverages only at break times.

When a new five-session group began, all parent participants who were to be invited or reinvited were again asked to sign the written agreement regarding attendance at the next five sessions. The advantage of limiting the agreement to five sessions is that the parents have a good chance of successfully meeting such a commitment, thereby reinforcing the making and keeping of commitments related to their child. Putting the rules in writing increases compliance with staff and peer expectations.

## *Providing Reminder Prompts Before Meetings*

After a group meeting, one of the staff members responsible for that meeting wrote a letter to all of the invited parents, whether or not they had attended. Highlights of the meeting were described in a positive manner that included personal and social news about the parents and staff members in the group. The letter also included a reminder of the time, date, and place of the next group meeting, and any information that the parents might need before it took place.

In addition, group leaders or PS/CL's personally telephoned each invited participant on the day before or day of the meeting. They talked about any reasons the parents might give for not attending the session, which often resulted in the elimination of the reasons. Even when parents were not able to attend the meeting, the group leaders continued their positive relationship with the parents and encouraged them to attend the next scheduled meeting. The agency's secretary initially made these telephone calls but reported frustration with the results. Many parents were unwilling to come to the phone (although they came to the phone when the group leader called), and on some occasions the secretary overhead parents instruct children to say that they were not at home.

## Transportation Assistance

The financial circumstances of many of the families involved in the parent group precluded ownership of a car and, in some cases, money for bus fare. For some, the distance was considerable (although never beyond 30 minutes' travel). Staff members transported some parents to and from the meeting; this practice was especially common for new participants. In other cases, the agency reimbursed bus fare. In addition, a pick-up place was arranged where staff members could help with the last part of the journey and shorten travel time. The staff also arranged sharing of rides with some parents who had cars and reimbursed the car owner for the cost of gas.

## Babysitting Support

Parents often told the staff that they couldn't attend meetings because they had small children to care for. Some particularly eager parents brought children and babies with them, which disrupted the meeting. The agency therefore hired a babysitter—a teenage boy or girl—who was responsible for entertaining the children in another room close to the meeting room.

## Refreshments

Group night was frequently the only social contact of the parents with other adults and sometimes their only excursion out of the home. PRYDE provided good, substantial snacks and made leftover snacks available for parents to take home to their children. The refreshments became a popular feature of the group. On some occasions parents proudly cooked a special treat and brought it in, to much applause.

## Dinner Visits

Many parents had a difficult time seeing the relevance of their presence in the group to the progress of their child in a distant treatment home. Several parents had never attended meetings relating to their children and expressed unwillingness to do so. In these cases, the staff began arranging visits between parents and children in PRYDE offices two hours before the start of the meeting, with boxed food provided by the agency. During these visits, parents were able to interact with their child, discuss the child's progress, use the grounds for walks and long talks, and use the playground equipment. Many parents who came to visit were willing to remain an extra hour and a half to attend the group meeting. The child then returned to the treatment home while the parent attended the group session. Providing dinner was also a genuine help to those parents whose schedules kept them from having to choose between attending a meeting and having dinner.

These last four components, transportation, babysitting, refreshments, and occasional dinners, required a small increase in the cost of running the parent groups over the previous structured classroom format. Usually, each session cost $25 to $35 for these attendance supports.

### Defined Staff Role

To add structure to the group process and to eliminate redundancy and confusion, the roles of staff members attending the sessions were clearly defined. The group leader was responsible for whatever happened within the session. This responsibility included assisting parents in defining their goals and objectives; ascertaining that each objective set by a parent was observable, measurable, and realistic; identifying any skills required for the accomplishment of each objective; and ensuring that a PS/CL would teach skills in one-to-one follow-up sessions. The group leader interacted with each parent during the session, maintained the flow of the meeting, and made sure that each parent had a chance to speak. Group leaders were chosen from the staff for their ability to interact positively with parents and to respond rapidly and appropriately to each parent's verbal report. Group leaders were also expected to keep abreast of new developments in each child's case, so that they could confront a parent on inaccurate reports of events or goal achievement.

The group leader was assisted by another regular staff member who served as the logistics manager, responsible for all tasks that occurred between sessions. These tasks included delivery of prompts for attendance, correspondence, transportation coordination, meal provision, babysitting provision, ensuring that all data on goal setting and achievement were collected, and that minutes of each session were written.

Logistics managers were occasionally assisted by university practicum students or other staff.

## Empowering Group Process

Each session was conducted so as to minimize the inherent threatening quality of the situation without eliminating demands on the parents. Group leaders empowered parents to take responsibility for their own actions by first providing supportive acceptance for honest self-disclosure, as described earlier. Second, the leaders were energetic, enthusiastic, and optimistic, trying to inspire hope that matters really could improve and to prompt parents' efforts to change through this encouraging and rather fast-paced style. Third, they treated each participant with respect by maintaining a realistic approach to each situation they described, minimizing neither the problems identified by the parents nor the parts the parents played in the problems. Parents were held individually responsible for their results with their children, and all verbal interactions within the group served to support that responsibility without blaming or implying guilt. Most parents were accustomed to the assumption that the child welfare system was responsible for their children. The use of empowerment strategies generally resulted in the parents' increased willingness to take some action related to their child. Fourth, parents chose their own global goals, so that the content of group participation was highly personal and relevant to them; however, these large goals were broken down into smaller objectives or steps that could be achieved in the two-week time period between sessions. Parents were able to see some measurable progress related to their participation in the group. This perception also allowed the staff to teach the necessary skills (in one-to-one follow-up sessions) in a timely fashion, when the parent was eager to try the new skill.

## Starting Where the Parent Is

During the first group attempt (structured parent training), many parents said that the staff's choice of topics did not reflect their own situations or needs. Although the staff taught skills that are widely recognized by professionals as effective with troubling children, skills that were clearly not a part of the parents' repertoire, the parents reported their frustration and insisted that they attend to the tasks at hand rather than discuss their problems. They asked, instead, that the group meetings deal with their current difficulties.

The group design necessarily turned to the parents' current needs. They set their own goals, and group leaders assisted them in reframing, identifying skills that would be necessary, and breaking down large goals into realistic small steps. Many times the initial goals related only peripherally to the child. Participants wanted help with housing problems, lack of income, marital or other relationship difficulties, adversarial relationships with the family court and the child welfare system, and lack of a network for social support. The staff addressed all of these issues, both in group and one-to-one sessions. Specific parenting and child behavior management skills were taught when they seemed relevant to the parents' concerns.

*Result*

The first criterion in evaluating the effectiveness of PRYDE's current group approach is that most, if not all, of the invited and expected families attended. In the initial group, for which there was a predetermined curriculum, the mean percentage of attendance of families invited was 21 percent of the total nine over the five sessions. The mean of families expected (i.e., parents confirmed their attendance during a phone call from staff) was 43 percent.

When the change to the current group procedure took place, the percentage of those invited rose abruptly, soon reaching more than 60 percent. Furthermore, of those actually expected, more than the targeted level of 80 percent usually came.

Several drops in attendance resulted from changing one of the group process features. First, on two occasions, the staff failed to send a letter prompt before the meeting, and attendance was lower on both of those occasions. On three evenings, the parents were informed in advance that the regular group leader would not be present; attendance fell in two instances and increased in another. On two of those evenings in which lower attendance resulted with a new leader, however, the group had also decided to try weekly meetings. It is likely that the reduced attendance was due to the increased frequency rather than a change in leaders, particularly since there was a noticeable increase in attendance after cessation of weekly meetings and resumption of bimonthly meetings.

When the group leader was unable to interact adequately with the growing numbers of parents who attended, two groups were created.

Each group was limited to 12 families or fewer than 20 parents. Attendance by those expected was maintained at a high level through these various changes. Before the split into two groups, it averaged 58 percent (range 24–88 percent). After the split, one group averaged 53 percent attendance, with a range of 45–70 percent; the second group averaged 57 percent (range 41–75 percent). Attendance of those invited, however, fell somewhat after the first nine or ten sessions, probably because the excitement about the group's success was leading the staff to invite a broader variety of parents, including parents who were not likely to attend even with the level of support provided for attendance. In addition, the PRYDE program was growing rapidly, and invitations may have been extended somewhat prematurely, before, the development of a sufficiently influential relationship between the PS/CL and the parents

From these data it seems that the reminder letters, commitments to a limited number of sessions, the avoidance of abrupt changes in leaders, and making certain that families are not prematurely invited, help to maintain high attendance.

The second criterion of effectiveness for the group process is that the persons attending participate. The staff measured four types of participation by seven families over 33 of the sessions for a one-year period. "Sharing a story" occurred a mean of 9.18 times per session among these families, with the highest family averaging 13.13 such sharings and the lowest family, 7.29. "Offering a solution" to another parent's problem or to their own averaged 2.53 times per session per family, with families ranging in their rates from 0.09 to 3.0. "Giving feedback" to parents (such as "You're on the right track with that time-out idea" or "That'll never work with a 15-year-old") occurred an average of 4.18 times per session per family, with a range of 2.60 to 5.33. Finally, "participating in a role-play" averaged only .09 per family per session, with a range of .08 to .40.

We judge these figures as evidence of a rather high level of various kinds of participation. Obviously, the relating of vignettes is a relatively high-frequency behavior. These stories provide a realistic context for analyzing results of different parenting behaviors and how alternative behaviors might yield more favorable results. Staff leaders used the stories to model problem solving and teach good behavior management skills.

A third criterion of effectiveness is that for which the group was developed: to produce behavior change among its members that would

positively affect the youngsters. The primary measure used for evaluation was whether parents completed the next small step they set for
themselves between one group meeting and the next. The kinds of goals
ranged from very small—calling a realtor about getting a better place to
live or spending some time with their youngster—to large—getting a
job, remaining sober every day, or applying their child's point motivation
system on a weekend home visit.

Table 1 illustrates the small-step completion results of seven parents,
selected by the staff's subjective rating of parents' progress and choosing
the top two, the two who had progressed the least, and the three whose
progress seemed average. Parents set achievable objectives at each meeting and they reported on completion of these at subsequent meetings.
PS/CLs confirmed the truthfulness of the reported completion since
they saw or called the parents between meetings. Six of the seven
parents completed at least 42 percent of their objectives (range 42–
83 percent). The seventh parent, who completed only 20 percent of her
objectives, dropped out of the group after eight sessions due to a change
in her work schedule that made attendance impossible. The other six
attended the group for 12 to 23 sessions.

The most frequently identified objectives related to the general goals
of "improving home visits with the child," "improving housing," "completing an educational program of some sort," "getting a job," and
"improving contact with their child." Improving home visits was the
most frequently set goal—99 times over all the sessions (and parents
reported achieving this goal on 76 percent of the visits). The remaining
objectives (those that related to improving housing, getting a job, and so
on) were achieved 75 percent of the times they were set at a group
session.

A secondary means of evaluating whether the group improved the
parent-child relationship is the degree to which attendance at the group
influenced a child's return home. Several informal measures of this effect
were examined. Of the 16 families who participated in the group, discharge planning began for five children primarily because of parents
achieving goals in the group, and the PRYDE program discharged 17
children, nine of whose families were in the group. Of these nine, four
continued to attend sessions during follow-up: in one case, the judge
recommended that the parent continue to participate in the group; in two
cases, the public agency made this recommendation; in one case, the
parent stated in court his intention to continue group participation.

Due to the frequency with which home visit goals were set the
PRYDE staff also examined the results of home visits for all group

## TABLE 1
### Goal Completion by Parents Attending Support Group

| | Objectives Set | % Completed | Sessions Attended |
|---|---|---|---|
| Parent 1 | 14 | 64 | 23 |
| Parent 2 | 7 | 57 | 13 |
| Parent 3 | 9 | 56 | 18 |
| Parent 4 | 9 | 44 | 12 |
| Parent 5 | 12 | 42 | 14 |
| Parent 6 | 6 | 83 | 17 |
| Parent 7 | 5 | 20 | 8 |

members as a measure of the effect of the group on the parent-child relationship. Five of the 16 families in the group first began having home visits with their children, after they had been unwilling or unable to host visits. Nine families reported an improvement in both the behavior of their child and their own ability to enjoy the presence of the child. These reports were confirmed by the PS/CLs involved with those families. We judged that home visits were positively influenced for 88 percent of the group participants.

## Summary

Although the staff members of People Places and PRYDE do not believe that a powerful method for changing families has evolved from their services to biological families—certainly not comparable to that reported by Kinney et al. [1977], in which professionals often spend many hours daily in the family's home—both programs find that they have moderately favorable effects on most of the families with whom they are working. The data from PRYDE tend to support such a conclusion. Furthermore, the group procedure used in PRYDE is something that maintains interaction between at least two staff members and the families, whereas individual contact in the home or office by a single staff member tends to be at a low frequency unless the parents are unusually cooperative and motivated.

### REFERENCES

Aponte, H. J. Underorganization in the poor family. In Guerin, P. J. (ed.), Family Therapy, Theory, and Practice. New York: Gardner Press, 1976.

Braukmann, P. D. The foster-care of children: A literature review. Unpublished manuscript, University of Kansas, 1979.

Butehorn, L. A plan for identifying priorities in treating multi-problem families. Child Welfare LVII: 365–372, 1978.

Haapala, D. Perceived Helpfulness, Attributed Critical Incident Responsibility, and a Discrimination of Home-Based Family Therapy Treatment Outcomes: Home-Builders Model. Report prepared for the Department of Health and Human Services. Washington, D.C.: Administration for Children, Youth, and Families, 1983.

Hawkins, R. P.; Freemouw, W. J.; and Reitz, A. L. A model for use in designing or describing evaluations of planned interventions in mental health or educational intervention programs. In McSweeney, A. J., Freemouw, W. J., and Hawkins, R. P., (eds.), Practical Program Evaluation in Youth Treatment, Springfield, Illinois: Charles C. Thomas, 1982.

Kadushin, A. Myths and dilemma in child welfare. Child Welfare LVI: 141–153, 1977.

Kazdin, A. Treatment of antisocial behavior in children: Current status and future directions. Psychological Bulletin 102 (2): 187–203, 1987.

Kinney, J. M.; Madsen, B.; Fleming, T.; and Haapala, D. A. Homebuilders: Keeping families together. Journal of Consulting and Clinical Psychology 45: 667–673, 1977.

Larson, C. C., and Talley, L. K. Family resistance to therapy: A model for services and therapists roles. Child Welfare LVI: 121–126, 1977.

Patterson, G. R. A Social Learning Approach: Vol. 3, Coercive Family Process. Eugene, Oregon: Castalia Publishing Company, 1982.

———, Reid, J. B.; Jones, R. R.; and Conger, R. E. A Social Learning Approach to Family Intervention: Vol. 1, Families with Aggressive Children. Eugene, Oregon: Castalia Publishing Company, 1975.

Schaefer, C. E.; Briesmeister, J. M.; and Fitton, M. E. Family Therapy Techniques for Problem Behaviors of Children and Teenagers. Washington, D.C.: Jossey-Bass, 1984.

Stuart, R. B. Behavioral contracting within the families of delinquents. In Lovaas, O. J., and Baucher, B. D. (eds.), Perspectives in Behavior Modification with Deviant Children. Englewood Cliffs, New Jersey: Prentice Hall, 1974.

Wolf, M.; Braukmann, C. J.; and Ramp, K. A. Serious delinquent behavior as a part of a significantly handicapping condition: Cures and supportive environment. Journal of Applied Behavior Analysis 20: 347–359, 1987.

# 9

# Evaluating Therapeutic Foster Care

## Robert J. Jones

PROGRAM EVALUATION IN THE FIELD of human services delivery is difficult to do well and usefully and, as a topic for discourse, it can be imprecise because the concept means many different things to different people. For sociologists, other social scientists, and economists, program evaluation normally implies a systematic comparison—ideally employing a true experimental (or at least a quasi-experimental) research design—of the relative merits and weaknesses of two or more approaches to a specifiable human services problem or population. For a small direct-service agency, at the other extreme, any nominal effort to ensure that agency policies are being carried out with some semblance of regularity may constitute program evaluation. Between these extremes, a wide variety of human services activities has been undertaken, correctly or not, under the rubric of program evaluation.

The program evaluation efforts of the programs that are the subject of this volume can be found in this middle region of the program evaluation continuum. The elaborate and methodologically sophisticated comparative analyses mentioned above are usually energetic, if not arduous, and almost always expensive; they are generally beyond the means of small, new, or demonstration-level programs. The People Places, Professional Parenting, and PRYDE programs are all, like the concept of therapeutic foster care (TFC), in their relative infancy, and none has yet enjoyed the luxury of outside support for comprehensive program evaluation research. Each of the programs has marshalled sufficient resources, however, to mount program evaluation activities that exceed the level of simple staff or policy accountability.

As has been pointed out by Hawkins and Meadowcroft [1985], program evaluation within the means of most service organizations can accomplish important and multiple objectives. They have described an approach to program evaluation within the limits of regular TFC resources that serves to *(1)* improve the program, *(2)* fulfill requirements imposed from outside the program, *(3)* create general knowledge and technology, and *(4)* promote the program itself.

The following broad definition may not be universally acceptable, but it does capture the concept of program evaluation as it has been used by the three focal programs: Program evaluation, for present purposes, will refer to any systematic effort to use information gathered from within a program for internal purposes (for example, to assess, control the quality of, or refine the program) or to meet external goals and requirements (for instance, to comply with outside data-reporting requirements or to assist other agencies and organizations wishing to implement similar programs).

Since each program has undertaken evaluation activities for both internal and external purposes, this discussion will be organized around these two types of activities. In each evaluation category, the objectives are substantially the same, whereas the methods and results vary considerably among the programs. The goal of internal evaluation at each site, for example, is to ensure that the children are receiving the most effective, least restrictive treatment possible within the program. The methods of internal evaluation adopted by PRYDE, however, are substantially more formal than the approaches taken by People Places, which, in turn are more formal than those of Professional Parenting.

Similarly, each program has gathered information that may be useful to outside individuals and organizations. Although each program has made its own choices concerning what kinds of information might be most useful and in what format that information would be best offered, there are categories of information, such as cost data, that are common to, and maintained by, each program and, thus, lend themselves to cross-site analysis.

One last category of information—presented later under Program Evaluation for External Use and Dissemination—represents the first effort of the three programs at more formalized, cross-site data collection. This information does permit a direct comparison of the characteristics of the children and foster parents from the three programs, considered together, with the children and teaching parents who populate several hundred teaching family model group homes around the nation.

## Internal Program Evaluation

Each core program has a vested interest in providing high-quality services to problem children and in refining program strategies and components whenever it is apparent that revised methods might further this goal. Each has, as well, exhibited an abiding attachment to the need for program and staff accountability and continual quality control. As was mentioned, however, this unity of purpose has not generalized to a consensus on methods, except at the less formal level of internal evaluation.

The less formal methods are accomplished in the context of the supervision and consultation services provided by the staff to the treatment parents. All services in any program serve an evaluation function to the extent that systematic, documented information or data gleaned from a service guides program revisions. All three programs provide treatment parents with frequent home supervision, phone consultation, and in-home training, and consistently document these interactions. This material can then be reviewed at staff supervision meetings or with clinical consultants to determine *(1)* revisions in a child's day-to-day treatment and long-range goals, and/or *(2)* the necessity of additional training with increased supervision for the treatment parents.

### *Professional Parenting's Internal Evaluation*

Internal evaluation at this informal level is exemplified in the in-home supervision and consultation provided by the Professional Parenting program (though the uses of information derived from treatment parent supervision are quite similar across the three core programs).

In the Professional Parenting program, internal program evaluation—or treatment parent performance assessment—is viewed as an adjunct to training and is accomplished informally in connection with regular staff consultation with treatment parents. In-home training and consultation visits begin immediately after the pre-service training workshop. Since the strengths and weaknesses of the professional parent couple have been identified and addressed in this workshop, the in-home training can be highly individualized from the outset. The staff consultant's relationship with the treatment parents is that of a friend and colleague. The consulting visits are designed to provide these parents with feedback and suggestions to make their family relationships mutually satisfying and effective. It allows them someone to talk with who is thoroughly familiar with their situation and the problems of the children in their care.

The consulting sessions, which last from one to two hours, consist of observing the treatment parents interacting with the placed child to assess their abilities in communicating with, relating to, and teaching the child. Family integration and togetherness are also observed. The consultant addresses in addition issues or problems that have occurred but may not have been observed directly (e.g., problems in working with schools, agencies, or particular types of problem behaviors). Moreover, the consultant reviews with the treatment parents the individual treatment goals for the child and his or her progress. The content and outcome of these consulting visits are documented on a "Professional Parenting Program Consulting Visit Form."

A final aspect of these in-home visits, and one that serves an important evaluation function, is the periodic private interview with the child. Usually, the consultant takes the child out for a meal. While these meetings are informal and often characterized by the sharing of positive information concerning the child's progress and recent activities, they afford an opportunity for the child to express both satisfactions and dissatisfactions concerning the placement and his or her perspective on the foster family. This information, when necessary, is cycled back to the couple in the form of constructive feedback and suggestions.

All treatment parents are contacted by phone at least once a week. Although comparatively brief, the calls may, as required, approximate the intensity and comprehensiveness of the in-home visits. The substance of all phone consultation contacts is also documented. These records are reviewed at staff meetings and by the appropriate consultant before the next in-home visit to assure continuity and to record the progress of both child and treatment parent.

Finally, beyond the regular record-keeping noted above, Professional Parenting uses a trainee performance assessment system that permits the staff members to keep a running record of their subjective impressions of each couple's performance on selected variables that appear to be directly related to children's progress and success in placement. These variables include the couple's *tolerance* of (i.e., inclination to persist in the face of) untoward child behaviors, their willingness to *implement feedback* suggested by the staff, and an estimate of the couple's *overall performance*. This information is collected during the weekly, staff-initiated phone contacts using a compact rating instrument called the "Professional Parenting Performance Assessment Sheet" and is added to other information gathered through regular consultation.

### The People Places Approach

Internal program evaluation at People Places is embedded in routine procedures aimed at systematic placement supervision and general treatment accountability. The agency's method is somewhat less formalized than that used by PRYDE, and a degree more formalized than that just described for Professional Parenting. In addition to the evaluative functions of in-home treatment parent supervision and consultation, People Places uses self-monitoring data generated by treatment parents and progress data on children maintained by case managers.

Placement monitoring and documentation are carried out by case managers, who are trained and required to record the purpose, nature, and content of all contact with the clients, their foster families, their biological families, and other significant adults. Some of this information is documented by code. In describing the purpose of each contact, for example, case managers select from a list of 15 different purposes, including such coded designations as "seeking information," "providing training," and "handling logistics." Case managers rehearse the use of the coding protocols until their code choices consistently agree with a standard constructed by the agency director.

Conversely, no uniform coding system is used to record changes in client behaviors. Instead, in the interest of individualization, case managers design and implement for each child a tracking system that reflects the particular child's presenting problems and also considers the individ-

ual abilities of the treatment parents with whom the child is placed. This
information, along with the aforementioned contact data, is dictated on
to a cassette tape by case managers and is subsequently transcribed,
entered into a computer base, and summarized for use by case managers
in planning future supervisory contacts with each foster family.

In addition to these staff-initiated evaluation procedures, treatment
parents track their own daily performance with their foster child. They
are expected to spend at least ten minutes each day of positive, non-
contingent time with their foster child and to record brief descriptions of
these experiences, along with comments about the general quality of
their interactions with the child that day, on a simple form. Only two or
three minutes are required to complete the form each day, and treatment
parents earn a "bonus" of $10 for submitting properly completed forms
at the end of each week. These self-report data complement the contact
and progress information gathered by case managers and, along with less
formal evaluation methods similar to those described earlier for Professional Parenting, constitute continual internal program evaluation at
People Places.

### Internal Evaluation at PRYDE

PRYDE's internal program evaluation is the most detailed and formal of the three programs. It is fashioned after the teaching parent
performance evaluation that has evolved from the nationally organized
teaching family model of group home treatment for delinquent, difficult,
or otherwise problematic adolescents. PRYDE's energetic and relatively
formalized approach has been detailed in various reports and materials
available from that organization. The formal components of PRYDE's
internal program evaluation focus on the daily progress of children and
treatment parents.

Daily progress of children is regularly evaluated by staff members
and treatment parents reviewing the results of a child's daily point system
records. The staff constructs an individualized daily point system that
reflects a child's entering problems. Point losses and gains for each
treatment behavior can be observed daily from the records that treatment
parents keep. Trends in treatment can be seen from the treatment parents'
weekly summaries of these records. Thus if a child persistently engages
in a misbehavior, the staff will learn of this action from informal observations in home supervision and consultation and see the extent and fre-

quency of the behavior from more formal daily point sheets and weekly summaries.

Treatment parents routinely evaluate their own performance by completing each day a Log of Daily Events. These logs require treatment parents to report on daily use of parenting skills (e.g., positive reinforcement, certain communications/counseling strategies, and discipline techniques). In addition, treatment parents rate the child's interactions with the family for that day, write a brief summary of important incidents, and list the child's activities for the day on the log. The logs are collected every week or two by the treatment family's supervisor or are mailed in for periodic review by the program staff.

A formal periodic treatment parent evaluation is conducted by a staff member other than the foster family's treatment supervisor (in the interest of objectivity) after each foster family has been in the program for six months, after 12 months, and again every subsequent 12 months. During these periodic evaluations, the evaluator observes in the home all required treatment skills and general interactions between treatment parents and foster child. Each evaluation addresses the five following performance areas for each treatment parent: direct treatment and parenting, family environment, indirect treatment, administration (completion of paperwork), and the performance of the child.

Numerical ratings from $-2$ (poor performance) to $+2$ (excellent performance) for each of these categories are determined on the basis of the evaluator's direct observation, a review of accumulated logs, the daily records of the child's point gains and losses, a child satisfaction questionnaire, and ratings by the treatment parents' supervisor. Overall ratings of $-2$ to $+2$ in each of the five evaluation areas are calculated, and descriptions of the treatment parents' strengths and weaknesses are listed in an evaluation report.

The evaluation determines several actions: the amount, if any, of pay raise the treatment family will receive (up to $2.00 per child per day in treatment) for that evaluation period; the extent and areas of in-home treatment parent training needed to improve the overall evaluation for the next period; and the necessity and nature of changes in a child's treatment plan, including continued placement in that home setting.

Another formal method of assuring quality services is the use of a daily child-incident tracking procedure, called "the morning report." This procedure requires treatment parents (and/or staff) to report on the occurrence of 50 possible events, such as a supervised visit with a biological parent (SV), runaway (RUN), police contact (PC), suspension from school (SUSP), accidental physical injury—no staff involved (API-NSI), allegation by the child of sexual misconduct (YA-SM), or transfer from one PRYDE family to another (TRAN). Before noon each day, a program secretary compiles a list of children's names and events called in that day, dates the report, and distributes it to staff members, including the team managers, site director, and PRYDE director. This method allows the program to know of each child's whereabouts, the particular status of a child, and prompts supervision follow-up. It also permits computing trends in various critical incidents across time and PRYDE program offices. Finally, it is a management tool for assuring that agency incident reports are completed and submitted for review by the agency child protective task force, a committee composed of staff members from all of the different treatment programs at the Pressley Ridge Schools.

PRYDE also formally conducts annual follow-up evaluations on all children discharged from its treatment homes. Each summer, low-cost staff members are hired to contact by phone all children who were discharged within the past year. These staff members ask a set of questions to determine how well the child is doing. Where is the child living? Is he or she attending school or employed? What have been the incidents of antisocial behavior such as police contacts? These one-year follow-up reports indicate that 86 percent of the 110 discharged children between July 1983 and June 1987 were contacted. Of these, 76 percent were living in less restrictive settings one year after discharge (43 percent home or adopted, 26 percent in independent living, 6 percent in regular foster care). In addition, few children had had police contacts (21 percent), alcohol or drug usage (16 percent and 17 percent, respectively), or engaged in aggressive acts (31 percent). Finally, 77 percent of the children were either in school or employed. The follow-up staff members contact at least one additional reporting source for verification of the information on a random sample of at least 25 percent of the discharged children. Although these data are not of the highest scientific quality, they are consistently collected and obtained in a replicable fashion. The data are used to determine generally how the program affected children it served, where the program needs to improve (e.g., are many of the children needing extra help in avoiding drug problems or completing school), and whether the program should provide special intervention services for a child who may be at risk for recidivism.

## Program Evaluation for External Use
## and Dissemination

Scriven [1972] has suggested the term "formative" to describe the kinds of program evaluation data discussed thus far, in that the data are used internally to form, guide, and refine the treatment parameters of a program. We shall now move on to the second category of program evaluation activities—those that are intended, or are at least able, to serve needs and requirements external to the day-to-day operation of human services programs. The distinction between internal and external program evaluation is rarely precise, and products of either activity can often serve both internal and external purposes. For example, a survey of the treatment parents' satisfaction with Professional Parenting's support services was prompted primarily by the staff's genuine interest in what the treatment parents felt (an internal function). The results also served a formative function in that the staff made several changes and adjustments based on them. The data were, in addition, of interest to colleagues outside Professional Parenting and will be presented later.

One fairly reliable distinction between the two categories of program evaluation is that external-use evaluations tend to assume the approximate character of formalized research. As such, they are characteristically addressed to questions concerning matters like program viability, durability, effectiveness, and cost. Each of the three programs has attempted to gather and assemble data that address aspects of these questions in a pilot or preliminary way.

The remainder of this chapter is devoted to a review of data, gathered by the three programs, that, considered collectively, shed preliminary light on program efficacy. It should be borne in mind that each program independently developed data collection procedures, and although the programs have occasionally (and coincidentally) sought answers to similar questions, they have equally often addressed different questions. Each site, for example, has been concerned with the important question of program effect on clients served, and each has looked to its own placement and discharge data for estimates. In such instances, data from all three programs are arrayed together (though not combined, as we chose differing means and methods of collecting these data). Conversely, some questions of interest have been addressed by one program but not by the other two. People Places, for instance, has assembled some data on youth convictions during treatment. When presented, such discrete data sets must be viewed as representing only the program that generated them.

The questions and issues that have been the subject of evaluation at one or more of the three programs include the following: *(1)* TFC as an alternative to institutionalization; *(2)* the effects of a placement on the life routines and social activities of the treatment family and the placed child; *(3)* the satisfaction of treatment families with the extent and quality of program support services; *(4)* influence and outcome affecting children (as evidenced by placement and discharge data, target behavior improvement, and youth convictions during treatment); and *(5)* relative costs. In addition, results of the three programs' joint participation in the National Data Base sponsored by the National Teaching-Family Association are presented.

### *TFC as an Alternative to Institutionalization*

In an era that has eschewed the wholesale incarceration of minors, one of the most compelling arguments for treatment in the foster care environment is that it can serve as an effective alternative to institutional care. This statement, of course, begs the question: Can it? Failing to find a clear answer to this question in the child-care literature, Bryant [1984] undertook analyses of two sets of data gathered at People Places. The first involved a sample of client discharge data from eight TFC programs, including People Places, and PRYDE; these data are discussed later under placement and discharge data.

The second analysis entailed an examination, albeit informal and retrospective, of ". . . an institution and [a] TFC program operating at the same time in the same community and serving roughly the same client group." This examination was occasioned by the coincidental establishment of People Places and the DeJarnette Center for Human Development (a state-run residential treatment facility) in Staunton, Virginia, in the mid-1970s. Although the children entering the two programs were not randomly assigned to their respective placements, interviews with senior staff members at the two programs revealed that ". . . the client populations of the People Places and DeJarnette programs in 1976 were essentially the same in terms of presenting problems and diagnosis." Both programs reported "adjustment reaction to adolescents" and "acting-out behavior" as the most frequently diagnosed presenting problems among their clients, and, for both, the average period of treatment was approximately 18 months.

The question of interest to Bryant was: Were those children who, largely capriciously, entered the less restrictive therapeutic foster placements able to be sustained in those placements and to be returned to normal or minimally restrictive environments? In other words, did the TFC program serve as a true substitute for the residential program or simply as a temporary holding place for children who would eventually require institutionalization after all? The answer: Of the 26 clients who were discharged from People Places in 1977, only 11 percent went on to institutional programs. Of the remainder, 46 percent returned to their biological families, 31 percent were placed in regular foster care, and 12 percent moved on to independent-living arrangements [Witters and Snodgrass 1982]. Although these data represent only a small piece of the final picture, they do suggest that at least one application of the TFC model was able to divert a large majority of its clients from more restrictive settings. (Bryant adds incidentally that the average per-client per-day cost of the institutional program during his assessment was exactly double that of the People Places program—$52 versus $26, respectively.)

PRYDE's experience adds further validity to Bryant's earlier results. By maintaining a simple tracking form on all children referred to PRYDE since 1981, the program was able to answer the question as to whether it served as an alternative to institutionalization. In 1985 and 1986, PRYDE Pittsburgh received 376 referrals, of which 39 (10 percent) were either rejected as inappropriate or whose later dispositions were not known. Of the remaining pool of 337 referrals, 61 children (18 percent) returned home without further placement. From the final referral pool of 276 children, PRYDE placed 59 (21 percent). Most of the remaining youngsters (143, or 52 percent) were placed in group homes or residential facilities at a cost range of $60 to $110 a day (as compared to the PRYDE per diem at the time of about $50).[1]

## Placement Adjustment

One of the greatest initial concerns among Professional Parenting staff members was whether the recruited treatment families would be able to tolerate the pronounced and often multiple behavior problems of the children long enough for treatment strategies to begin to control the problems. Part of this concern related to how the presence of a troubled and troubling child might affect the functioning of the family in which the child was placed. Data collection instruments were devised that allowed Professional Parenting to assess the effect of placement on own and foster children and treatment parents in terms of their satisfaction with various aspects of their daily lives that were most likely to be influenced by the abrupt change in the family configuration brought about by the placement per se. The basic plan called for pre-placement and post-placement collection of data, using a straightforward questionnaire in a telephone or face-to-face interview format. The impetus for the assessment arose from initial apprehensions that, despite efforts to prepare treatment families and the children for the kinds of difficulties the placement would produce, various lifestyle disruptions might interrupt the placements. Professional Parenting staff members reasoned that if they could identify the sources of such disruptions early, in the future they might be better able to anticipate and defuse them. Initially the data were to be gathered from the treatment parents, the foster child, and all the biological children over age ten in the treatment family before each placement and at six-month intervals thereafter for the duration of placement. Because the collection process proved time-consuming (and unpalatable to some treatment parents) and because the staff members were, at that time, trying desperately to mount and hold the program together, the actual assessment was substantially less ambitious and was finally terminated altogether early in the third program year. The data that were assembled are, nonetheless, illuminating, if not definitive.

*Assessment Method*     Usable information was gathered from a total of nine couples and from 15 foster children. (The couples, more often than the foster children, said that they were inconvenienced by the interviews.) The pre-placement foster parent interviews required each spouse to respond to questions concerning their satisfaction, during the year just past, with 15 social, recreational, occupational, and marital aspects of their lives. From two to six months after the placements, these same couples were asked to respond to an expanded version of the same questions. The foster children were interviewed, using similar forms of the same three questionnaires.

*Results*     Only the rating data, using a scale defined by "Completely Satisfied" (rating seven) to "Completely Dissatisfied" (rating one), are presented here. Table 1 shows the average adjustment, in terms of pre-placement and post-placement change scores, on each of the lifestyle questions included in the treatment parent questionnaires. These data indicate that both husband and wife were largely satisfied with the measured aspects of their lives during the one-year baseline period, and that comparable levels of satisfaction were reported at the post-placement interviews. This general absence of major change is the most notable feature of the table. Minor noteworthy changes are the average drop in male satisfaction with the amount of their personal free time and a nearly equal gain in satisfaction with the level of their social and leisure contacts. Also, both spouses became less satisfied with the wife's job outside the home, and both felt better about the behavior of their own children.

Youth adjustment data shown in table 2 are also notable only to the

## TABLE 1
*Professional Parent Adjustment to the Placement of Foster Children*

| | Mean Satisfaction Ratings | | | | | |
|---|---|---|---|---|---|---|
| | Baseline | | Internal | | Change | |
| Adjustment Area | Males *(n)* | Females *(n)* | Males *(n)* | Females *(n)* | Males | Females |
| Amount of free time | 6.56(9) | 6.11(9) | 5.56(9) | 6.11(9) | −1.00 | .00 |
| Social contacts with friends | 6.33(9) | 6.00(9) | 6.56(9) | 6.33(9) | .23 | .33 |
| Social and leisure contacts | 5.11(9) | 6.22(9) | 6.33(9) | 6.22(9) | 1.22 | .00 |
| Jobs outside home | 6.50(8) | 6.14(7) | 6.63(8) | 5.43(7) | .13 | −.71 |
| Contact with relatives | 5.89(9) | 5.78(9) | 5.67(9) | 5.22(9) | −.22 | −.56 |
| Relationship with spouse | 6.89(9) | 6.78(9) | 6.67(9) | 6.56(9) | −.22 | −.22 |
| Resolving problems with spouse | 6.67(9) | 6.56(9) | 6.67(9) | 6.44(9) | .00 | −.11 |
| Spouse's job outside the home | 6.00(7) | 6.38(8) | 5.43(7) | 6.25(8) | −.57 | −.13 |
| Relationship with children | 6.78(9) | 6.56(9) | 6.67(9) | 6.11(9) | −.11 | −.45 |
| Children behaving | 6.11(9) | 6.22(9) | 6.56(9) | 6.67(9) | .45 | .45 |
| Resolving problems with children | 6.44(9) | 6.33(9) | 6.56(9) | 6.67(9) | .11 | .34 |
| Children's progress in school | 5.89(9) | 6.11(9) | 6.00(9) | 6.00(9) | .11 | −.11 |
| Children's relationships with friends | 6.44(9) | 6.00(9) | 6.44(9) | 6.22(9) | .00 | .22 |
| Children's happiness | 6.11(9) | 6.11(9) | 6.00(9) | 5.89(9) | −.11 | −.22 |
| Own happiness | 6.22(9) | 6.44(9) | 6.56(9) | 6.22(9) | .34 | −.22 |
| Overall average | 6.26(9) | 6.25(9) | 6.29(9) | 6.16(9) | .02 | −.09 |

TABLE 2
*Program Youth Adjustment to Professional Parenting Placement*
*(N = 15 Youths)*

| Adjustment Area | Mean Satisfaction Ratings | | |
|---|---|---|---|
| | Baseline | Interval | Change |
| Amount of free time | 6.20 | 6.10 | −.10 |
| Amount of personal space | 5.50 | 6.30 | .80 |
| Time with friends | 5.80 | 5.90 | .10 |
| Relationships with friends | 6.30 | 5.90 | −.40 |
| Performance in school | 6.10 | 6.50 | .40 |
| Attention from parents | 6.50 | 6.30 | −.20 |
| Activities with family | 6.50 | 6.50 | .00 |
| Rules in the home | 6.30 | 5.90 | −.40 |
| Say in making decisions | 6.00 | 5.80 | −.20 |
| Parental discipline | 5.90 | 6.10 | .20 |
| Fair treatment by parents | 6.50 | 6.60 | .10 |
| Resolving problems with parents | 5.50 | 5.90 | .40 |
| Relationship with parents | 6.50 | 6.50 | .00 |
| Parents' happiness | 6.30 | 6.50 | .20 |
| Own happiness | 6.30 | 6.60 | .30 |
| Overall average | 6.10 | 6.20 | .10 |

extent that they portray no systematic or significant change in satisfaction from pre-placement to post-placement on any of the interview questions.

*Discussion*    If these results are valid (and there is no reason to believe that they are not) and representative (there is less certainty about this, owing to the small numbers involved), the major import of these data lies in their failure to support staff expectations that placements with treatment parents would probably produce major, if not debilitating, disruptions in the life routines of the treatment families. The staff had no reason, of course, to expect positive change scores and were delighted with the overall absence of major change among this small sample from pre-placement to post-placement.

### Trainee Satisfaction with Program Support Services

If TFC programs are distinctive from previous and current applications of traditional foster care, they are distinguished by the quality and intensity of training and support services to program families. These support services are important not only because they may be unique but also because they account for approximately half of all costs associated with this treatment approach. It has proven imperative, for all three of the core programs, that the expense of these support services be justified by their utility. During its fourth year of operation, Professional Parenting undertook to assess the value to the trainees of its support services by conducting a formal survey of the impressions of past and current Professional Parenting couples.

*Method*    A Support Services Questionnaire was mailed to all individuals with whom a foster child was, at the time of the survey, in placement, or who had previously provided either regular (full-time) or weekend (part-time) placement for a child served by the program. The questionnaires were accompanied by a letter explaining the purpose of the survey, describing the method by which respondents would not be identified with their data, and instructing spouses to mark their questionnaires independently. Questionnaires were sent to 19 couples and to one single woman then providing full-time placements, to 17 couples who had previously had a full-time placement, and to nine couples and one single woman who had previously provided part-time placements.

*Results and Discussion*    As was expected, most of the current program families returned their questionnaires; only a handful of those with whom the agency had had no recent contact returned theirs. Among those returned, some items were not completed.

Three different categories of responses were solicited on the questionnaire. The majority of the items required an ordinal rating on a seven-point satisfaction scale similar to that which has come into standard use within the teaching family model. Some of these questions were followed by a clarification question requiring a yes/no or other nominal response. At the end of each subsection of questions, respondents were invited to offer spontaneous comments.

The results of all responses to the nominal and ordinal items among the questionnaires that were returned are summarized in table 3. For each satisfaction question, the number of individuals responding, the range of the responses, and the mean responses are shown. For the ordinal questions, the sum of individuals responding to the question, the number of responses in each response bin, and the percentage of all responses appearing in each response bin are presented.

Data are broken down by sex of the respondents, and the responses

TABLE 3

*Professional Parent Satisfaction with Program Support Services*

| Survey Questions: Source | | Satisfaction Ratings | | | |
|---|---|---|---|---|---|
| | | Current Females | Current Males | Previous Females | Previous Males |
| *Program Orientation and Licensure* | | | | | |
| How satisfied were you with the orientation and information you received about the program before you decided to become a Professional Parent? | $n=$ | 14 | 15 | 5 | 4 |
| | range $=$ | 5–7 | 5–7 | 5–7 | 5–7 |
| | $\bar{x}=$ | 6.71 | 6.47 | 6.00 | 6.00 |
| How satisfied were you with the information and assistance you received from program staff in obtaining your foster care license? | $n=$ | 14 | 14 | 3 | 3 |
| | range $=$ | 3–7 | 5–7 | 5–7 | 6–7 |
| | $\bar{x}=$ | 6.57 | 6.64 | 6.33 | 6.33 |
| *Pre-Service Training* | | | | | |
| How satisfied were you with the amount of time you spent in training? | $n=$ | 14 | 15 | 5 | 4 |
| | range $=$ | 1–7 | 1–7 | 3–7 | 6–7 |
| | $\bar{x}=$ | 6.43 | 6.27 | 5.40 | 6.75 |
| | $\Sigma n=$ | 13 | 15 | 5 | 4 |
| Would you recommend a longer or shorter period of training? | $n$ (%) : | | | | |
| | longer $=$ | 0(0) | 3(20) | 0(0) | 0(0) |
| | shorter $=$ | 1(8) | 2(13) | 1(20) | 0(0) |
| | no change $=$ | 12(92) | 10(67) | 4(80) | 4(100) |
| How satisfied were you with the amount of material covered in training? | $n=$ | 13 | 14 | 5 | 4 |
| | range $=$ | 1–7 | 2–7 | 3–7 | 6–7 |
| | $\bar{x}=$ | 5.92 | 6.43 | 5.60 | 6.25 |
| | $\Sigma n=$ | 14 | 15 | 4 | 2 |
| Would you recommend that we cover more or less training material? | $n$ (%) : | | | | |
| | more $=$ | 2(14) | 4(26) | 0(0) | 0(0) |
| | less $=$ | 1(7) | 1(7) | 2(50) | 0(0) |
| | no change $=$ | 11(79) | 10(67) | 2(50) | 2(100) |
| How satisfied were you with the choice of topics covered in training? | $n=$ | 14 | 15 | 5 | 4 |
| | range $=$ | 1–7 | 3–7 | 4–6 | 6 |
| | $\bar{x}=$ | 6.36 | 6.13 | 5.70 | 6 |

## TABLE 3 *(Continued)*

| Survey Questions: Source | | Satisfaction Ratings | | | |
|---|---|---|---|---|---|
| | | Current Females | Current Males | Previous Females | Previous Males |
| How satisfied were you with the way the topics were presented? | $n =$ | 14 | 15 | 5 | 4 |
| | range = | 1–7 | 1–7 | 3–5 | 5–6 |
| | $\bar{x} =$ | 6.36 | 6.70 | 5.00 | 5.75 |
| How satisfied were you that your pre-service training prepared you for your role as a Professional Parent? | $n =$ | 14 | 15 | 5 | 4 |
| | range = | 1–7 | 2–7 | 2–6 | 5–6 |
| | $\bar{x} =$ | 6 | 6.07 | 4.80 | 5.75 |
| *Placement Arrangements* How satisfied were you that you were given enough background information on the children being considered for placement in your home (prior to their placement)? | $n =$ | 15 | 15 | 5 | 4 |
| | range = | 2–7 | 1–7 | 1–6 | 1–7 |
| | $\bar{x} =$ | 6.13 | 5.93 | 4.80 | 5.50 |
| Were you able to have trial weekend visits with the children prior to deciding on their placement in your home? | $\Sigma n =$ | 15 | 15 | 4 | 4 |
| | $n(\%)$ : | | | | |
| | yes = | 12(80) | 12(80) | 4(100) | 4(100) |
| | no = | 2(13) | 2(13) | 0(0) | 0(0) |
| | (yes/no) = | 1(7) | 1(7) | 0(0) | 0(0) |
| If yes, how satisfied were you that there was enough time for these visits before a placement decision was made? | $n =$ | 13 | 12 | 4 | 4 |
| | range = | 6–7 | 5–7 | 4–7 | 4–7 |
| | $\bar{x} =$ | 6.85 | 6.67 | 5.50 | 5.75 |
| How satisfied were you that you were given ennough information concerning any special arrangements for the children (such as doctor visits, school meetings, probation requirements, parent visitation, etc.)? | $n =$ | 15 | 15 | 5 | 4 |
| | range = | 4–7 | 1–7 | 5–6 | 6–7 |
| | $\bar{x} =$ | 6.40 | 5.87 | 5.40 | 6.25 |

## TABLE 3 *(Continued)*

| Survey Questions:<br>Source | | Satisfaction Ratings | | | |
|---|---|---|---|---|---|
| | | Current<br>Females | Current<br>Males | Previous<br>Females | Previous<br>Males |
| *Staff Consultation* | | | | | |
| How satisfied are (were) | | | | | |
| you with the frequency | $n =$ | 15 | 15 | 5 | 4 |
| of visits to your home by | range = | 6–7 | 5–7 | 4–7 | 4–7 |
| program staff? | $\bar{x} =$ | 6.87 | 6.87 | 6.20 | 5.50 |
| | $\Sigma n =$ | 14 | 14 | 5 | 3 |
| Would you recommend | $n(\%)$ : | | | | |
| more or less frequent | more = | 2(14) | 1(7) | 1(20) | 2(67) |
| visits? | less = | 0(0) | 0(0) | 0(0) | 1(33) |
| | no change = | 12(86) | 13(93) | 4(80) | 0(0) |
| How satisfied are (were) | | | | | |
| you with the amount of | | | | | |
| time staff members | | | | | |
| spend (spent) with you | $n =$ | 14 | 14 | 5 | 4 |
| when they visit(ed) your | range = | 6–7 | 5–7 | 3–7 | 3–7 |
| home? | $\bar{x} =$ | 6.79 | 6.86 | 5.40 | 5.75 |
| | $\Sigma n =$ | 15 | 15 | 5 | 3 |
| Would you recommend | $n(\%)$ : | | | | |
| longer or shorter visits | longer = | 0(0) | 1(7) | 2(40) | 1(33) |
| by staff members? | shorter = | 0(0) | 0(0) | 1(20) | 0(0) |
| | no change = | 15(100) | 14(93) | 2(40) | 2(67) |
| How satisfied are (were) | | | | | |
| you with the frequency | $n =$ | 15 | 15 | 5 | 4 |
| of staff telephone | range = | 7 | 4–7 | 1–7 | 1–7 |
| contacts with you? | $\bar{x} =$ | 7.00 | 6.80 | 5.20 | 5.00 |
| | $\Sigma n =$ | 14 | 15 | 4 | 2 |
| | $n\%$ : | | | | |
| Would you recommend | more | | | | |
| more or less frequent | frequent = | 0(0) | 1(7) | 1(25) | 1(50) |
| phone contacts? | less | | | | |
| | frequent = | 0(0) | 0(0) | 0(0) | 0(0) |
| | no change = | 14(100) | 14(93) | 3(75) | 1(50) |
| How satisfied are (were) | | | | | |
| you that you can (could) | | | | | |
| reach a staff member for | $n =$ | 15 | 15 | 5 | 4 |
| help or advice at any | range = | 1–7 | 5–7 | 4–7 | 7 |
| time? | $\bar{x} =$ | 6.60 | 6.87 | 6.20 | 7 |

## TABLE 3 *(Continued)*

| Survey Questions: Source | | Satisfaction Ratings | | | |
|---|---|---|---|---|---|
| | | Current Females | Current Males | Previous Females | Previous Males |
| How satisfied are (were) you with the quality of the help, advice, and suggestions you have received from program staff? | $n=$ | 15 | 15 | 5 | 4 |
| | range = | 2–7 | 2–7 | 2–7 | 5–7 |
| | $\bar{x}=$ | 6.27 | 6.40 | 5.40 | 6 |
| How satisfied are (were) you that program staff have been pleasant and have shown genuine concern in their contacts with you? | $n=$ | 15 | 15 | 5 | 4 |
| | range = | 5–7 | 1–7 | 3–7 | 6–7 |
| | $\bar{x}=$ | 6.73 | 6.47 | 5.80 | 6.50 |
| *In-Service Training* How satisfied are (were) you with the frequency (every six months) of our in-service meetings? | $n=$ | 13 | 14 | 3 | 2 |
| | range = | 1–7 | 4–7 | 4–7 | 6 |
| | $\bar{x}=$ | 5.85 | 6.00 | 5.67 | 6.00 |
| | $\Sigma n=$ | 13 | 14 | 3 | 2 |
| Would you recommend more or less frequent meetings? | $n\%$ : more frequent = | 6(46) | 7(50) | 0(0) | 2(100) |
| | less frequent = | 0(0) | 1(7) | 0(0) | 0(0) |
| | no change = | 7(54) | 6(43) | 3(100) | 0(0) |
| How satisfied are (were) you with the amount of time scheduled for each in-service meeting? | $n=$ | 12 | 14 | 3 | 2 |
| | range = | 6–7 | 4–7 | 4–7 | 6–7 |
| | $\bar{x}=$ | 6.92 | 6.43 | 5.67 | 6.50 |
| | $\Sigma n=$ | 13 | 14 | 3 | 1 |
| Would you recommend longer or shorter in-service meetings? | $n(\%)$ : longer = | 0(0) | 3(21) | 0(0) | 1(100) |
| | shorter = | 0(0) | 1(7) | 0(0) | 0(0) |
| | no change = | 13(100) | 10(71) | 3(100) | 0(0) |
| How satisfied are (were) you with the usefulness of the information | | | | | |

## TABLE 3 *(Continued)*

| Survey Questions: Source | | Satisfaction Ratings | | | |
|---|---|---|---|---|---|
| | | Current Females | Current Males | Previous Females | Previous Males |
| provided at the in-service meetings you have attended? | $n =$ | 12 | 13 | 3 | 1 |
| | range = | 6–7 | 2–7 | 4–7 | 6 |
| | $\bar{x} =$ | 6.92 | 6.08 | 5.67 | 6 |
| *Compensation* How satisfied are (were) you with the amount of the monthly payment provided to Professional Parents? | $n =$ | 15 | 15 | 5 | 3 |
| | range = | 1–7 | 2–7 | 5–7 | 5–6 |
| | $\bar{x} =$ | 6.00 | 6.33 | 5.00 | 5.67 |
| If you feel the amount of the payments should be increased, indicate what monthly amount you think would be more suitable. | $n =$ | 3 | 5 | 0 | 1 |
| | range = | $400– | $400– | | |
| | $\bar{x} =$ | $625 | 600 | — | $450 |
| | | $542 | $490 | — | $450 |
| *Staff Assistance with Other Agencies/Individuals* How satisfied are (were) you with the amount of help you receive(d) from program staff in dealing with people such as D.S.S., court, and school personnel, and with the parents or other relatives of your elective child? | $n =$ | 15 | 15 | 4 | 3 |
| | range = | 1–7 | 1–7 | 3–7 | 6 |
| | $\bar{x} =$ | 5.87 | 5.93 | 5.50 | 6.00 |
| *The Support Services Overall* How satisfied are (were) you that the program support services, considered together, are meeting (did meet) your needs as a Professional Parent? | $n =$ | 15 | 13 | 5 | 4 |
| | range = | 4–7 | 3–7 | 3–7 | 4–6 |
| | $\bar{x} =$ | 6.33 | 6.38 | 5.40 | 5.50 |

How satisfied are (were) you that the program support services,

TABLE 3 *(Continued)*

| Survey Questions: Source | | Satisfaction Ratings | | | |
|---|---|---|---|---|---|
| | | Current Females | Current Males | Previous Females | Previous Males |
| considered together, are helping (did help) you meet the needs of the youths in your care? | $n=$ | 15 | 13 | 5 | 4 |
| | range $=$ | 4–7 | 2–7 | 3–7 | 4–6 |
| | $\bar{x}=$ | 6.53 | 6.31 | 5.80 | 5.50 |
| How satisfied are (were) you with your overall experience as a Professional Parent? | $n=$ | 15 | 13 | 5 | 4 |
| | range $=$ | 4–7 | 5–7 | 2–7 | 6 |
| | $\bar{x}=$ | 6.27 | 6.38 | 5.40 | 6.00 |

of current and previous or past treatment parents are shown separately. (It should be noted that the seven-point satisfaction scale is familiar to anyone working with the teaching famiy model, and that "criterion performance" on teaching parent and staff evaluations has come, conventionally, to be set at the level of six or above on this scale.)

While no attempt is made here to discuss the responses of the couples to each question on the survey, results of several specific items are noteworthy, and several generalizations about these data, considered together, are of interest.

The suspicion that many elements of the support services package were initially flawed or deficient was borne out by the differences between the reported satisfaction levels of the previous treatment parents and those of the current treatment parents (who were exposed to more refined versions of these services). Compared by sex of the respondents, only in rare and isolated cases do the reported mean satisfaction levels of previous participants exceed those of the current or more recent couples. Data from even more recent couples, gathered since this analysis, continue to bear out this generalization. It is also true, in this same connection, that most of the averaged ratings that fell below the level of 6.00 (the arbitrary standard of acceptability) were from previous rather than current couples.

A preponderance of all current treatment parents reported substantial levels of satisfaction (6.00 or above) with most of the support services. Exceptions occurred in the following areas: *(1)* current females were slightly less than satisfied (5.92) with the amount of material covered in pre-service training (though 79 percent of them recommended no change in that amount); *(2)* current males were slightly less than satisfied (5.93) with the amount of background information provided before the placement of the child and with the amount of information provided concerning special arrangements for doctor appointments, school visits, and the like (5.87); *(3)* current females were slightly dissatisfied with the frequency of the in-service training sessions, with 46 percent of them recommending more frequent meeetings; and *(4)* both current females (5.87) and males (5.93) were less than satisfied with the amount of help they received from staff members and with the biological parents or other relatives of the child.

Averaged responses from current couples to all other response categories, including the three important items in the Support Services Overall category, were at or above 6.00.

The general atmosphere of satisfaction among current couples is also reflected in most of their responses to the several items that called for a recommendation. Ninety-two percent of the females and 67 percent of the males recommended no change in the duration of the pre-service training. Similarly, 79 percent of the females and 67 percent of the males recommended no change in the amount of material covered in these workshops.

In terms of staff consultation, no change in the frequency of in-home visits was recommended by 86 percent of the females and 93 percent of the males. Those who differed on this item recommended more frequent visits. Also, all but one of the current trainees recommended no change in the duration of these visits. Frequency of phone consultation was also satisfactory to all but one respondent, who wished to be contacted more frequently.

As indicated previously, responses of both males and females to the item concerning frequency of in-service training sessions were about equally divided between "no change" and "more frequent" meetings. All of the females and 71 percent of the males, however, recommended no change in the duration of these meetings.

Finally, it was a pleasant surprise to the agency that most of the current couples were satisfied with the amount of monthly stipends. Both females (6.00) and males (6.33) indicted general satisfaction with the stipend and only eight individuals felt that the amount should be increased.

### Effect on Children and Outcome

All three programs have gathered various kinds of data that bear on the general question of program effectiveness or effect on children served.

Although the categories of data are in some cases similar across programs, the sampling methods, time factors, and other data collection specifics were sufficiently different to preclude either the combining of data between programs or directly comparing them. Nevertheless, groupings of similar data from the different programs were possible in the following subgroupings: *(1)* discharge data, *(2)* placement data, *(3)* improvement during treatment of targeted behaviors, and *(4)* frequency of convictions of youths during treatment.

*Discharge Data*     One broad indicator of the overall effect on children served in TFC is the environment to which the child is discharged. Can the program release or discharge the child under favorable circumstances to minimally restrictive settings—to the child's own family or relative, to an adoptive home, to a traditional foster home, or into independent living? Or does the program see many of its children discharged to more restrictive settings because the program was unable to meet their needs? Each of the three programs maintains discharge data on the clients they serve to indicate outcomes and to strive continually for success.

Based on the data of each program, developers and consumers of TFC services should expect or aim for a 75 percent successful discharge rate of children served. If a program is providing the supervision and support it must, it will succeed with a majority of the children it serves. If the program is serving a seriously troubled population of older children and adolescents, then it is unlikely to succeed with all children.

In table 4, discharge data for seven years' operation in PRYDE show that of the 114 children discharged, 72 percent were able to go to settings less restrictive than the PRYDE home. It is encouraging to note that the rate of successful discharges increases over time. In the first year of operation, with few children served and few discharged (only two), the rate of successful discharges was quite low (50 percent, or one child). As the program served more children and learned from its mistakes, it was able to discharge more children successfully. By 1987, the seventh year of operation, PRYDE Pittsburgh discharged 86 percent of its children successfully.

People Places assembled similar discharge status data concerning 26 and 45 children discharged during the years 1977 and 1981 [Witters and Snodgrass 1982]. The authors note: "The pattern of placement is similar for the two years represented, although in the 1981 sample a larger percentage of children fall in the category of 'other' placements. This is due in large measure to the fact that this sample contains more 17- and

TABLE 4
*Discharge Data Across All Three Programs*

| PRYDE Pittsburgh | 1981 | 1982 | 1983 | 1984 | 1985 | 1986 | 1987 | Total |
|---|---|---|---|---|---|---|---|---|
| No. Successful discharges | 1 | 3 | 15 | 25 | 14 | 12 | 12 | 82 |
| No. Unsuccessful disharges | 1 | 4 | 7 | 8 | 6 | 4 | 2 | 32 |
| % Successful discharges | 50 | 42 | 68 | 75.7 | 70 | 75 | 86 | 72 |

| People Places | 1977(%) | 1981(%) |
|---|---|---|
| Living Arrangements | | |
| Biological family | 46 | 31 |
| Foster family | 31 | 33 |
| Institution | 11 | 14 |
| Other (independent living) | 12 | 22 |
| | (n = 26) | (n = 45) |

| Professional Parenting | No. | % (n = 24) |
|---|---|---|
| Minimally Restrictive Placements | | |
| Biological family | 8 | 33.3 |
| Independent living | 7 | 29.2 |
| Traditional foster care | 3 | 12.5 |
| Relative/other family member | 1 | 4.2 |
| Total | 19 | 79.2 |
| | | |
| More Restrictive Settings | | |
| Temporary placement in jail, juvenile detention, emergency shelter | 2 | 8.3 |
| Psychiatric hospital or child-care institution | 2 | 8.3 |
| Training School or wilderness camp | 1 | 4.2 |
| Total | 5 | 20.8 |

18-year-old children who were emancipated rather than returned to the custody of a family or agency." It is noteworthy that 89 percent of the 1977 sample and 86 percent of the later sample were discharged to settings less restrictive than People Places homes.

Also in table 4, comparable data from Professional Parenting depicts the effect of the program on children's discharge status. Of 24 children discharged, 79 percent were released to their parents, relatives, traditional foster care, or independent living; only 21 percent of the discharges resulted in placements in restrictive settings such as psychiatric hospitals, detention centers, or training schools.

*Placement Data*     Another broad indicator of program success is the ability of the program to sustain a child in placement; chronic runners, for example, who cannot be sustained in a program, cannot benefit from the treatment the program affords. Successful placements are, therefore, defined as children successfully discharged during a reporting period as well as all other youngsters remaining in program homes during that period. An unsuccessful placement would be any child who is unsuccessfully discharged during the reporting period. Both PRYDE and Professional Parenting provide data on placement status of children.

Table 5 shows PRYDE placement data from program inception to its seventh year of operation, including the total number of successful placements and percentages of chidren successfully sustained during each year. As more children were served and more children were successfully discharged, the rate of successful placements increased. In the seventh year of operation, PRYDE Pittsburgh served 98 children, of whom only two failed. All other 96 children (98 percent) were either successfully main-

TABLE 5

*Placement Success: Effectively Maintaining Children in Treatment Homes*
*PRYDE Pittsburgh*

|  | 1981 | 1982 | 1983 | 1984 | 1985 | 1986 | 1987 |
|---|---|---|---|---|---|---|---|
| Total placements | 17 | 33 | 70 | 94 | 80 | 88 | 98 |
| Successful placements | 16 | 29 | 63 | 86 | 74 | 84 | 96 |
| % of successful placements★ | 94 | 88 | 90 | 91 | 92.5 | 95 | 98 |
| % of unsuccessful placements | 6 | 12 | 10 | 9 | 7.5 | 5 | 2 |

★Successful placements include all children maintained in the program and successful discharges.

tained in the program or were discharged to settings less restrictive; only 2 percent of the children served that year were unsuccessfully maintained by the program.

Of the first 44 children who entered Professional Parenting for extended placement, almost 90 percent were able to depart the program to less restrictive placements within their home communities or successfully remain in program homes (table 6). Unfortunately, the program was unable to maintain 11 percent of the total population served; these youngsters were released to institutional placements. Nevertheless, a successful placement rate of 89 percent is impressive for programs serving seriously troubled children and adolescents.

Considered together, these independently gathered data show remarkable similarity. They indicate (albeit not comparatively with other treatment modalities) that properly mounted TFC programs can, indeed, effectively sustain greater than 90 percent of the difficult children they serve and successfully discharge a convincingly large majority, 75 percent to 80 percent.

*Target Behavior Improvement*    Another relevant index of program efficacy is the degree to which client behaviors targeted for treatment actually improve as a function, or at least during the period, of that intervention.

At People Places, major referral or target behaviors of each child are documented at the time the child is admitted to the program. Clients enter that program with an average of four to five specified problem behaviors. Later, at discharge, staff members rate each child on each of the initially targeted behaviors, using the following scale: "no problem," "some problem but improving," "some problem and getting worse," and "major (continuing) problems." Data depicting the target behavior improvement for the same two samples of children shown in table 4 (those discharged from that program in 1977 and in 1981) are assembled and arrayed under two headings, *Significant Improvement* and *Continuing Problem,* in table 7.

The two headings reflect a merging of the two positive rating statements and the two negative rating statements.

Witters and Snodgrass [1982] comment on these data:

Because of the subjective nature of the responses and the lack of independent verification, the results can only be suggestive of the occurrence of actual behavior. Given this rather serious limitation, the

TABLE 6

*Placement Success: Effectively Maintaining Children in Treatment Homes*
*Professional Parenting*

| Minimally Restrictive Community Placement | No. | Percentage of Total Placements |
|---|---|---|
| Continue in program with initial Professional Parent family | 12 | 27.3 |
| Continue in program with second Professional Parent family | 8 | 18.2 |
| Biological family | 8 | 18.2 |
| Independent living | 7 | 15.9 |
| Traditional foster care | 3 | 6.8 |
| Relative/other family member | 1 | 2.3 |
| Total Successful Placements★ | 39 | 88.7 |

| Significantly Restrictive Non-Community Placements | No. | Percentage of Total Placements |
|---|---|---|
| Temporary placement in jail, juvenile detention, or emergency youth shelter | 2 | 4.5 |
| Psychiatric hospital or child care institution | 2 | 4.5 |
| Training school or wilderness camp | 1 | 2.3 |
| Total Unsuccessful Placements | 5 | 11.3 |

★Successful placements include all children maintained in the program and successful discharges.

perceptions of continued improvement in target behaviors were encouraging. An average of better than 75 percent of the behaviors were rated as significantly improved in both the 1977 and 1981 samples. The target behaviors of enuresis, hyperactivity, and poor self-help skills were behaviors which were treated reliably by this program. Noncompliance and runaway behavior on the other hand were more difficult to deal with. Some of the children for whom runaway behavior was a continuing problem did not remain in the program long enough to reap any treatment benefits from it.

*Convictions During Treatment*    A final, and pressing, societal concern about any program purporting to serve delinquent adolescents is whether the program, apart from its effect on other troublesome behaviors, is able to interrupt its clients' pattern of delinquent behavior. On this subject, Bryant [1984] has raised the concern that, if TFC programs

TABLE 7

*Ratings of Treatment Effectiveness on Target Behaviors of 1981 Discharged People Places' Clients*

| | %<br>Significant<br>Improvement | %<br>Continuing<br>Problems |
|---|---|---|
| Poor peer interaction | 87 | 13 |
| Non-compliance | 50 | 50 |
| Runaway | 58 | 42 |
| Aggression | 67 | 33 |
| Tantrums | 78 | 22 |
| Stealing | 69 | 31 |
| Lying | 75 | 25 |
| Enuresis | 100 | 0 |
| Hyperactivity | 100 | 0 |
| Sexual misconduct | 86 | 14 |
| School problems | 70 | 30 |
| Poor self-help skills | 100 | 0 |
| Destructive | 83 | 17 |
| All target behaviors | | |
| For 1981 ($n = 191$) | 76 | 24 |
| For 1977 ($n = 156$) | 83 | 17 |

are the least restrictive of community-based alternatives and if their populations include children who have been adjudicated as delinquents, might they not also provide the least security (protection against subsequent criminal acts) to the communities they serve? Looking to the literature for a minimal answer to this question, he further notes, "If there is little data to show that institutions provide more security than community placements, there is even less comparing various community placement options."

In an effort to shed at least preliminary light on this issue, Bryant analyzed juvenile convictions data from the city of Staunton, Virginia, gathered by the Commonwealth's Attorney's office in 1980. The data concerned the rate of convictions, during that year, of the clients of three local community-based programs serving juvenile offenders. The programs included People Places, a halfway house for male juvenile offenders, and a group home for girls. During that year, one conviction was recorded for the girls' group home, five for the boys' halfway house and six for clients of People Places. Cast as a percentage of each program's average census, the comparative conviction rates for the three programs were [Bryant 1984]; 17 percent for the girls' group home, 42 percent for the boys' halfway house, and 12 percent for People Places.

Bryant observes that these three programs are ". . . basically non-comparable except in their common status as community-based alternatives to institutional care," and adds, "Differences in the conviction rates shown . . . are likely to reflect more on the question of which client populations are most safely served in community settings than on what type program works best." (All of the halfway houses clients were adjudicated delinquents referred from the Department of Corrections, whereas only 15 percent of People Places clients can be so described.) "Nevertheless," Bryant concludes, "the statistics do suggest that therapeutic foster care in this case may be 'safer' or less 'risky' than other community options for the client population it serves."

### Client and Parent Characteristics: A National Comparison with Group Homes

We have apologized throughout this chapter for the virtual absence of systematically gathered data that would permit direct comparisons on almost any dimension, of programs using the TFC model with other, currently accepted treatment alternatives. We have also noted that joint, or collaborative, data collection among the three core programs has not yet been undertaken. Happily, there is one significant exception to this state of affairs, occasioned by activities initially outside the purview of the core programs.

In late 1982, proponents and members of the National Teaching-Family Association, the professional organization of programs around the nation using the teaching family model of group home treatment, established a computer-based system for gathering, storing, and analyzing data from the several hundred group homes using this treatment home model. The method and procedures for the system were developed by the research staff of Father Flanagan's Boys Town, and the data repository is located there. The system is called the National Data Network (NDN) and it has been in continuous operation since its implementation. The NDN was intended as a central clearing house of information on programs using the teaching family model and focused, initially, on descriptive data—client demographic characteristics, teaching parent (group home treatment providers) characteristics—and on the problems at admission of clients entering participating homes. The data base is updated bimonthly and has already amply served the purpose of informing association members of the broad, national status of the teaching family enterprise [Fabry et al. 1983; Beier et al. 1984].

Late in the second year of NDN collection, the three TFC programs of this book were offered the opportunity to participate in the enterprise. The three programs were interested for two reasons. The behavioral treatment technologies used at the teaching family model group home sites had much in common with those used by the three TFC programs; and the three programs had set out to serve a population of children who might overlap with the difficult children served by the teaching family model around the nation. This offer was a valid opportunity to see how the two populations of children compared and, at the same time, to compare the program treatment families with group home teaching parents around the nation. Secondarily, participation in the NDN would allow some uniform data collection among the three programs.

The three programs began submitting data (using forms only slightly revised from those used by the teaching family model group homes) to NDN in December 1983. The remainder of this section focuses on data from a representative recording interval (January–February 1984) comparing TFC children and treatment parents with a nationwide sample of teaching family model group home children and their teaching parents.

*Characteristics of Treatment Providers*    It is immediately apparent from the demographics of treatment parents in the two samples (table 8) that TFC parents are, as a group, older (38 years old versus 31) and somewhat less well educated than the teaching-parents. Most teaching family model group homes require that one or both parents of prospective teaching parent couples have at least a bachelor's degree; none of the TFC programs imposes such a requirement, though most TFC parents have at least a high-school education. Given the average age differences of both the males and females in the two groups, it is not surprising that the TFC parents who are married have been married longer and have more children of their own than do teaching family couples. The TFC programs also appear to employ a greater percentage of black providers than do the teaching family homes, but this datum is largely accounted for by the fact that the large PRYDE Pittsburgh program works with about 60 percent black families. Neither of the other TFC programs exceeds a 75:25 white:black ratio. Finally, the average duration of services is only slightly longer for TFC than for teaching parents—about two to three

## TABLE 8
*NDN Characteristics of Treatment Providers During the January–February 1984 Reporting Interval*

|  | Group Home Teaching Parents | Foster Home Treatment Parents |
|---|---|---|
| Age in Years: Females |  |  |
| (Total *n*) | (113) | (96) |
| Mean | 31.58 | 38.66 |
| Standard deviation | 7.49 | 10.61 |
| Range | 23–62 | 15–77 |
| Age in Years: Males |  |  |
| (Total *n*) | (110) | (82) |
| Mean | 33.44 | 39.71 |
| Standard deviation | 7.56 | 10.40 |
| Range | 23–64 | 15–67 |
| Education: Females |  |  |
| (Total *n*) | (79) | (96) |
| Elementary | 0.0% | 4.1% |
| Secondary | 1.3% | 15.5% |
| High school | 19.0% | 29.2% |
| High school+ | 21.5% | 30.4% |
| Associate | 5.1% | 6.3% |
| Bachelor | 35.4% | 11.5% |
| Bachelor+ | 11.4% | 1.0% |
| Advanced | 6.3% | 1.0% |
| Advanced+ | 0.0% | 0.0% |
| Doctoral | 0.0% | 1.0% |
| Education: Males |  |  |
| (Total *n*) | (79) | (83) |
| Elementary | 2.5% | 6.0% |
| Secondary | 0.0% | 15.7% |
| High school | 7.7% | 32.5% |
| High school+ | 23.1% | 15.8% |
| Associate | 9.0% | 7.2% |
| Bachelor | 34.6% | 12.0% |
| Bachelor+ | 19.2% | 0.0% |
| Advanced | 2.6% | 8.4% |
| Advanced+ | 1.3% | 1.2% |
| Doctoral | 0.0% | 1.2% |

## TABLE 8 *(Continued)*

| | Group Home Teaching Parents | Foster Home Treatment Parents |
|---|---|---|
| Years Married for Couples | | |
| (Total *n*) | (92) | (87) |
| Mean | 8.01 | 12.63 |
| Standard deviation | 6.31 | 9.57 |
| Range | 1–28 | 0–41 |
| Number of Biological Children | | |
| (Total *n*) | (158) | (95) |
| Mean | 1.41 | 2.24 |
| Standard deviation | 1.15 | 1.91 |
| Ethnic Distribution: Females | | |
| (Total *n*) | (104) | (95) |
| Caucasian | 75.0% | 62.1% |
| Black | 22.1% | 37.9% |
| Hispanic | 1.9% | 0.0% |
| American Indian | 0.0% | 0.0% |
| Oriental | 1.0% | 0.0% |
| Other | 0.0% | 0.0% |
| Ethnic Distribution: Males | | |
| (Total *n*) | (103) | (83) |
| Caucasian | 73.8% | 66.3% |
| Black | 22.3% | 33.7% |
| Hispanic | 1.9% | 0.0% |
| American Indian | 0.0% | 0.0% |
| Oriental | 1.0% | 0.0% |
| Other | 1.0% | 0.0% |
| Duration of Service in Months | | |
| (Total *n*) | (172) | (96) |
| Mean | 22.00 | 24.52 |
| Standard deviation | 19.32 | 26.54 |
| Range | 0–88 | 1–125 |

years. The range of tenure is much greater for the foster parent groups, however, most likely because some of the foster families work with children, sometimes in their early teens, who require a treatment home until they reach the age of 18.

*Client Demographic Characteristics*      A comparison of the sex, age, and race of almost a thousand children in teaching family group homes with over 100 TFC children is shown in table 9. Although both categories of programs serve more boys than girls, the client sex ratio is more nearly equal in the TFC sample. Children in TFC are, on average, about one year younger than their teaching family counterparts, although the extensive range of age of clients in the group home sample is much greater (seven years old to a few disabled older adults) and thus greatly influenced the higher average age. Again, the apparent difference between the groups in the ratio of black to white clients is substantially influenced by the fact that PRYDE's clients are about equally divided between those races. Neither program group has so far served substantial proportions of clients of other races.

TABLE 9

*NDN Client Characteristics of Youth in Treatment During the January–1984 February Reporting Interval*

|  | Group Home Youth | Foster Home Youth |
|---|---|---|
| Sex Distribution | | |
| (Total *n*) | (942) | (127) |
| Males | 78.2% | 59.1% |
| Females | 21.8% | 40.9% |
| Age in Years | | |
| (Total *n*) | (933) | (125) |
| Mean | 15.07 | 14.02 |
| Standard deviation | 3.51 | 2.91 |
| Range | 7–51 | 2–17 |
| Ethnic Distribution | | |
| (Total *n*) | (935) | (127) |
| Caucasian | 70.9% | 63.8% |
| Black | 20.9% | 33.8% |
| Hispanic | 4.9% | 0.0% |
| American Indian | 2.5% | 0.0% |
| Oriental | 0.4% | 1.6% |
| Other | 0.4% | 0.8% |
| Duration of Treatment in Months | | |
| (Total *n*) | (944) | (130) |
| Mean | 13.33 | 12.19 |
| Standard deviation | 13.56 | 11.19 |
| Range | 0–89 | 0–65 |

Comparative duration in treatment of clients is shown in the last portion of the table. Although both program modalities are currently serving the average client for just over one year, this average duration in treatment among TFC children may gradually increase during subsequent data-reporting intervals. This change may occur because all teaching family model group homes are geared to returning clients to their own families and have historically witnessed average treatment durations of just over a year. Conversely, many TFC placements may span the placed youths' remaining teen years and thus produce longer lengths of stay as the programs mature, or at least wider ranges of length of stay. For example, PRYDE, with a primary goal of successful reunification with the child's family for about half of its clients, has an average length of stay of 18 months over several years of service, yet shows an increasing range of length of stay from three months to 18 months in its second year of operation to two months to 66 months in its seventh year of operation.

On these broad dimensions, there appear to be more similarities than significant differences between the populations of clients served by the two program categories.

Another, perhaps more illuminating, question about program clients that can be addressed via the data submitted to the NDN is, "Where did they come from?" This question relates to the relative severity of problems between the two client groups. Table 10 identifies the placements, or living circumstances immediately before admission, of over 500 teaching family model group home children and over 100 TFC clients. Most notable among the data are the similarities, in the percentage columns, of program referrals/admissions accepted from previous placements other than the children's relatives. In the previous placement categories of foster home, teaching family model group home or shelter, detention facility, institution, psychiatric inpatient, and training school, the two groups are almost identical, with small differences, where they exist, usually showing larger percentages of TFC children coming from the more restrictive previous placements. A substantial 25 percent of TFC children originating from a "different treatment home" are children moved between program families within a TFC program. (The author has not yet determined the nature of the rather large difference—38 percent for teaching family youth vs. 21 percent for TFC youths—originating from unspecified "other" placements.)

*Children's Problems at Admission*    Perhaps the most compelling evidence that the three programs in this volume are serving children from the same population as those receiving teaching family model group home intervention lies in the NDN data comparing problems at admission shown in table 11. Group home teaching parents and the case managers of each of the three TFC programs identified the four most serious problems of each child in treatment during the reporting interval. The preponderance of all clients in both groups were categorized as "troublesome youth." For most problems, including most of the more serious, antisocial difficulties, percentages of children so characterized from each group were within a few points of one another. Two exceptions bear mention. First, greater proportions of TFC (10 percent and 8.5 percent) than teaching family children (2.1 percent and 2.0 percent) were described as having problems with physical and verbal aggression.

TABLE 10

*NDN Previous Placement Data for Youths in Treatment During the January–February 1984 Reporting Interval*

| | Group Home Youth (n = 513) | | Foster Home Youth (n = 130) | |
|---|---|---|---|---|
| | n | % | n | % |
| With both parents | 38 | 7 | 5 | 4 |
| With one parent and stepparent | 24 | 5 | 4 | 3 |
| With mother | 56 | 11 | 5 | 4 |
| With father | 6 | 1 | 0 | 0 |
| With grandparent(s) | 7 | 1 | 0 | 0 |
| With relative(s) | 2 | 0 | 1 | 1 |
| Foster home | 20 | 4 | 4 | 3 |
| Wilderness camp | 2 | 0 | 3 | 2 |
| Another family home | 3 | 1 | ★ | ★ |
| Non-family home or shelter | 41 | 8 | 11 | 8 |
| Detention facility | 12 | 2 | 4 | 3 |
| Institution | 38 | 7 | 13 | 10 |
| Psychiatric inpatient | 11 | 2 | 3 | 2 |
| Training school | 5 | 1 | 4 | 3 |
| Readmission | 5 | 1 | ★ | ★ |
| A family home | ★ | ★ | 8 | 6 |
| Different treatment home | ★ | ★ | 33 | 25 |
| Other | 15 | 3 | 27 | 21 |
| Unknown or no information given | 227 | 44 | 3 | 2 |

★Not applicable

TABLE 11

*NDN Youth Categories and Problems at Admission During the January–*
*February 1984 Reporting Interval*

| | % Group Home Youth (n = 164) | % Foster Home Youth (n = 128) |
|---|---|---|
| *Categories* | | |
| Troublesome youth | 97.1 | 96.4 |
| Autistic youth | 1.2 | 0.8 |
| Retarded youth | 0.0 | 0.0 |
| Emotionally disturbed adult | 1.6 | 0.0 |
| Retarded adult | 0.1 | 0.0 |
| *Four Most Serious Problems at Admission for Troublesome Youth* | | |
| Adjudicated felony/violent offender | 0.7 | 1.3 |
| Adjudicated misdemeanor/status offender | 4.1 | 2.3 |
| Pre-delinquent | 1.2 | 3.4 |
| Physically agressive youth | 2.1 | 10.0 |
| Verbally aggressive youth | 2.0 | 8.5 |
| Fire-setting | 0.2 | 0.8 |
| Running away | 1.9 | 3.8 |
| Peer relationship problems | 4.2 | 5.3 |
| Sexual adjustment problems | 1.3 | 3.6 |
| Physiologically dependent on drugs | 0.1 | 0.0 |
| Drug or alcohol problems | 2.2 | 0.6 |
| Emotionally disturbed | 2.1 | 3.8 |
| Depression/withdrawal problems | 1.3 | 3.4 |
| Suicide attempts/threats | 0.5 | 1.3 |
| Self-injurious behavior | 0.2 | 0.2 |
| Hallucinations/delusions | 0.1 | 0.6 |
| Hyperactive problems | 0.5 | 3.2 |
| Encopresis/enuresis | 0.3 | 2.1 |
| Low IQ | 0.5 | 2.1 |
| Orphan | 0.1 | 0.4 |
| Outgrew last placement | 0.7 | 1.1 |
| Failed previous nonresidential placement | 0.6 | 0.4 |
| Failed previous residential placement | 1.0 | 1.1 |
| Unmanageable by parents | 7.7 | 11.5 |
| Parental neglect | 1.4 | 3.8 |
| Parental rejection | 18.3 | 3.2 |

TABLE 11 *(Continued)*

| | %<br>Group Home Youth<br>(*n* = 164) | %<br>Foster Home<br>Youth (*n* = 128) |
|---|---|---|
| Parents withdrew support | 1.0 | 1.1 |
| Parental overprotection | 7.3 | 0.2 |
| Parental skill deficiency | 2.8 | 2.8 |
| Physically abused | 1.3 | 1.7 |
| Sexually abused | 1.0 | 2.1 |
| School attendance problems | 7.4 | 3.4 |
| School behavior problems | 8.0 | 6.8 |
| School learning academic problems | 5.0 | 3.0 |
| School suspension | 0.2 | 0.4 |
| Serious physical disability | 0.1 | 0.6 |
| Serious problems with all authority | 0.6 | 0.0 |
| Alcoholism in family | 0.0 | 0.0 |
| Parents preoccupied with own problems | 8.6 | 0.0 |
| Other | 0.0 | 0.0 |

Second, larger differences between the groups occurred in several problem areas relating to parental or family difficulties. Larger percentages of teaching family than TFC children were described as suffering from parental rejection (18.3 percent vs. 3.2 percent) and overprotection (7.3 percent vs. 0.2 percent). But a slightly greater percentage of TFC children were described as unmanageable by their parents (11.5 percent vs 7.7 percent).

Thus, while there appear to be some reliable differences, notably on the dimensions of age and education, between the treatment parents who serve the two categories of programs, the clients served by the two modalities tend to be more similar than different. The generalization concerning clients appears to hold for the previous placement histories and presenting problems of both groups of children as well as for their respective demographic characteristics, with possibly those in TFC homes being more aggressive and difficult to manage. If the two groups of clients do, as these data appear to suggest, emerge from the same population, the implications are apparent. Teaching family treatment is both inherently more restrictive and, as is in the next section, more expensive than TFC for difficult adolescents. If TFC placements can be shown to be more effective than, or even as equally effective as, teaching family placements, the choice between the two treatment models would clearly favor the former. And although no definitive data can be presently brought to bear on the important question of comparative effectiveness, there is no reason to suspect that TFC programs serve their clients less well than they might be served in group homes (all NDN data were adapted from Jones et al. [1984]).

### Comparative Cost of Treatment

Because start-up conditions and, thus, start-up costs are so variable from program to program, they constitute an unwieldy method for assessing relative cost efficiency. A more meaningful, and certainly more convenient, dimension upon which the operational costs of residential programs can be compared is the total cost of services per client per day, excluding initial, one-time program implementation expenses. Bryant [1984] conducted just such an assessment of per-client-day costs of the three core TFC programs, among others. Though they were derived from budget records at different points in time, the per-client-day costs for the three programs were as follows: $26 for People Places (for 1976, exclusive of their special education program); $26.30 for Professional Parenting (1983); and $39 for the PRYDE program (1981). These cost data are offered not to emphasize differences between programs, but rather to establish a basis for comparing the modest cost range across these programs with other kinds of residential programs.

Bryant reviewed several national treatment cost studies done during the 1970s and recalculated all reported program costs in 1976 dollars. This review indicated that average per-client-day costs for residential youth treatment centers were $42.87 and for children's psychiatric hospitals, $89.90 (based on data from Witkin [1984]). Only group home ($32.42) and regular foster care ($5.69) per diem costs—again, in 1976 dollars—fell within or below the range of operational costs shown above for the core programs (based on data from Piasecki et al. [1978]).

It would seem, then, that the cost of TFC, allowing for some variability among such programs, may well represent the least expensive residential treatment for problem children and teenagers. The possible exception to this generalization would be traditional foster care, but such placements have proven historically untenable for the kinds of clients targeted by the special programs. The view of Snodgrass and Campbell [1981], that the cost of residential treatment correlates directly with the level of restrictiveness of the treatment and not treatment intensity, would appear to be borne out. TFC appears capable of serving children who otherwise would be treated in group care facilities, yet for less cost and with successful results.

## NOTE

1. These data impelled the PRYDE program to pursue and receive outside funds for a thorough review of nearly 800 children referred since 1981. The main purpose of this evaluation was to determine the success of this TFC model by comparing the children it has served with similar children referred to but not served by PRYDE due to lack of sufficient treatment homes. The dimensions of the comparison included *(1)* the restrictiveness of the setting in which the children were placed, *(2)* the restrictveness of the setting to which the children were discharged, *(3)* the frequency of negative incidents while in placement, *(4)* the frequency of incidents after discharge, and *(5)* a cost comparison (including length of stay). The project was designed to answer the major question "Do children do better, worse, or about the same if they are placed with their parents, in regular foster care, PRYDE, group homes, or group residential settings?" Results of this formal, comparative evaluation are available from the PRYDE program.

## REFERENCES

Beier, C.H.; Fixsen, D.L.; Blase, K.; and Thompson, L. Who are we and what are we doing? A data-based response. Paper presented at the 7th annual conference of the National Teaching-Family Association, Chicago, 1984.

Bryant, B. Special foster care: evaluation of an alternative to institutions for disturbed children. Unpublished master's thesis, University of Virginia, 1984.

Fabry, B.D.; Beier, C.H.; Fixsen, D.L.; and Blase, K. Who, by whom and how well? A look into the national data network. Paper presented at the 6th annual conference of the National Teaching-Family Association, Las Vegas, 1983.

Hawkins, R.P., and Meadowcroft, P. Practical program evaluation in a family-based treatment program for disturbing and disturbed youngsters. Unpublished manuscript. Pittsburgh, Pennsylvania: The Pressley Ridge Schools, 1985.

Jones, R.J.; Timbers, G.D.; Gross, N.; Judkins, B.L.; and Beier, C. Who indeed: Professional Parenting joins the National Data Network. Paper presented at the 7th annual conference of the National Teaching-Family Association, Chicago, 1984.

Piasecki, J.R.; Pittinger, J.E.; and Rutman, I.D. Determining the costs of community residential services for the psychosocially disabled. Mental Health Statistics Series D, No. 13. Rockville, Maryland: NIMH, 1978.

Scriven, M. The methodology of evaluation. In Weiss, C.H. (ed.), Evaluating Action Programs: Readings in Social Action and Education. Boston: Allyn and Bacon, 1972.

Snodgrass, R., and Campbell, P. Specialized Foster Care: A Community Alternative to Institutional Placement. Monograph available from People Places, Inc., Staunton, Virginia, 1981.

Witkin, M.J. Residential psychiatric facilities for children and adolescents; United States,

1971–1972. Mental Health Statistics Series A, No. 14. Rockville, Maryland: NIMH, 1984.

Witters, D., and Snodgrass, R. Past, present, and future of therapeutic foster care at People Places, Inc. Paper presented at the 8th annual convention of the Association for Behavior Analysis, Milwaukee, May 1982.

# 10

# Realizing the Potential of Therapeutic Foster Care

PAMELA MEADOWCROFT
AND
WM. CLARK LUSTER

THE PROGRAMS DESCRIBED IN THIS BOOK demonstrate that therapeutic foster care (TFC) can work for many children. The enthusiasm and hope that the model provokes in staff members, treatment parents, and consumers of its services should be apparent from earlier chapters. This final chapter summarizes why TFC should be developed for seriously troubled children; reviews critical issues that might be addressed to increase the likelihood of successful implementation of the model, including defining this model of care; and concludes with the special promise this model holds for many children.

## Why Therapeutic Foster Care Should Be Developed

Program developers, mental health professionals, and policy makers will want to consider TFC as a treatment model for children with diverse needs because it provides *(1)* a humane, normalized treatment environment; *(2)* highly individualized treatment; *(3)* flexibility in treatment programming; *(4)* rich staff-to-child ratio; *(5)* expansion and contraction capabilities to meet demand; *(6)* a sense of permanence and foster family connectedness; *(7)* more lasting learning because the setting is similar to the home/community setting that it is hoped the child will experience when leaving the treatment program; *(8)* post-discharge context of family relationships; *(9)* reduced administrative problems; and *(10)* lower cost than even less treatment-intensive services in a residential group care setting. (Hawkins and Luster 1982). Each of these advantages of the model is briefly described below.

### Humane, Normalized Treatment Environment

Most professionals would agree that, in the majority of cases, for children to be able to live at home with their own parents is preferable to any out-of-home placement. Unfortunately, in this less than ideal world, circumstances often create the need for removing youngsters from their own homes. In the majority of cases, the most humane and normalized alternative living situation for the child is then another home. For children with significant mental health problems or other handicapping conditions, TFC provides treatment within an alternative family. A family is the structure with which the child is most familiar and is the structure into which most children will move after treatment. The family model is less likely to cause trauma to the youngster, is most likely to avoid the contamination of large institutional populations, and is most likely to teach skills that will be useful in preparation for adulthood.

### Highly Individualized Treatment

The TFC model allows individual treatment. With one child living in a home with carefully selected, professionally trained, and intensively supervised foster parents, treatment can be targeted to problems in the same kind of environments in which the issues historically occurred. Less treatment time is spent in maintaining the protocol of the setting, as occurs in institutional programs; more time is spent in teaching skills.

### Flexibility in Treatment Programming

The model can serve a diversity of youngsters. The traditional residential treatment setting is often limited by physical design as well as by history and program philosophy to serve a narrowly defined population. The range of children and adolescents potentially served within TFC is limited only by the lack of an appropriate treatment family, by uncreative treatment technologies, or by inadequate professional supervision. Very young children, the older teen or teen mother and child, sibling groups, multiply handicapped children, and youngsters with unique problems and symptoms are readily accommodated in TFC.

### Rich Staff-to-Child Ratio

With the professional foster parent as the primary treatment agent working closely with the case management and clinical staff, the model provides for consistent and individualized treatment. With the back-up support of highly trained professionals representing psychology, psychiatry, social work, pediatrics, and other disciplines, a whole range of expertise is at hand to augment the primary treatment agents. A "staff"-to-child ratio (including treatment parents as staff) of two to one is possible while at the same time maintaining moderate cost.

### Expansion and Contraction Capabilities to Meet Demand

In contrast to group homes, residential treatment facilities, or inpatient psychiatric hospitalization, which are programmatically and fiscally related to critical levels of occupancy, TFC is readily able to expand or contract to meet population needs. On one hand, should the need for placements within a particular geographic area grow significantly, the model can meet that need through rapid recruitment, training, and supervision of treatment parents. Admittedly no easy task, TFC programs have been initiated and operational, each serving more than 25 children, within one year's time. On the other hand, should the number of placements decline or should funds be unavailable to support placement, reduction in program size can be accomplished with few complications and with minimal effect on the remaining program.

### A Sense of Permanence and Foster Family Connectedness

Permanency planning may be best thought of as "family-connectedness" [Forsythe 1987]. Although the goal of TFC is often to return children to their parents in the shortest possible period of time, the model is able to provide long-term placement if treatment or other circumstances require it. Often the staffing pattern, the program philosophy, and staff turnover in traditional group care settings limit the development of bonding between child and adult. Long-term placement within a group facility robs the child of any healthy family experience. The TFC model can serve as the foundation for long-lasting family connectedness. Even after treament has ended, the family relationship that was developed during the treatment phase often continues for many years, if only on an informal basis. In some cases, the treatment parents may welcome the youngsters into their homes on a long-term basis. Permanent adoption has materialized in a number of cases. In any case, to achieve a sense of permanence for the child in a treatment home requires of this model a commitment to either active involvement of the child's biological parents or quick resolution of the child's long-term placement needs.

## More Lasting Learning

Since treatment takes place within a family environment, and since the youngster actually "lives" rather than "receives" the treatment, the learning that occurs is likely to be more lasting. In addition, the skills targeted for enhancement as part of the treatment plan, as well as competencies learned incidentally through living in a family and within a neighborhood, are likely to be useful in later life. The environment of a treatment home is also the most appropriate place to allow problems to occur and be resolved.

## Post-Discharge Context of Family Relationships

In addition to the likelihood that the treatment parents are going to develop a long-term bond with the youngster in treatment, they are also likely to remain living in the same location after the child leaves their home. The youngsters know how to and often do remain in contact with the treatment parents, calling the treatment family on holidays, birthdays, or when they need words of encouragement. Since the treatment parents are often in close communication with the child's biological parents, they may become part of the youngster's extended family. Formal and informal relationships are relatively easy to maintain even after the official relationship is no longer needed. Support, crisis intervention, and general conversation unrelated to treatment issues all flow naturally from the relationship developed between treatment parent, biological parent, and youngster. The treatment family in this sense can strengthen the child's own family.

### Reduced Administrative Problems

Many of the administrative issues prevalent in residential treatment are significantly reduced. Capital costs are minimized. Zoning issues are usually eliminated. Relationships with neighbors and the local community are not usually an issue. Problems with staff such as maintenance and dietary personnel are eliminated. This reduction in peripheral distractions leaves more time and energy to focus on the child.

### Lower Cost

With a current cost structure of between \$35 and \$150 per day per child (\$36 to \$55 for the three programs described in this volume), TFC is significantly less expensive than inpatient psychiatric hospitalization. Although usually more expensive than regular foster family care, the model compares favorably in cost to group home or residential treatment. TFC also affords a significantly higher proportion of unit cost to direct treatment services than other models. Since treatment occurs in the homes of professional parents, capital investment is minimized. Office space for staff and standard office equipment are the only necessary capital costs associated with the model.

## Getting Started

TFC requires fewer resources to be started successfully than do residential programs. Buildings, a full staff complement, adherence to extensive regulations regarding group care, management, sprinkler systems, and so forth, are not necessary. Nonetheless, getting started—placing the first child in a treatment home—does require a start-up period to *(1)* create the local climate for the model; *(2)* design and develop the materials needed to define exactly what the program will be; *(3)* describe the population of children to be served; *(4)* recruit and train the first group of treatment parents; *(5)* hire sufficient staff members to allow for program growth; and *(6)* obtain funds to bridge the planning phase with the fiscal viability phase.

## Creating the Climate

The need for developing a TFC program may come from a loosely defined problem of insufficient bed space for children needing out-of-home care—or it may be as specifically defined as a need for 23 TFC beds as part of a continuum of care for children within a particular community.

When program developers respond to a general rather than a specific need, they may be faced with a skeptical audience. Many professionals and public policy makers are not sufficiently familiar with the TFC model to trust its effectiveness in dealing with a wide range of mental health, juvenile justice, special education, and child welfare issues. Unfortunately, many TFC programs grow out of the ineffectiveness of traditional foster family care in many cases; at first glance, the program looks like foster family care, and in some instances, the actual service developed may be only expensive foster family care.

Another aspect of the model that creates credibility problems is its lack of physical presence. Most of the program funds are by design used to support treatment activities rather than the physical plant, equipment, or buildings. Consequently it may be difficult to see treatment taking place in a variety of natural settings (homes, schools, restaurants, ball fields, and so on). Policy makers and many professionals within mental health too often confuse bricks and mortar with treatment intensity—they assume that intensive treatment requires larger buildings to house the clients and treatment professionals [U.S. Congress, Office of Technology Assessment 1986]. It may take a great deal of faith to believe that high levels of treatment intensity can take place in the natural environments of substitute families.

How does one convince the skeptics? How are faith and appropriate political climate developed? Program developers must first begin with an assessment of the sources of potential resistance or opposition to the model. A determination of the experience base for the objections, who will object and who will support, and a plan of action to confront the opposition are essential. Armed with research data for dissemination, the potential program developer would be wise to meet with the appropriate public policy professionals and even politicians to explain the model. Increasing the acceptance of TFC requires dissemination of information that describes program results and children served in existing models. Data on the population of children successfully served, outcomes in such terms as percentage discharged to lesser restrictive settings (e.g., home, foster family care), and follow-up outcomes (e.g., recidivism) will all be useful or necessary. Financial reports that illustrate cost effectiveness reinforce the value of the model. Personal testimonials by professional staff members and treatment parents can also give credence to the model as an effective treatment modality. Letters of endorsement and other kinds of positive communications from juvenile court judges or other public officials can help. Possibly the most convincing argument can be voiced by the youngsters and their anonymous consumer satisfaction ratings. Youngsters who have successfully experienced the positive outcome of having met treatment goals while living in a supportive family environment are the most able and convincing of persons for communicating the message. For example, a 17-year-old former PRYDE child wrote in a letter to his treatment parents:

> I wouldn't have made it without all your help. I'd be in the streets, dead, or worse. I'm sure there are lots more kids like me out there. And I'm sure there are families like yours who want to help. I just wish those two kinds of people could get together and share their love. I know it would work.

### Defining the TFC Model to be Implemented

TFC models will reflect the particular needs of the communities they serve and the expertise and personalities of the developers. Generally, however, TFC fits into two broad categories [Stroul and Friedman 1986]. The first category includes programs that provide the foster parents with a modest increase over traditional foster care payments, some general training, frequent supervision, and rely primarily on the family environment as the main therapeutic intervention.

The second category comprises programs that treat the foster parent more as an employee than as one with the anomalous status of the traditional foster parent. Foster parents in this category receive more technical training, have responsibilities for implementing treatment plans within the home and community, and are paid a stipend or salary that would be equivalent to a beginning child-care worker's pay. Even among treatment parents there is often a strong sense of departure from traditional foster family care, as reflected in the following quotation from Lee Blankenbicker, a PRYDE program parent for over five years:

> I don't consider myself a foster parent. I'm a treatment parent. That means I receive professional training, certification, and ongoing

supervision for working with a child who has serious problems. As a parent, I care for a troubled child in my home. As a treatment parent, I am a teacher and I teach the child a variety of adaptive behaviors such as how to get along with peers, how to do school work, how to express feelings, how to fit into a family, and how to succeed within a community. I really see myself as a professional.

Although there are variations in the program size, expectations of treatment parents, and degree of treatment intensity, all TFC programs should develop the ten features that follow [Pierce 1987].

*Safe, Nurturing Family Environment Usually for One or Two Troubled Children*     The most common characteristic of all TFC programs is the setting—within the private homes of substitute families—and the low number of children served in each treatment home. Treatment foster homes usually serve only one or two children so that the proper supervision and teaching of each child is assured, as well as the elimination of the deviant influence of other troubled peers. Because treatment parents must participate in extensive pre-service and in-service training and implement professionally developed treatment plans, those who become treatment parents are highly functioning, well-adjusted, strongly committed, and successful adults; these traits are exemplified in what one PRYDE program parent said about why she chose to become a treatment parent:

> I was put on this earth to perform one miracle. When Terry first came to our house, we knew we were his last chance before the decision would be to send him to a psychiatric hospital. They called him psychotic. To see Terry today playing with my other kids in the backyard is that one miracle I needed to perform.

*Low Caseloads*     The next most common feature of TFC is a necessary high ratio of staff members to children. Case management staff members, or program event supervisors, typically carry a caseload of no more than 12 to 15 children. Some programs report caseloads as low as five. Programs with low caseloads normally require the supervisors, in addition to supervising the treatment parents, to work with the child's family, assist with recruitment and training activities, and perform extensive liaison work with external resources (e.g., schools, juvenile court, child welfare/mental health).

*Frequent, Treatment-Oriented Supervision*     Low caseloads allow the supervisors to visit the treatment homes once a week or more often, if necessary, especially during initial placement and crises. Home supervision meetings can require up to three hours of interaction time to review the week's events, conduct in-home training of the treatment parents, provide a supportive ear to the treatment family, and meet with the child, if necessary. Phone consultation with the treatment families also consumes a great deal of time each week, with calls to or from the treatment family every day.

*Provision of Treatment*    In most instances, treatment parents have no formal training as youth care professionals, yet TFC requires that they be the main treatment agents for the child. They are responsible for providing the child with the interactions and activities that will increase the child's ability to live successfully within a family and community. They are responsible for implementing specified counseling strategies. Whatever model of training and service TFC developers adopt, it must include skills that are transferable to home settings and to couples who are not professionally trained youth care specialists. The programs described in this book have all used a treatment technology based on behavior analysis because it is easily transferred to a home setting and implemented by parents [Hawkins et al. 1966; Kirigin et al. 1982; Wahler et al. 1965].

Other treatment services for the child in a TFC home include initial and periodic assessment of the child's needs, and counseling or clinical consultation by a professional counselor/therapist. Not all of every child's counseling needs can be met by a treatment parent; however, the danger in employing counselors for any significant portion of TFC services is the usurping of the treatment parents' role as the main treatment agent. To counteract this, the goal for counseling services by professionals should be primarily to assess the child's situation and prescribe additional training of staff members and/or treatment parents that will enhance successful adjustment of the child in that treatment family. Therapists and counselors within the TFC model will function more as clinical consultants than as direct service providers.

TFC client records need to include documentation of treatment activities provided within the treatment foster home and elsewhere. If the full potential for serving seriously emotionally disturbed children in home settings is to be realized, and if TFC is to increase its credibility as a treatment model, programs must build in evaluation methods to demonstrate quality care and treatment of these high-risk youngsters [Fabry et al. 1987; Meadowcroft et al. 1982].

Finally, TFC programs must address the child's relationship with his or her own family as a treatment service. If reunification of the child with the family is possible, then effective means for involving the parents in the child's ongoing treatment and giving them needed skills for parenting their child become essential. If reunification is not possible, helping the child and the parents to define their relationship may become essential to the child's adjustment.

*Professionalizing Treatment Parents*     TFC regards its foster parents as extensions of its professional staff. The foster parents need to be well paid, receive regular evaluations, be regarded by the program staff with respect, and receive the types of training and opportunities that will enhance their own professionalism. If program developers cannot pay treatment parents at least twice that which local foster parents receive, then they will not be able to recruit, intensively train, and expect highly skilled treatment parents to work with the more seriously emotionally disturbed children.

*Crisis Intervention Services*     Crises will happen in the homes, communities, or schools where seriously emotionally disturbed children live. If a program does not experience any incidents of serious aggression, property damage, runaways, or other antisocial behavior, then they are not serving the more troublesome children for whom TFC is designed.

Yet a program should not be buffeted from one crisis to another. Taking appropriate preventive measures—careful selection of treatment parents, intensive training and supervision of each home, and careful, frequent documentation of in-home implementation of a treatment plan—helps to minimize the frequency and severity of these events. When crises do occur, the program must have ready well-developed crisis intervention components including *(1)* a 24-hour on-call service through which treatment parents can reach a professional staff member within minutes; *(2)* crisis intervention teams that can respond, if needed, within a short time and that includes appropriate expertise (suicide interventions, physical restraint, defusing conflict, drug abuse, and the like); and *(3)* back-up placement options for each child. An event may occur that requires removing the child from the treatment home. Until the crisis can be resolved and the child returned to that treatment home, alternative placement arrangements must be available (e.g., other treatment homes, a specially staffed treatment home designed for children in crisis, or prearrangements with local psychiatric or detention facilities).

*Training and Support of Treatment Parents* As with the staff at a residential treatment center, the program expects treatment parents to continue working with a child in their care even after a series of stressful interactions. These expectations and the needed skills to help the child are provided through intensive pre-service and in-service training, supportive supervision, and a wide array of additional support services for the treatment family. Pre-service training must be of sufficient length for staff members to get to know the foster parents' strengths, and for the foster parents to acquire the necessary skills and attitudes to be successful with a seriously troubled child. In-service training must be frequent and meet the immediate training and support needs of the treatment families (including all members of the family living in the treatment home). Programs have to plan on budgeting and staffing for additional support services, including family counseling, planned respite, 24-hour on-call, support groups, professional opportunities (e.g., career ladders), bonuses, and social events.

*Educational Liaison* TFC can fail if a child fails within his or her school placement. Most of the children placed within TFC will have special education needs, and therefore the potential for school problems is high. Program developers must plan for strong educational liaison services that include assuring appropriate educational placement, assisting the school with behavior management problems, and, when necessary, having the capability of providing alternative educational experiences if community resources are exhausted.

*Staff Training* Currently no educational programs exist that will prepare prospective supervisors of treatment parents. Certainly, training within social work is helpful. Experience as a provider of direct child-care services, such as a residential child-care worker, is valuable. Advanced training in psychology and special education will help staff members to learn the teaching skills that treatment parents need in working with a seriously troubled child. Experience as a parent or a foster parent can increase one's sensitivity and credibility among treatment parents. But each of these areas of training fails to train individuals in the other disciplines' skills. Thus, program developers must anticipate staff training needs and program to meet them. Receiving training and consultation from experienced providers of TFC will help. Developing training materials that include staff expectations, the program's goals and values (e.g., "Never give up on a child"), and clinical intervention materials will also help orient, rapidly develop, and expand the knowledge and skills of new members. The best training includes modeling by experienced supervisors of treatment families: style of interaction and creative problem solving are all too often poorly communicated through written training materials.

*System Linkages*      TFC requires thoughtful planning for external program linkages, unlike self-contained residential/hospital programs for emotionally disturbed children. Particular attention, during start-up, to establishing linkages with other services will reduce later obstacles. Developers will need to form working relationshps with personnel from educational and vocational services; case management staff from child welfare and/or mental health; professionals providing specialized services such as drug and alcohol counseling; sex abuse counseling, job-training programs; the local police; the staff of community programs that provide recreational activities for special-needs children during non-school hours; (especially in the summer), and with medical and health care professionals. Even after careful linkages are instituted with the necessary external services, coordination of all these services for each child has to be established. Determining which services are needed, who is responsible for making sure the child receives these services, and that the services change when the child's needs change require good communication and coordination across agencies that traditionally have not worked well together [Stroul and Friedman 1986]. For example, a boy in a treatment home may also be attending a day treatment program for his education needs, working at a neighborhood restaurant after school, receiving family counseling through a local mental health center, and be a member of the Boy's Club. Special education teachers, mental health professionals, the employer, child welfare caseworkers, and staff members of the TFC program will need to confer frequently to be certain the child is making progress in all areas of development.

## Defining the Client Population

Initially a TFC program must narrowly define the population of children it will serve. Will the program focus on delinquents, status offenders, developmentally delayed adolescents, or young children? A major advantage of TFC is that it can serve a diverse population of children, as demonstrated by the three programs described in this book. Diversity of the population at the beginning of the program, however, will produce initial program weaknesses and strains. Referral sources will be confused by the program's lack of definition and will fail to focus their referral process. If very young children are accepted initially, or children who have no significant behavior problems, then initial program credibility will be weakened, and treatment parents will be inclined to wait for the younger or less difficult child. Finally, if diverse children are accepted initially, self expertise will be strained. Since the staff must be able to teach treatment parents how to teach and support the troubled children in their care, they must have depth of skills in working with a particular population of needy children. Of course, once a program has established a credible track record for a particular population of troubled children, then adaptations of the models for serving younger children, children with severe physical handicaps, or medically involved children can follow, as long as the program brings in the necessary staff expertise and modifies the treatment parent training accordingly.

### Recruiting Exceptional Foster Parents

The biggest obstacle to overcome during start-up is recruiting a corps of excellent treatment parents. The initial set of foster parents will strongly influence the future success of the program, since future treatment parents will probably be recruited through present treatment parents.

During start-up, TFC developers must be willing to make recruitment of highly skillful foster parents a top priority. Recruitment will have to be done throughout the start-up phase, daily, evenings, and weekends. Strategies for recruitment are described in earlier chapters and elsewhere [Grealish et al. 1987], but primarily what distinguishes successful from unsuccessful recruitment is the degree of time, energy, enthusiasm, and follow-up a program can invest in it.

### Commitment to Sufficient Program Growth

Program developers should assess the degree of their commitment to the TFC model. A program size of at least 20 children seems more practicable than smaller programs [Update 1986]. It permits a full-time, professional staff of at least four—one administrator and three supervisors—plus support personnel and consultants. Though a full complement of staff members is not needed in initiating TFC, as it is in residential group care services, at least two staff members must initially be hired. Two to three staff members allow for program identity, shared areas of expertise, continuing feedback, and the enthusiasm that can be generated from work with a committed team. As important, two to three staff members allow for the diverse planning, recruiting, training of treatment parents, and pursuit of licensure and funds that are all necessary for launching a TFC program. A program size of at least 20 children also permits a sufficient number of treatment parents with whom to match referred children, provide respite, and make necessary internal moves of a child.

*Setting a Realistic Time Schedule*

Developers of TFC should plan for a three- to 24-month start-up period. The time from initial consideration of starting TFC to placement of the first child will vary depending on obstacles encountered within each of the five areas of start-up described earlier (creating the political climate, defining the model, defining the client population, recruiting appropriate foster parents, and hiring a sufficient staff). It will also vary depending on such additional factors as the developing agency's current strengths and the availability of leadership to launch the development effort. Constraints on rapid implementation will occur if developers or the initial staff members are writing training materials for treatment parents, overcoming sentiment against foster care for seriously troubled children, having difficulty in obtaining sufficient funds to pay treatment parents suitably, or failing to recruit talented foster parents. Under these circumstances, placing the first child may take as long as 24 months. If, however, developers hire highly committed, experienced staff members, adopt existing training materials or existing models, and produce immediate interest among skillful, potential treatments parents, then the time schedule can be compressed into just a few months.

A reasonable time schedule for fiscal adequacy will also vary. A major advantage of TFC is its fiscal flexibility, because funding primarily covers only personnel costs and treatment parent fees, which will be low if population is low. Thus start-up and early expansion costs will be for personnel and office space. From placement of the first child to a cost break-even point will take about an additional year, if the program is funded on a fee-for-unit-service basis. This schedule would not apply, of course, if the service were program funded or were an approved budget-funded arrangement.

## The Future of Therapeutic Foster Care

TFC has the potential to encompass a wide range of treatment issues. On the one hand, a single child's needs could be the catalyst for developing the model becuase the child may be so multiply handicapped that conventional service models may be excluded. On the other hand, the model can also be developed or adapted to serve a wide range of youngsters. For example, within Pennsylvania during 1988, on a daily basis over 2,000 children were in special foster care homes instead of residential group care settings. Two agencies, for example, had an average population of over 300 youngsters each, with TFC as the only program component within the agencies. Another provided TFC as one service component on a continuum including residential treatment and day treatment. Yet another agency provided primarily foster family care and developed a special form of foster care for up to ten children with AIDS [Pierce 1987].

No one program is ever likely to meet the total needs of a highly troubled population, especially not an out-of-home placement program; however, special foster care can become an increasingly strong service component in a continuum of service offerings.

Special foster care can be a short-term shelter service for youngsters who are abandoned, in need of detention, shelter, or protective custody. Instead of placement in a shelter facility, the youngsters would reside in shelter or treatment homes for short-term family reconciliation, to await longer-term placement or adoption, or simply to receive shelter and care until their own home environment stabilizes and the child's family is again able to care for the youngster. This service is currently being offered by a spinoff from PRYDE called PRESS (Pressley Ridge Emergency Shelter Services). The county in which PRESS is located discovered that most of the adolescents in crisis who they originally thought could only be housed in group shelters can in fact be more successfully sheltered in crisis stabilization homes.

Special foster care can be a diversionary program for youngsters who are targeted for placement. In cases where the system responsible for placement is overburdened, where waiting lists exist, or where there is a lack of confidence in the cost-benefit ratio of traditional residential placements, the model may be implemented on an experimental or even an ad hoc basis. In fact, these conditions may offer the ideal opportunity to overcome some of the roadblocks to easy initiation of the model as the treatment of choice.

TFC can be a highly intensified individualized treatment program for special populations. By coupling the standard TFC model with various layers of professional staff members and support services, atypical cases such as the autistic child, the developmentally disabled, dually diagnosed youngster, or the seriously violent child can receive long- or short-term treatment in the least restrictive setting. Within West Virginia PRYDE, six children are being served in so-called intensive PRYDE homes because of the seriousness of their violent behavior. These children represent beginning efforts within that state to bring back to West Virginia over 100 children placed in expensive, out-of-state institutions and psychiatric hospitals because of the seriousness of the children's difficulties. Within each intensive PRYDE home, the children must be within eyesight of an adult 24 hours a day. Treatment parents receive higher pay, the assistance of a rotating staff of foster parent assistants within their homes, and professional support of staff members whose caseloads are yet smaller than the regular PRYDE model described in this volume—three to four children.

TFC can provide medical foster care. Children with serious medical needs can be well served within a therapeutic foster home. Special medical services for individual children can be finely tuned by the treatment parents' focus on one child's needs. Medical foster care provides a good home environment to a child who would otherwise be hospitalized for an extended time. The child's physical well-being is assured by recruiting nurses or others with medical backgrounds to serve as the treatment parents, paying them a salary comparable to that which they would receive through hospital employment, and providing the home with all the necessary medical equipment, all for a fraction of hospital costs.

But the exciting potential of TFC is not without its negative side. Many programs may develop as alternatives to traditional foster care and be unnecessarily expensive, overly restrictive for a child, and occupy the time of treatment parents who could be serving more troublesome children. Furthermore, this model could mistakenly develop as an alternative to more intensive services in the child's own home. Since the technology exists for parents to assist their own emotionally disturbed children, program developers must always retain a bias toward keeping the child with his or her own family and giving the family the training and supports needed. In-home treatment models do exist (e.g., Homebuilders) and show that seriously troubled or delinquent children can be maintained at home as long as the family is open to intensive services [Kinney et al. 1977] and the child's safety is not jeopardized.

To ensure that TFC continues to develop as an alternative to more restrictive residential care, providers of this service need to contribute actively to revolutionizing children's mental health care. Professionals and policy makers continue to confuse treatment capability and intensity with the location of the service; that is, institutional settings are considered inherently more treatment-intensive than a family setting. To redress this bias, providers of TFC must be willing to serve only those children who cannot be served in traditional foster care. They must be ready to demonstrate, through adequate assessment of the children's needs and continued maintenance of program data, that in fact their population of children are the neediest. They must include the ten features of TFC described above to be distinct from traditional foster care, to demonstrate treatment within the foster home home setting, and to be able to serve more successfully a difficult population of children. Finally, TFC must be willing to take risks and take extraordinary steps in protecting the children, treatment parents, and the community when placing chidren who are at risk.

### REFERENCES

Fabry, B.; Meadowcroft, P.; Frost, S.; Hawkins, R.P.; and Conoway, R. Low cost, high validity, multiuse data: Practical program evaluation in a family-based treatment program. In Wesch, D.W. (chair), Evaluating Behavior/Agencies in Community Setting: Successes and Future Directions. Symposium conducted at the Association of Behavior Analysis Convention, Nashville, Tennessee 1987.

Forsythe, P.W. Foster care and the permanency continuum. Keynote presentation at the First North American Conference on Treatment Foster Care, Minneapolis, Minnesota 1987.

Grealish, E. M.; Hunt, J.; Lynch, P.J.; and James, M.M. Professional Parent Recruitment: Effective Methods for Family-Based Treatment Programs. Paper presented at the Southeastern Psychological Association Convention, Atlanta, Georgia, 1987.

Hawkins, R. P. and Luster, W. C. Family-based treatment: A minimally restrictive alternative with special promise. In Behavior treatment of youth in professional foster homes, chaired by E. L. Phillips. Symposium presented at The American Psychological Association Convention, Washington, D.C. 1982.

Hawkins, R.P.; Peterson, R. F.; Schweid, E.; and Bijou, S.W. Behavior therapy in the home: Amelioration of problem parent-child relationships with the parent in the therapeutic role. Journal of Experimental Child Psychology 4: 99–107, 1966.

Kinney, J.W.; Madsen, B.; Fleming, T.; and Haapala, D.A. Homebuilders: Keeping families together. Journal of Consulting and Clinical Psychology 39: 905–911, 1977.

Kirigin, K.A.; Braukmann, C.J.; Atwater, J.D.; and Wolff, M.M. An evaluation of teaching family (Achievement Place) group homes for juvenile offenders. Journal of Applied Behavior Analysis 15: 1–6, 1982.

Meadowcroft, P.; Hawkins, R.P.; Trout, B.A.; Grealish, E.M.; and Stark, L. Making family-based treatment accountable; The issue of quality control. In Phillips, E.L. (chair), Behavioral Treatment of Youth in Professional Foster Homes: An Alternative. Symposium presented at the American Psychological Association Convention, Washington, D.C., 1982.

Pierce, J. Summary Report of Meeting of Special Foster Care Programs in Pennsylvania, Harrisburg, Pennsylvania: Pennsylvania Council of Children's Services, 1987.

Stroul, B.A., and Friedman, R.M. A System of Care for Severely Emotionally Disturbed Children and Youth. Washington, D.C.: CASSP Technical Assistance Center, Georgetown University, 1986.

Update. Therapeutic Foster Care. Update 2, (1): 8–10, 1966.

U.S. Congress, Office of Technology Assessment. Children's Mental Health Problems and Services. Washington, D.C.: Government Printing Office, 1986.

Wahler, R.C.; Winkel, G.H.: Peterson, R.F; and Morrison, D.C. Mothers as behavior therapists to their own children. Behavior Research and Therapy 3: 113–124, 1965.

# The Editors

PAMELA MEADOWCROFT is Deputy Executive Director of The Pressley Ridge Schools, a multi-service agency serving over 400 troubled and troubling children and adolescents in Pennsylvania, West Virginia, and Maryland. Her teaching, administrative, clinical, and research interests reflect her commitment to institutional alternatives for the neediest of people. She received her Ph.D. in Psychology from the University of Pittsburgh in 1978, served on the faculty of West Virginia University until returning to Pittsburgh in 1981 as the director of a newly emerging alternative to institutionalizing troubled children: PRYDE, foster family-based treatment. PRYDE has grown from a pilot project to one of the largest, most successful institutional alternatives for youths in the region, annually serving over 200 children in PRYDE foster homes. Dr. Meadowcroft has provided technical assistance and consultation to many agencies across the country and state departments of mental health/social services in developing family-based treatment for children. She is on the faculty of the University of Pittsburgh, an adjunct member of the faculty of West Virginia University, a regular consultant to the National Institute of Mental Health, Child and Adolescent Service System Program (CASSP), a founding member of the Foster Family-based Treatment Association, and serves on the editorial boards of the journals *Community Alternatives* and *The Education and Treatment of Children*. She has authored and presented over 50 papers at national or regional conferences and is a frequent workshop presenter.

BARBARA A. TROUT is a clinical psychologist, licensed in the states of South Carolina and Pennsylvania. She obtained her Ph.D. in clinical psychology from West Virginia University in 1982. Dr. Trout assisted in the early development of the PRYDE Program at The Pressley Ridge Schools in Pennsylvania and then served as Coordinator of Research and Development for the agency from 1982 to 1986. Since April, 1986, she has served as Coordinator of Child and Adolescent Services for the

Santee-Wateree Mental Health Center in Sumter, South Carolina. Dr. Trout divides her time between direct clinical service to families, staff supervision, and program development. In addition to providing traditional family-focused outpatient services, Dr. Trout coordinates the implementation of home-based, crisis intervention services for children, adolescents and their families. Dr. Trout helped establish the South Carolina Young Sex Offenders Network, and she served as its first president from March 1988 to November 1989. Dr. Trout currently serves as Membership Coordinator for the Network, which seeks to develop and improve services to young sex offenders through education, advocacy, and resource development. Dr. Trout also served for two years as the chairperson for the Children and Youth Advisory Council of the South Carolina Department of Mental Health. Dr. Trout has served on several state and local task force committees to examine existing and needed services for youth in South Carolina.